TORAH AS OUR GUIDE

TORAH AS OUR GUIDE

Laws and customs for Jewish youth

BY WALTER ORENSTEIN
AND HERTZ FRANKEL

HEBREW PUBLISHING COMPANY
NEW YORK

ACKNOWLEDGMENT

We acknowledge our indebtedness to the following who were of help in various ways in the preparation of this work. Our sincerest appreciation to Mr. Joel Philips, Educational Director of the Oakland Jewish Center. His interest and devotion contributed greatly in making a reality of a book from what was once only a manuscript. To Rabbi Jacob J. Hecht, we are grateful for permission to make use of the many Torah inspired stories published by the Committee for Furtherance of Jewish Education under the auspices of the Merkoz L' inyonei Chinuch, stories that are certain to be a source of inspiration and enjoyment to our youth.

To Mrs. Gloria Horowitz, our thanks for her gracious contribution of two original stories: "The Lesson of Tisha B'Av" and "The Ride That Might Have Been," also for her version of the "Blood Spots" based on a folk tale. These stories are not only informative but also make fascinating reading. To Miss Toby Beer, for her creative suggestions. Mrs. Nellie Orenstein for the many hours she gave to the reading, correcting the manuscript, and clarifying many of the difficult passages and ideas. And, last but not least, we shall ever remain grateful to our parents, Rabbi and Mrs. Chaim Orenstein and Rabbi and Mrs. Menasheh Frankel, our first teachers in Jewish Laws and Customs and the love of learning.

CONTENTS

PREFACE

One of the most vital subjects taught in Hebrew schools is that of customs and ceremonies, or traditions and observances. Unless the teacher is successful in developing a positive attitude in his pupils toward Jewish practices, toward frequent visits to center and synagogue, toward active and intelligent participation in Jewish communal life, all other subjects will become meaningless and ultimately will be forgotten. By close association with his synagogue, center, the Jewish adolescent will continue to relate himself to the Jewish heritage, will become immersed in a Hebraic environment, and will eventually mature into an adult, qualified to take an active role in guiding the destiny of his immediate Jewish community.

However, the teaching of customs and ceremonies is most difficult because it often tends to be an object of controversy. Many children who attend either an all-day or afternoon school come from non-practicing homes, or from homes in which Jewish observances are practiced in varying degrees. Parents may often disagree with a school or teacher for having made their youngster aware that they are negligent in some of their religious duties.

It is the duty of the parents to study and try to understand the important practices that the child has been taught in the school. They should encourage the child to observe these practices and try to make gradual changes in their own observances. Such an approach is necessary so as to minimize conflict in the child, and so that neither parent nor Hebrew school falls in the esteem of that child.

While there are already many fine texts dealing with the subject of Jewish customs and ceremonies, the authors have prepared this book on the basis of their experiences and the incorporated suggestions of their colleagues, thus making the text more readable and meaningful to the student, as well as a ready source for research and classroom reporting. To the teacher it will prove to be most utilitarian as it presents the subject in a definite order and in a logical sequence. The readings of a chapter or topic should lead to class discussion, wherein the teacher can elaborate upon the material by supplementary readings which will enhance the comprehension and retention of the material.

No book, no matter how well written, can replace the motivation and the personal attachment of a teacher to his class. Hence, to achieve best results, a teacher must inject his personality, sincerity, and careful lesson planning into the presentation. Only then will children become imbued with the contents of this book, will develop positive attitudes, and above all, have their interest aroused.

The approach used is sound psychologically, for we achieve greater reward from encouragement than from threats. The handling of this delicate matter should prove to be acceptable to all schools of religious instruction whether they be orthodox, modern orthodox, conservative, or moderately conservative, as the treatise is developed along traditional lines, in the historical continuity to which all segments of the Jewish faith adhere.

As aids to student and teacher, the authors have prepared a calendar to mark pictorially and chronologically the events of the year. The dictionary of terms will also prove to be a handy reference for the pupil. While it is not suggested that teachers utilize every exercise in the book, they can nevertheless serve as a guide for further elaboration in accordance with the ability and level of the class. Although the authors prepared the text primarily for 11–14 year olds, teachers of younger classes may avail themselves of the material and present it on the comprehension level of their younger pupils.

This text is the product of actual day-to-day contact with teaching situations. I am confident the profession will greatly appreciate the labor and efforts expended on this work and will find the book helpful to them in class, library, and school.

JOEL PHILLIPS, B.A., M. S. IN ED.
Educational Director
Oakland Jewish Center, Bayside, N. Y.

TO THE TEACHER

It is our purpose in this volume to present to children of ages eleven through fourteen a comprehensive study of Jewish laws and customs. The text has been written from a traditional viewpoint, based on the Torah and Rabbinical interpretations.

Although the topics are arranged in chapters, they have been sub-titled to afford the teacher maximum flexibility, to choose particular sections if he does not find it feasible to cover the entire chapter.

Of use to the student as well as the teacher are the stories at the end of some chapters. These stories are appropriate to the topic and will be of much value if integrated within the lesson or read by the teacher aloud as motivation.

At the end of the book you will find an appendix containing English-Hebrew and Hebrew-English vocabularies of terms used in the text. These vocabularies are of particular value to the child who does not cover the textbook chapter by chapter. Often Hebrew terms that were explained in English or translated literally, in previous chapters, are used only in the Hebrew later on. The child who has skipped chapters, who would ordinarily be hampered by words he has not learned, can easily find their meaning by looking them up in the appended "dictionary."

Another feature of the appendix is a list of all the blessings in each chapter. The blessings are listed in Hebrew and in English. By having the child refer to these blessings at home and in class, he will familiarize himself with them and learn their meaning.

Of practical importance in the appendix are the exercises for each chapter. They have been varied (multiple choice, fill in, matching and essay type) to contribute to the motivation and interest of the student. All questions of the objective type tests were carefully constructed to have only one correct answer, although some of the alternatives in the multiple choice and matching exercises are *constructively misleading*. The essays are based, generally, on the introductions of each chapter. They have been composed to be thought-provoking and, as much as possible, relate to the child's experience.

KEY TO PRONUNCIATION OF TRANSLITERATED HEBREW TERMS

Ei in Kohein — as in heir or neighbor
Ch in Chanukah — as in German Ich
I in Bimah — as ee in see
A in Aliyos — as in art
O in Oleinu — as ou in rough
U in Succos — as oo in too

TORAH AS OUR GUIDE

TAKING G-D INTO OUR HOMES

AWAKENING IN THE MORNING. When we awake in the morning, and all through the day, we must always remember that we are in the presence of the Almighty G-D. Wherever we go, even in the most hidden places, He is always near us. What does this mean? Does it mean that we should always be afraid of Him? Should we sit and pray to Him all day long? No! It only means that we should behave and try to fulfill His wishes. If we were in the presence of a great king, how would we act? Wouldn't we watch our language and manners? Wouldn't we try to find favor in his eyes? Certainly we would. How much more so should we watch our actions if we are in the presence of the greatest of all kings, Almighty G-D, the King of kings.

When we awake in the morning, the first thing we do is thank G-D for helping us to rise fresh and ready for a full day. We thank Him by reciting the "Modeh Ani" prayer, "I thank Thee, O living and eternal King, for returning my soul to me. Thy faithfulness is very great."

WASHING THE HANDS. When we wake up in the morning with new freshness and vigor, we are in a sense new persons. We must wash ourselves and be clean. Just as in the days of the Temple, the priest washed his hands from a vessel before he began his service to G-D, so we wash our hands before

1

beginning our service to Him. We must also wash our hands before eating. Our Sages tell us that the table upon which we eat is like an altar before G-D. We must approach it with clean hands. Another important measure of cleanliness is to wash our hands after leaving the bathroom.

OUR PLACE OF WORSHIP AND STUDY AT HOME. How do we prepare for an important guest? In what room of the house is he usually entertained? We all know the answer. The house is arranged exceptionally well; it is spotlessly clean. We use our best silverware and dishes. We dress in our best clothes and await our guest. When he comes, we take him into our living room, the nicest room in the house.

Shouldn't we act the same way when we take G-D into our homes by praying to Him or by studying His Law. Whenever we are doing anything that is Holy, it must be done with respect. We must do it in a proper place. Whether we are reciting prayers, studying the Torah, doing our Hebrew homework or practicing our Bar Mitzvah studies, we are reading the words of G-D and should show proper respect. It is forbidden to pray or perform any religious study in the bathroom. Any other room of the house would be considered proper. Let us always remember to give our religious studies the respect and honor they deserve.

LAWS OF THE BROCHOS. When we receive a gift from a relative or a friend, we show our appreciation by thanking him in some way. If the gift is given by our parents, we may show appreciation by listening to their advice or by making a resolution to behave well among guests, so that they will be proud of us. How do we show our appreciation to the Father of us all who has given us the greatest gift of all, the gift of life and all the wonders of the world? Surely He deserves some credit and appreciation on our part. We show our appreciation to Him just as we show it to our friends and relatives;

we thank Him. We recite "Brochos," "blessings." We recite these "Brochos" at every occasion we have for giving thanks. Don't you feel it is the proper thing to do?

Because these blessings are so important, we must always concentrate upon what we are saying. Imagine the impression it would make upon our relatives if we were to thank them for a gift while we were watching a TV program or reading the comics in the newspaper. They wouldn't think that we appreciated the gift very much. Would they? When we recite a "Brocha" to G-D, therefore, we must learn the proper blessing beforehand, so that when we recite it, we do it without hesitation and with meaning. It must come from our hearts. When we recite a "Brocha," we should be careful not to mention the name of G-D (which is in the middle of the blessing) and then change our mind about reciting the "Brocha." For example: If we wanted to eat fruit and recited the blessing, or part of the blessing for the fruit, and then changed our mind about eating the fruit and put it away, we would be reciting a "Brocha" in vain. Mentioning the name of G-D in vain would be disrespectful and, therefore, against the Law. We must make up our mind before we recite a "Brocha" for anything. In this way, we can avoid disrespect to G-D.

When someone recites a "Brocha" and we are nearby, we should make it a habit to answer "Amen." The Hebrew letters of "Amen" are the initials of "El Melech Ne-emon," "G-D is a faithful King." It is a way of saying that all we heard is true. (See Appendix Chapter One for "Brochos" recited on various occasions.)

THE FOOD THIEF

The boys broke up their football game on the vacant lot where they used to play. It had started to thunder, lightning flashed in the distance, and it looked as though a heavy downpour was due any moment.

Joe, too, prepared to leave and he was very pleased when Sidney said to him, "I'll walk you home, Joe."

Joe was a Yeshiva student, and when he joined the boys of the neighborhood in their games, he wanted this fact to be known. Not that he wished to boast about it, although he was very proud, but he wanted to impress upon the other boys how important it was for every Jewish boy to get a Jewish education. He was sorry that so many Jewish boys knew so little about Torah and "Mitz-vos." He used to invite some of them to his house on Friday nights or "Shabbos" afternoons. In the course of time several boys joined the Yeshiva thanks to Joe's influence. There would have been many more but for one boy, Sidney.

Sidney, or Sid the Kid, as he liked to be called, was a real tough guy. He was the captain of his team and many a boy wanted to belong to it. Sid was not a bad kid and he did not turn his team into a gang, like many other tough kids. Dishonesty was a serious crime in Sid's opinion, which at once disqualified any dishonest boy from belonging to his team. Yet, Sid was not in favor of a Yeshiva education because, first of all, his parents never expected it of him, and secondly, because he knew that going to a Yeshiva meant giving up some of the things he wanted to do.

Joe often thought that if he could win Sid over, he would win his entire team. But that was not easy, for Sidney could see no sense in laws like making a "Brocha" before eating anything, or not playing ball on "Shabbos." Secretly, however, Sidney admired Joe's faith and steadfastness and courage. Joe always had his head covered, always made a "Brocha" before and after he ate anything, never was tempted to play ball on "Shabbos," and the like.

And today Sidney's admiration for Joe turned to awe, when Joe stopped in the middle of the game to make a "Brocha" over a flash of lightning in the distance. Joe had just broken through the tough line of defense held by Sid's team, and saw the field clear for a touchdown, when he suddenly stopped to recite the "Brocha." Sidney and the other boys were so amazed that they just gasped.

Now, Sidney had offered to walk home with Joe, and Joe was glad of it, for he longed for an opportunity to talk to Sidney.

"That's swell, Sidney," replied Joe eagerly, and the two boys walked on.

"Some trick you played on us, Joe, when you stopped with the ball in your hands in order to make a 'Brocha' over the flash of lightning," Sidney remarked. "Whoever heard of throwing away a game like that? Boy, that was something!"

"It only goes to show you, Sid, that it is always necessary to have your head covered in order to be prepared for a 'Brocha'."

"Oh! you and your 'Brochos'," said Sidney impatiently.

The boys walked on silently for a moment, Joe trying to think what would be the best line of conversation on the subject. Nearing the corner they noticed a little crowd of people gathered near a brightly lit restaurant. The boys joined the crowd to find out what it was all about. At that moment they saw a man getting up from the ground, and brushing the dust off his clothes. In the doorway of the restaurant stood an attendant, tall and tough looking. Wagging his finger at the man, he shouted: "Don't ever try to snatch a meal that way again, you loafer!" And addressing the crowd that had gathered around, he said: "The impudence! The guy orders a full course dinner and a drink, too, if you don't mind, and when it comes to paying the bill, he says, 'Ain't got no money, bud!' The sneaky thief!"

Everybody turned away from the man in disgust. The boys, too, went on their way.

"I feel sorry for the man," Joe said. "Maybe he is poor and was hungry."

"Nah!" replied Sidney, "he didn't look poor. He is just mean. He wanted to get something for nothing."

"Would you ever do a thing like that, Sid?"

Sidney was indignant. "You know I would never do a thing like that, Joe."

"Well, I saw you do a thing like that. In fact more than once!" Joe said.

Sidney stopped suddenly. "That's a lie, Joe, and you know it. Say, what's the big idea, do you want to pick a fight?"

"No, Sidney, I don't want to fight. But I'm serious. Listen for a moment and then decide for yourself."

Sidney was puzzled, but he was prepared to listen.

"Well, Sidney, you were Bar Mitzvah, when was it, two years ago?"

Sidney nodded.

"Okay, then you still remember a few things. Well, it is written in our Torah 'To G-D belongs the Earth and all things upon it.' It is also written 'The heavens are G-D's but the Earth He gave to the children of man.' The two statements do not agree, obviously, but there is an explanation. The whole world is like a beautiful restaurant with the nicest things in it, food and drink and everything. G-D created this beautiful 'restaurant' and permitted the people to enjoy the things He created. However, He expects a price for them, just as the restaurant owner expects a price for his dinner. The price which we have to pay to G-D for our food is a 'Brocha.' It is a price which everybody can afford, don't you think so? It is so easy to make a 'Brocha' before eating anything and to recite Grace after meals. And that makes all the difference between the honest man who would not eat anything unless it is paid for, and the man we saw in the gutter, thrown from the restaurant because he would not pay for his meal."

Sidney listened attentively, but did not reply. He was thinking how right Joe was. In his mind he began to revive the blessings which he had once learned. He was very glad that he remembered every one of them.

From the corner of his eye, Joe looked at his friend and saw him smile. Joe smiled too.

THREE RELIGIOUS SYMBOLS

LAWS OF THE FRINGES AND THE TALLIS. All of our laws come to us from G-D. Some are found in the Torah, the "Chumosh," and some were handed down orally from generation to generation. The laws of the fringes are written in the "Chumosh." As a matter of fact, there is a whole paragraph devoted to this law. What is this law? What makes it so important? Let's try to find out.

The "Chumosh" tells us that G-D spoke to Moses and told him that the Israelites should make fringes on the corners of their garments. One of these fringes should contain a blue thread. The Israelites should look upon these fringes and remember all the "Mitzvos," the commandments of G-D, and observe them. They should not just do whatever they feel like doing. These fringes should serve as a reminder to do all the "Mitzvos" of G-D and in that way be holy to Him.

What do we learn from this paragraph? Firstly, that the Israelites in the time of the Bible wore cornered garments. Secondly, that among the fringes there was one thread of blue color. (Our tradition tells us that this color was a perfect sky blue so that when the Israelites looked at it, they would think of the sky, of G-D and of holy things. Unfortunately, the exact color of the dye and how it was made, is no longer known, and we no longer have a blue thread among our fringes.) Thirdly, and most important, we learn that the

8

purpose of these fringes was that they should serve as a sign, a reminder.

Do you remember the story of the boy who tied a string around his finger to remind him that he had an errand to run? Whenever he looked at the string, he reminded himself of what he had to do. It helped didn't it? Well, that is the purpose of the fringes, or "Tzitzis," as they are called in Hebrew. Whenever we look at them, we remind ourselves of the "Mitzvos" commanded to us by G-D. We remind ourselves that we must always try to do the right thing according to the Will of G-D as He has written in the Torah. What a wonderful world this would be if everyone were to wear "Tzitzis" and always remembered to do the right thing.

THE ARBA KANFOS. How do we fulfill this commandment nowadays? If you remember the paragraph from the "Chumosh" about the "Tzitzis" you also remember that we are told to put them on the corners of our garments. But we don't wear cornered garments now. So what do we do? We make a four-cornered garment and put "Tzitzis" on each corner. We make this garment by cutting a hole, big enough to put our head through, in a rectangular-shaped piece of cloth. Once the "Tzitzis" are put on the garment, it is ready for use. This garment is called in Hebrew, "Arba Kanfos," which means "four corners." It is worn only by males. The "Arba Kanfos" is worn under our shirt, all through the day. Some pious Jews wear the "Arba Kanfos" as an outer garment so that they may see the "Tzitzis" at all times and in that way remember to act justly and follow the laws of G-D at all times. When we look at the "Tzitzis" on the four corners of our "Arba Kanfos," we are reminded that G-D is everywhere in the "four corners of the earth."

THE TALLIS. The "Tallis" which is the prayer shawl that we see worn in the synagogue is really a larger form of the "Arba

Kanfos." It has "Tzitzis" on its four corners and is worn around the shoulders. "Taliyos" come in silk and wool, they may differ in size from a small scarf-like "Tallis" to a large one that reaches to the floor.

Why do some people wear such large "Taliyos"?

Why do some of the congregants cover their heads with them?

If we read the prayer recited when putting on the "Tallis" we can answer the first question. "Blessed art Thou, O Lord our G-D, King of the universe, who hast made us holy by Thy commandments and hast commanded us to enwrap ourselves in the 'Tzitzis'." (See Appendix, Chapter 2.) Many Jews feel that it is necessary to enwrap oneself entirely in the "Tallis" in order to fulfill the commandment properly. These people want to be exceptionally careful not to recite the blessing in vain. Do you remember the importance of not reciting a blessing in vain? Look back and reread the section on "Brochos."

There is also a good reason why some people cover their heads with the "Tallis." It is very easy to be distracted in the middle of a prayer by someone or something in the synagogue. By covering their heads with the "Tallis," they can concentrate better on what they are saying.

The "Tallis" is worn during the morning service. It is only worn by males. It is customary among many Jews not to wear a "Tallis" until they are married. A person serving as Cantor wears a "Tallis" in the morning on weekdays and at all three services on the Sabbath and holidays, whether he is married or not. Although all through the year the "Tallis" is worn by the congregation only in the morning, on Yom Kippur Eve, at the "Kol Nidre" service, due to the holiness of the occasion, all the males wear "Taliyos."

There is an interesting law about the "Tallis" that teaches us a wonderful lesson. It is permissible to take a "Tallis" belonging to someone else and pray in it even though the owner is unaware of it and cannot give his permission. The borrower must not take it out of the synagogue, however, and he must return it to its proper place when he is finished praying.

Wouldn't this be stealing?

How could the law give permission for such a thing?

The answer is really quite simple. The law tells us that no man would object to the use of his property to fulfill a "Mitzvah" as long as the use of it does not damage it in any way. On the contrary, he would be proud to have been of help in the fulfillment of a "Mitzvah."

We must always remember that the "Tzitzis" on our "Tallis" or our "Arba Kanfos" are holy since they are being used for a holy purpose. Even when they are too old to be used or by accident they fall off a "Tallis," they must not be thrown away. An old "Tallis" or "Arba Kanfos" must not be thrown away either. It must be brought to the synagogue to be taken care of by the rabbi. Each of the "Tzitzis" must have eight strands, no more and no less. If one is missing, or there is one too many, it should be fixed, and until then another "Tallis" should be used. The "Tallis" and every other religious article should be handled with respect. It should be used with clean hands and no part of it should touch the ground.

ANOTHER SIGN: THE TEPHILLIN. Just as the idea for the "Tzitzis" originates in the Torah, so the idea for the "Tephillin" also originates in the Torah. It is found in a paragraph that we recite three times a day; a paragraph you have recited many times in Hebrew school. Here it is in a simplified form: "Hear O Israel, the Lord our G-D, the Lord is One. And you should love the Lord your G-D with all your heart, with all your soul, and with all your might. And these words which I command you this day shall be upon your heart. You should teach them well to your children, when you are sitting at home, when you are traveling, when you lie down and when you arise. And you shall bind them as a sign upon your hand and they shall be as bands between your eyes. And you shall write them on the doorposts of your house and on your gates."

Surely, you have recited this paragraph more than once, perhaps even in the English version. But did you ever ask yourself the meaning of the sentence: "And you shall bind them for a sign upon your hand and they shall be as bands between your eyes"? This is the sentence from which we learn the law of the "Tephillin." We are told in this paragraph that the law that G-D teaches us should be put on our hand and between our eyes. Our Sages learned from tradition that we should put the "Tephillin" on our left hand, the one near our heart. They taught us that the way in which we can fulfill this law properly is by putting the words of G-D into two cubes, or square boxes, and strapping one of them to our arm facing our heart and the other on our head between our eyes. In this way the "Tephillin" serve as a sign, just as the "Tzitzis" do, to remind us to act in the ways of G-D, to love Him, and to teach His laws to our children.

The "Tephillin" are two black cubes from one to two square inches in size. They have black leather straps attached to them. One is called "Shel Rosh"; it is for the head. The other is called "Shel Yod"; it is for the arm. The "Shel Rosh" contains four pieces of parchment, in four separate compartments, upon which four chapters of the Torah are written. One of these prayers we read in the beginning of this chapter: the "Shema." In the "Shel Yod" these same chapters are written on one parchment, for the "Shel Yod" has only one compartment.

The "Tephillin" are worn during the morning services only. They are worn every day except on the Sabbath and holidays. On the Sabbath and holidays, they are not necessary since the observance of those days already serves as a sign that we walk in the ways of G-D and love Him. We must remember that the "Tephillin" are not only worn in the synagogue when we recite the morning service with a "Minyan," but they are also worn when we recite the morning service at home, by ourselves.

PUTTING ON THE "TEPHILLIN." The "Tephillin" are put on in a certain order, and it should be followed exactly to fulfill the Mitzvah properly. To show due respect for the "Tephillin" we must stand during the whole procedure. Even when we take them out of the Tephillin bag, they must be taken out carefully, the "Shel Yod" first, and then the "Shel Rosh." The "Tephillin" are taken off after the service in the opposite way: the "Shel Rosh" first and then the "Shel Yod." It is important to make sure that when the "Shel Yod" is put on, the polished side of the strap is facing upward. During the entire procedure of putting on the "Tephillin," we must concentrate on what we are doing. No talking is allowed. It is even forbidden to recite "Amen" upon hearing someone recite a "Brocha" during this time. The "Shel Rosh" must be put on the head and not on the skullcap, and the front part of it should touch the beginning of the hairline. (The "Brochos" for the "Tephillin" are found in the Appendix, Chapter 2.)

It is a beautiful custom to touch the "Tephillin" whenever we mention them in our prayers. When we say, "And you shall bind them as a sign upon your hand," we touch the "Shel Yod" and kiss the hand. When we say, "And they shall be as bands between your eyes," we touch the "Shel Rosh" and likewise kiss the hand. The "Tephillin" must be opened and examined every few years by a qualified person, a "sofeir," to correct any faded letters.

Why do you have to be thirteen to put on "Tephillin"? Well, the answer is quite simple. Would you give your younger brother or sister your precious baseball mitt? Would your mother lend you her diamond ring to play with? Would your father let you wear his best tie to school? Definitely not. Why? Because valuable things are loaned only to people who know the value of them. If we do not know the value of something precious, we will not know how to take care of it. We might lose it or spoil it. We have to be of a certain age to be able to appreciate value.

The same is true of the privilege of putting on the "Tephillin." Only a boy of thirteen is old enough and mature enough to be given the honor of wearing them.

What should the "Tephillin" mean to us?

The "Tephillin," in addition to what we have already mentioned, symbolize our devotion of hand and heart to the will of G-D. They remind us that we should give Him praise and honor by praying to Him, for prayer is one of the best ways we have to convey these thoughts.

If we put on the "Tephillin" properly and faithfully, they will always serve us as a reminder and a guide to lead our lives in the ways of G-D according to the true spirit of the Torah.

THE LAW OF THE MEZUZAH. The "Mezuzah" is another reminder. It is taken, as the "Tzitzis" and the "Tephillin," from the Torah. As a matter of fact, it is taken from the same paragraph as the "Tephillin." Remember the last sentence of that paragraph? "And you shall write them upon the doorposts of your house and upon your gates." What do we learn from this sentence? The Torah tells us that the laws of this chapter should be written on our doorposts. Well, let's enumerate these laws.

1. The belief that there is only one G-D.
2. To love G-D with all our heart, soul and might.
3. That these words of G-D be upon our heart.
4. That we teach these words to our children.
5. That we discuss and speak of these words in our homes, when we are traveling, when we awake and when we go to bed.

6. That we put these words upon our arms and between our eyes.
7. That we write these words upon our doorposts and gates.

A "sofeir," "scribe," writes this paragraph, which contains all these laws, on a piece of parchment. He uses the Torah script which is a bit different from our regular script. This piece of parchment is rolled up and put in an oblong case. The case is then attached to the doorpost. Now we have fulfilled the commandment properly.

WHAT ARE SOME OF THE LAWS OF THE "MEZUZAH"?

1. It is a commandment to put a "Mezuzah" upon every doorpost of every room except the bathroom. If a room has many doors, each door must have a "Mezuzah."
2. If a court, a Jewish city or province is surrounded by a gate, the gate must have a "Mezuzah."
3. The "Mezuzah" is put upon the right side of the entrance. It is put upon the upper third of the doorpost. When we put on the "Mezuzah," we recite a special blessing honoring the name of G-D, who has commanded us to put up the "Mezuzah." (This blessing is found in the Appendix, Chapter Two.) The "Mezuzah" should be put closer to the outside of the doorpost and it should be slanted with the top pointing inward.
4. If one moves from his home and he knows that a Jew will be moving in after him, he must not remove the "Mezuzah." He may leave it as a gift or ask the new tenant to buy it.
5. It is a custom to touch the "Mezuzah" and kiss the hand, when we enter and leave a house. In this way we can always be reminded of G-D and remember to follow His ways.

Our Sages tell us that a person who follows the laws of
"Tzitzis," of "Tephillin" and of "Mezuzah" properly and with
a perfect heart, can hardly ever sin, since he is constantly reminded of the right way of life. What a wonderful effect
these laws could have upon the world, if everyone were to
follow them. We would probably be blessed with everlasting
peace.

THE TALLIS MAKER

In the city of Bagdad lived a pious Jew by the name of Gershon. He was an excellent weaver of the tallis. The tallis, as most of you know, is a large woolen cloth with "tzitzis," or a bunch of specially prepared strings, attached to each corner. It is put on by grown-ups (Jews) when they pray. It was such cloths that Gershon wove on his loom, which hummed busily all day in one of the rooms of his small dilapidated house. But Gershon did not prosper; he made barely enough to live on. Often his family went hungry, and did without sufficient clothing.

But Gershon always kept a happy disposition, for he and his family were leading religious, righteous lives, according to the commands of G-D, and he was certain that the Almighty would not forsake them. But he had one bad habit: he would always say, "Everything the Almighty wants to do with me, let Him do. But two things He will never do: He will never make a tallis as beautiful as I do, and He will never make me a rich man." His wife would scold him when she heard this, for she was afraid that these brazen words would bring ruin to them, but Gershon would only smile and go on with his work.

One Friday afternoon, Gershon finished the last tallis for the day, closed up the workroom, and prepared for the coming Sabbath. He washed, dressed, and toward evening went to "Shul" to pray. In the "Shul" someone whom he had never seen before, an old man with a handsome beard, sat down beside him. As the man was obviously a stranger, Gershon approached him after the prayers, and invited him to spend the "Shabbos" at his house.

"We are poor," he said to the stranger, "but you are welcome to share with us the little that we have." The stranger thanked him heartily, and together they went to Gershon's house.

They made "Kiddush," that is, they blessed the Sabbath over wine, washed, and sat down to eat. In the course of the conversation, Gershon told the old man about his work and his struggle to make a living, and soon he repeated his old saying, i.e., that G-D couldn't make as beautiful a tallis as Gershon, and that the Almighty couldn't make Gershon a rich man. The old man looked at Gershon strangely for a moment, and then began talking about something else.

Later, the old man began talking about the Torah, bringing out thoughts that had never occurred to Gershon, for when Gershon learned the Torah, he only learned the obvious meanings. The old man revealed to Gershon beautiful ideas in the Torah. Obviously this stranger was a profoundly learned man. On and on the man talked, and Gershon listened eagerly. The stove made the room snug and comfortable, and the candles gleamed brightly on the table. Soon, the wife and the children of Gershon became drowsy, and they went off to bed. Gershon and the old man remained alone at the table.

Soon the room became too warm, and Gershon began to feel drowsy . . . "Come, let us go outside and take a little walk in the cool air and then we'll go to sleep," said the old man.

They walked slowly through the early-spring night. A refreshing cool breeze blew gently through the sleeping city of Bagdad. They came to a stream and walked along it. Suddenly, the old man grasped the hand of Gershon, spread his cloak over the two of them, and began rising upward, heavenward. Gershon felt no fear, he stared at the heavens in wonder, as new beauty, unseen from the earth, unfolded before him.

Soon they stopped. "Look down," said the old man. Gershon looked at the earth far below him. The sight that met his eyes took his breath away. What was this? Were his eyes deceiving him? The part of the earth that he saw seemed like the most exquisite tallis in the world. To the north flowed the River Chidekel, and, reflecting the white, silver moonlight and the twinkling stars, it looked like the piece of embroidered silk put at the top edge of a tallis. The forests, meadows, hills and valleys; the streams, creeks, rills and rivulets were so arranged, in such a beautiful design that the whole world formed a tallis. At the four corners tall palm and willow trees seemed to be the "Tzitzis," the fringes. The scene held Gershon enchanted, as he drank in the strange beauty of it all. Soon he became aware that the old man was speaking to him. The voice sounded full and majestic. "You who have sinned against your Creator, look down and see the tallis that the Lord has made. And just as easily, can your Creator make you rich, if you are worthy and deserving."

The next minute Gershon was standing alone at his house. And as he prepared to go to bed, Gershon thought about what had just happened to him. And, to the end of his days, Gershon remained a deeply religious Jew, and he never repeated his old saying.

Gershon, living his usual, everyday life, knew there was a G-D. But he had not realized to what extent G-D controls the world; he had not realized how all-powerful G-D is. Only when he was shown G-D's earth in its splendor did he realize that there is an all-controlling Ruler who rules the universe with wisdom and kindness.

CARE OF THE TORAH AND
OTHER HOLY BOOKS

THE BIBLE. Do you know what book has been the most popular since it first appeared? The Bible! More than five million copies are sold each year in the United States alone. The Bible has been the greatest treasure of humanity. It is recognized as the greatest work of literature ever written. This gift was given to humanity by the Jewish people. It has been our contribution to the world. The Bible has been translated into almost every known language. Why do you think this was done? People all over the world study the Bible and try to learn its wisdom. It is interesting to note that many laws of our government as well as of governments of other countries, are based upon the Jewish law, the Bible.

The first part of the Bible, the Five Books of Moses, is called the Torah. What should be our approach as Jews to the Torah as the most sacred symbol of our faith?

THE TORAH SCROLL. The Torah scroll must be given the utmost respect and honor. It must be kept in a special place in the synagogue and taken out only when it is to be used or repaired. When the Torah is carried during the service, we must rise as a sign of respect. When the Torah is read in the synagogue, we must remain quiet and follow the reading in a Bible.

It is one of the greatest honors to be called up to the Torah to recite the blessings. Every time we are called up to the Torah we recite a blessing to G-D thanking Him for giving it to us. We affirm our belief that the Torah is truth and we bless His name for giving us the privilege of teaching Torah to the world.

Lastly we thank Him for giving the blessing of everlasting life to the Jewish nation so that it can continue throughout the generations to teach the right way of life to the world.

It is a great "Mitzvah" to donate a Torah scroll to the synagogue. It is an even greater "Mitzvah" to copy a Torah oneself.

When someone carries the Torah scroll in the synagogue, he must be very careful for, if he drops it, he, and all who are present are obligated to fast or redeem their fast by giving charity.

HOLY BOOKS. It is the duty of every Jew to buy holy books such as: the Bible, prayer books for various holidays, and books of Jewish Law. One should set aside a certain period of the day to study these books. It is a great "Mitzvah" to lend holy books to friends so that they, too, may learn about their religion. What did we learn about the law of the "Tallis" that is similar to this law?

All holy books must be given proper respect. It is forbidden to place them on the floor. They must not be thrown about. They must be placed right side up when they are carried or put on the table. A holy book may be used only for the purpose for which it was made—for study.

When a Torah scroll is no longer fit for use, it is forbidden to throw it away or burn it. It must be brought to the rabbi, who will bury it according to Jewish law. This law also holds true for holy books.

Above all, let us always remember that a holy book contains the words of G-D and His Name. When we handle it with respect, we are showing respect to G-D. When we handle it with disrespect, we are showing disrespect to Him.

THE STRANGE PAWNSHOP

Yossi spent much of his spare time in the old pawnbroker's store. Somehow this half-dark, musty store filled with a thousand and one things—small and big, old and new—had a powerful attraction for him. Each drawer seemed to house mysterious secrets; and wondrous tales of adventures must have been attached to the swords, armor, and trophies which crowded every inch of the narrow store. Even the pawnbroker himself, Sam Gold, seemed as old as some of his precious possessions.

Sam Gold, however, was a friendly man with a wise word or two for each occasion. It was for this reason that the poor and needy, who were forced by circumstances to pawn their valuable possessions, preferred Sam Gold. For he, more often than not, paid prices far above the true value if he knew that the owner really needed the money.

Sam Gold was a simple and pious Jew. His only regret was that in his youth he did not have an opportunity to study the Torah. Every now and then his young friend Yossi came in and taught him the Dinim (laws) that he had learned at the Yeshivah. In exchange, Sam Gold taught Yossi much about the history of the world as told through the antiques in his pawnshop. Sometimes he pulled out the large drawer which contained the coin collections, or the drawer with the valuable stamps, and Yossi heard names of men and places he was first to meet years later while studying history at the State University.

Sam Gold was really at his best when he described the background and the personal history of his pawnshop customers. His warm description changed them, in Yossi's eyes, from ragged beggars or worried workers into personalities with interesting worlds all of their own. Very often they emerged from Sam Gold's stories as men with courage—men able to stand up fearlessly despite their bitter fate.

There was one man whom Sam Gold pictured as an angel of righteousness and as a great scholar. This was an old, bent Jew who looked pathetic as he hobbled into the store on his usual once-a-week visit, with books always bulging out of every pocket of his oversized coat. Whenever Yossi saw this old man leaning on a stick that had once been the stem of an umbrella, he would want to break out in laughter. But Sam usually gave him one of his rare, serious looks and Yossi quickly understood. And he thereupon looked with respect and awe at the hunched little man, who with a pair of thick-lensed glasses before his half-blind eyes, looked over the newly acquired books in Sam Gold's pawnshop.

Sam Gold explained to Yossi that this old man, Reb Yankel, was a great scholar, and that he spent his time salvaging old manuscripts. He told him that Reb Yankel spent all his money in buying back Hebrew books from pawnshops and second-hand book stores, so that the old and sacred Hebrew books should not fall into unfriendly hands and be treated in an unworthy manner.

The old man, although considered by many as one of the greatest experts on Jewish literature, refused to accept an important University position because he felt that he did not want to earn his living by utilizing his knowledge. When Yossi heard the story he respected the old scholar still more. Occasionally he even had the courage to ask him questions about the "Gemorrah" or the passage in "Tanach" he had recently learned.

One day Reb Yankel hobbled in even slower than usual. Instead of browsing through the books, as was his custom, he went directly to Sam Gold, pulled an old book out of his coat pocket and offered to sell it for a dollar. "Why, I think I could sell this for three dollars," said Sam after a brief glance at the book. "One dollar is all I paid for it, and I will not take a penny more," replied the old man in a trembling voice. Without saying another word Sam Gold pulled a dollar bill out of his pocket and gave it to Reb Yankel.

"I simply can't understand it," he muttered as the old man left his store. "This has been going on for the past few days. Reb Yankel who never gives a book away, comes in day after day to sell one of his precious possessions. Seems to me like he must be starving. I offered to give him all the money he needs on condition that he should pay me back whenever he can, but he refuses. He claims that he is too old to borrow or to accept gifts."

"Listen," he suddenly turned to Yossi, "go over to Yankel's house and find out what's behind his new and strange behavior."

Of course Yossi was eager to learn the cause of the change in Reb Yankel. Stealthily he followed him until he saw the old man enter a drug store. A few minutes later he came out with a small bottle in his hand, and hobbled back to the old house where he lived. Yossi, at a safe distance, watched closely. He noticed that Reb Yankel, instead of going into his own apartment, went into the one next door. As he did not close the door completely, Yossi, now in the hallway, was able to overhear the conversation.

"Here is your medicine, old mother," he heard Reb Yankel's voice. "Oh, thanks a million," replied the weak voice of a woman. "I told you, you should not do it for me. I am an old scrubwoman and am going to die anyway. Why should you sell your precious books to buy medicine for me?"

"Don't worry, mother. I told you a thousand times, a human life is worth more than all the books in the world."

Yossi was deeply touched. Rushing back to Sam Gold, he told him about Reb Yankel's kindness. Sam Gold smiled a knowing smile. After giving Yossi three ten-dollar bills, he told him to try and get the old woman to take this donation. The old lady accepted, only after Yossi convinced her that the money came from a distant relative.

Of course after this, on Reb Yankel's next visit, she told him that she didn't need his help any more.

The following week, Reb Yankel came back to the pawnshop to redeem two of his books. Sam Gold readily returned the books and his eyes moistened as he saw with what love Reb Yankel fondled them, as if he had just found a long-missed treasure.

Three days later the neighborhood was shocked to hear that Reb Yankel had died. It was unfortunate that this tragedy happened before Reb Yankel had a chance to redeem all of his treasured books. Reb Yankel, however, had already made his choice when the proper occasion presented itself.

Later on in life when Yossi grew up, he never forgot the simple lesson in charity and kindness that Reb Yankel had taught him. Many were the times when it seemed to him that he could hear Reb Yankel arguing with the old woman, and finally convincing her to use the medicine which he bought by selling his last precious possession—his sacred books. That day Yossi would not count as lost, for he would try to be like Reb Yankel, good and kind to people in need.

THE DIETARY LAWS

Is there a Jewish child who has not heard the word "kosher" at some time or another? This word has often been used by Jewish children without knowing its true meaning. The word "kosher" means "fit for use in accordance with Jewish law." This word, therefore, may be used in reference to religious articles such as a Torah scroll, a "Tallis" or a pair of "Tephillin," and may also be used in reference to foods or anything else that may be utilized by a Jewish person. It is the use of this word in reference to food that we will concern ourselves with in this chapter.

"Dietary laws" is the name given to the laws in the Bible dealing with the foods which we are permitted to eat and the foods which we are forbidden to eat. When we talk about a diet we picture a chart or an outline of special foods that we must eat for a certain purpose. It may be to improve our health after a long and serious illness or to keep our bodies healthy so that we can avoid illness. We are all on some sort of diet even though we may not be aware of it. In school, the dietician sees to it that the meals we are served are nutritious and well-balanced. At home, mother does the same thing.

In the Torah we are given a very basic diet. It does not outline for us the proper foods to balance our daily meals, but it gives us the foods from which we should choose our daily diet. It tells us which animals, which fowl and which fish we are permitted to eat. The diet given to us by the Torah must have an important purpose, for we know that anything given to us by G-D is given for very good reasons. Unlike many other laws in the Torah, the reason for these laws is not given. Learned men of every generation have tried to explain them, but to this day no one has found the reason for them. But we observe these laws because they are the will of G-D. Perhaps some time in the future it may be G-D's will to reveal to us the reason for the dietary laws and grant us the wisdom to understand them.

What did you eat for supper last Friday night? A piece of fish for an entrée? A piece of meat or some chicken with some vegetables for a main course? Well, if you did, then you ate a typical Friday night meal. What processes did these foods have to go through before they came to your plate if they were prepared in a kosher way?

FISH. The fish that you ate had to have two signs in order to be considered kosher. It had to have fins and scales; one of these signs alone would not be enough. If it had these qualifications, it had all that is necessary according to Jewish law. Fish can be caught and prepared in any way you wish. However, they may not be cooked with meat in the same pot.

MEAT. Let us now go to the main course. Meat goes through a number of processes before it can be eaten. The Torah tells us that an animal to be considered kosher must have two qualifications: it must chew its cud (that means that it digests its food in a certain way) and it must have split hoofs. Just as we said about fish, any animal that has only one of the qualifications is not a kosher animal. After we choose an animal with these qualifications, we have met the first requirement. Next we must make sure that it is slaughtered according to the Jewish law. It must be done by a man well acquainted with the Jewish laws of slaughter. He is called a "shochet." Although we are permitted to eat animals and fowl, Jewish law tells us that they must be killed by a special method. Through this method they suffer the least amount of pain possible. After the animal is slaughtered by the "shochet," it is inspected very carefully to find out whether it was diseased in any way. After inspection, some animals may be found to have been diseased or slaughtered incorrectly. These animals are not permitted for Jewish consumption. They are not kosher. If the animal is found to be kosher then it is cut up and the kosher parts are selected. (The hind quarters of the animal contain many tiny blood vessels that must be removed by an expert. Since this would take too much time and bother, the hind quarters are not eaten.)

SALTING PROCESS. The next stop is the butcher shop where the cut meat is trimmed of its veins and goes through a special salting process. The Torah tells us that blood is forbidden to be eaten by Jewish people. In order to eat meat, we must see to it that all the blood is taken out first. Our Sages taught us a method for removing the blood while the meat was still raw. Salt has the ability to draw blood out of meat. The meat is first softened in water for a half hour and then it is salted with coarse salt. When the piece of meat is completely covered, it is allowed to remain on a grated drain board for one hour and then it is thoroughly rinsed. After this process the meat is completely kosher. It is ready to be cooked and served. This process is not necessary if the meat is to be broiled since fire itself draws out the blood.

The law of blood also applies to eggs. Nowadays, most eggs are candled so there is little chance that you may find an egg with a blood spot. If, however, one is found, it is forbidden to eat it. When eggs are opened for cooking or baking, they should be examined for blood spots.

FOWL. If your main course was chicken, it had pretty much the same treatment. The Torah tells us that there are twenty-four families among the birds and fowl that are forbidden as food. Any bird or fowl not of those families can be eaten. We know by tradition that certain birds are kosher because they do not belong to these families. They are: geese, chickens, turkeys, pigeons and ducks. After your chicken was chosen, it went through the same slaughtering and salting process as the meat, mentioned above.

OTHER FOODS. Vegetables and fruits have no qualifications, but they must be checked to make sure they have no worms or insects. We may use any vegetable or fruit and prepare it in any way we choose.

Lobsters, crabs, clams and mussels are prohibited according to the Torah. They are mentioned specifically.

MEAT AND DAIRY. The Torah tells us that meat and dairy products may not be cooked together. The law appears in three different places in the Torah to emphasize its importance and to teach us that we are not only forbidden to eat such a combination, but we are also forbidden to cook it, or to get any use out of it. Our Sages said that we must wait six hours after a meat meal before we are allowed to eat dairy and a half-hour after dairy before we can eat meat. In order to make sure that these products are never mixed, even in the smallest amounts, we are told to have separate dishes and separate utensils. Many people have separate tablecloths and dish towels. Products which are neither meat nor dairy are called "Pareve." Such products may be used either with meat or with dairy.

We know very little about the reasons for the Jewish dietary laws, but there is one thing about them that is quite obvious. Kosher food means clean food. Even Gentiles often prefer to buy kosher food for that very reason. The care and thorough inspection that is given to meat before it can be called kosher guarantees us that this meat has met the highest sanitary and health standards. A kosher home is a home of which to be proud. It will earn the respect and admiration of all who enter it.

THE BLOOD SPOTS

Like a magnet pulling metal to itself the stranger drew the eyes of everyone sitting in the dining room of Polokoff's Inn. In that poor working town in Poland it was a rare sight to see a stranger and one so beautifully dressed was an even rarer sight.

"Are you the mistress of this inn?" he politely inquired of the woman wearing an apron.

"I am sir. May I be of service to you?"

"Thank you madam. I have come a long way and I'm very hungry. I can pay well if you would be kind enough to prepare a small meal for me. And then I must be off for I have business with your mayor."

"I have a special treat for the gentleman. This morning we received a wonderful surprise, a whole dozen eggs! Oh! perhaps sir, you are not aware that in this part of Poland eggs are very scarce these days?"

The stranger smiled. "I live just a few kilometers from here," he said, "and eggs are hard to get in our city too. I would be truly grateful, Madam Polokoff, if you would be kind enough to prepare an omelet for me."

"I feel it my duty to warn you that under the circumstances the eggs will be quite expensive."

"Expense can be no barrier if a man is hungry and has an opportunity to eat a delicacy," the stranger answered. He took off his gloves and then hung his coat on the rack.

The stranger watched, first with anticipation and then with

mounting curiosity as the mistress of the inn prepared his meal. She broke the first egg carefully, poured the contents from one half shell to the other and then threw the egg away. She repeated this strange process seven times, each time throwing the egg away after she had inspected it. At last she put two eggs into the bowl and proceeded to make the omelet. The stranger could not contain himself any longer.

"Why did you throw away those expensive eggs?" he practically shouted.

"Unfortunately, I had to, sir," the woman replied. "All the eggs I threw away had blood spots. The Torah, our Supreme Law, forbids Jews to eat blood in any form."

"But I am not of your faith and have no objections to eating eggs with blood spots. At least allow me to compensate you for the eggs you wasted on my account."

"Thank you, sir, but I cannot accept any money. The eggs belong to me and if I cannot use them for my customers it is my loss. Taking money from you for this would be a violation of my principles."

The stranger finished his omelet and expressed his amazement at this law that did not allow anyone the use of blood. On his journey home the stranger again thought about the Jewish law concerning blood. Two years passed before he again had occasion to remember it.

One morning, two years later, John Stephanski, Governor of one of the largest provinces in Poland (our "stranger" of the inn), read with amazement the screaming headlines in the leading newspaper of his province, "Jews are killing Christian children to provide blood for their Passover Matzos. . . . The populace is enraged. . . . Taking matters in their own hands, the mob killed 152 Jews." The governor read the article that detailed the blood accusation and its aftermath in horror.

No, they are wrong. I know they are wrong! Now, clearly remembering his visit to the Jewish inn and the "egg omelet," he decided to stop this slaughter of the innocent. He called his servant and told him to hasten and saddle his horse. I must ride into the city immediately, he told himself.

When he arrived he saw that the streets of the city were red with blood and that many bodies were strewn around. He rushed to the home of his friend the mayor. He had no time for preliminaries.

"What is the meaning of these mass slaughters?" he shouted.

"The town has gone wild," answered Mayor Kruchensky. "These Jews should be tried in a court before they are killed."

"Before they are killed? What are you talking about! The Jews are innocent. I can prove it."

"How, tell me."

Governor Stephanski then told Mayor Kruchensky the incident which had occurred at Polokoff's Inn two years before, and he explained about the law against using blood in any form, for any reason, making it impossible for Jews to want to use blood in baking their Passover "matzos."

Mayor Kruchensky then called a town meeting and asked Governor Stephanski to speak before the group. Governor Stephanski then explained to all the townspeople about the Jewish law forbidding the use of blood at any time. "In the name of justice," he pleaded, "stop accusing the Jews and then murdering them, for the Jews are truly innocent."

And so ended the blood accusations and the mass murders in this little city in northern Poland.

CIRCUMCISION AND REDEMPTION OF THE FIRSTBORN

CIRCUMCISION. It is a positive commandment in the Torah that every Jewish male must be circumcised on the eighth day after his birth. It is done either by his father, if he is qualified, or another man well versed in the laws of circumcision, called "Moheil." This law was given for the first time to Abraham who circumcised himself and all the males in his household. The Torah tells us that circumcision is a treaty between G-D and Israel. It is a sign of our allegiance to Him and His Law, and of His promise to be with us, to protect us and to bring us blessing throughout the generations.

G-D promised Abraham that he would be the father of a great nation. He would be given the land of Canaan, part of which is today known as Israel. It is the act of circumcision that brings every male child into the ranks of the Jewish people and for this reason the circumcision, or as it is called in Hebrew, the "Bris," ceremony is always celebrated with joy and festivity.

The "Bris" ceremony is so important that it must be performed on the eighth day after the child is born no matter what day it may happen to be. Should the eighth day fall on a "Shabbos" then the "Bris" is performed on that day and it is not considered to be a violation of the "Shabbos." The same rule holds true for Yom Kippur. The feast that usually follows the "Bris," however, may not be held on Yom Kippur; it being a fast day, only the ceremony is permitted.

If for any reason the "Bris" may not be performed on the eighth day because the child is not well, it may be postponed until he recovers. In this case, the "Bris" may not be scheduled for a "Shabbos" or holiday.

Circumcision has been recognized by the world as a valuable health measure. It is advised by most doctors and is performed on many non-Jewish children. This is one more proof that the Bible shows the wisdom of G-D. What human being could have known the value of such a law so many years ago?

REDEMPTION OF THE FIRSTBORN—ANOTHER SYMBOL

"And it came to pass that at midnight the Lord killed all the firstborn in the land of Egypt, from the firstborn of Pharaoh that sat on the throne to the firstborn of the captives that were in the dungeons; and all the firstborn of cattle."

As you have learned in the previous chapters of this book, the Jews are a people of symbols. For example, in our religion we have many laws that are given to us to help us remember certain ideas about G-D and man. The "Tephillin," the "Mezuzah," as well as the "Tzitzis" are good examples of these symbols.

The law of the redemption of the firstborn is another one of our symbols. It comes to remind us of the exodus of the Israelites from Egypt and the moral duties given to the firstborn son of every family because of this great event.

You remember from your study of Jewish holidays and history that the last of the ten plagues the Lord brought upon the Egyptians was the killing of the firstborn. As the Bible quotation at the beginning of this chapter tells us, all the firstborn, both of men and of animals were killed. The Israelites, as you know, were unharmed. This great miracle was so important that the Jew was told to remind himself of it at the birth of his firstborn son and the firstborn male among his flocks. Both must be dedicated to G-D. The firstborn male of his flocks was to be brought to the Temple in Jerusalem as a sacrifice to G-D. The firstborn son was also to be dedicated to G-D but in a different way. Originally he was to serve in the Temple as an aide to the priest, but later it was decided that he was to be redeemed from Temple service by his father and was to dedicate himself to the teaching of the ways of G-D to his own family. He was to serve as a representative of G-D's Law and its defender.

Today, since our Temple has been destroyed, we no longer have animal sacrifice. We can no longer bring the firstborn of our flocks to the Temple as a sacrifice to G-D. But it has to be given to a "Kohein" who keeps it till it sustains a blemish, after which he may use it. The beautiful ceremony of the redemption of the firstborn son, however, is still in practice.

It is necessary to have a "Kohein" (a member of the priestly family of Aaron) from whom to redeem the firstborn son and it is customary to choose a worthy "Kohein" for this great honor.

THE CEREMONY OF THE FIRSTBORN. The ceremony of the redemption of the firstborn son is performed on the thirty-first day after birth. If the thirty-first day falls on a Sabbath or holiday, then the ceremony is postponed until the next day.

The table is set for a meal. The opening blessing "Hamotsee," thanking G-D for our bread, is recited. The baby is brought in by his father, placed before the "Kohein" and the ceremony begins. The "Kohein" asks the father why he has come and the father replies, "I have come to redeem my son." The father takes out five silver dollars, holds them in his hand and recites the blessing, "Blessed art Thou, O Lord our G-D, King of the Universe who hast made us Holy by

Thy commandments and commanded us concerning the redemption of the firstborn." He then recites the "Shehecheyonu," a blessing that is recited when doing certain things for the first time. The father then gives the silver dollars to the "Kohein" who takes the money, holds it in front of the child and announces, "This money shall be in place of this child." The firstborn is then blessed by the "Kohein" with the traditional blessing of the "Kohanim," which dates back to the time of Aaron, the "Kohein."

At the end of the ceremony it is customary for the "Kohein" to return the money he received as a gift to the child. It is a noble custom to choose a "Kohein" who is needy and to allow him to keep the money. In this way one earns two "Mitzvos" at once.

If one knows for certain that he was not redeemed when he was a child, it is his duty to redeem himself (if he is a firstborn) even if he is an adult.

If the father is a "Kohein" or a "Levi," or the mother is the daughter of one, they do not need a redemption ceremony for their child.

The redemption of the firstborn son is one of the most colorful ceremonies of our tradition. In Hebrew we call it "Pidyon Habein."

DEATH TOOK A HOLIDAY

Shortly before the birth of Rabbi Judah Hanassi, the Roman emperor decreed that the Jewish people were not permitted to circumcise their children, on penalty of death.

When Rabbi Judah was born, his father, Rabbi Shimon ben Gamaliel, thought hard how to carry out the sacred commandment of the Torah without endangering his and the child's life. When the eighth day came, Rabbi Shimon did not hesitate long. "Why should I break a commandment of G-D because of a wicked decree by a human being," he decided, and disregarded the consequences, by circumcising his infant son himself.

Somehow the governor of the land of Israel, then under Roman rule, got wind of Rabbi Shimon's act of disobedience and had him brought before the court.

"Why did you act against the decree of the emperor?" he asked the widely revered sage. Rabbi Shimon replied that no decree of any earthly king could undo the laws made by G-D. And since G-D had ordered the circumcision, he had no choice but to obey the Divine command.

The governor had high respect for Rabbi Shimon who was the princely leader of the Jewish people. Yet there was no doubt that the patriarch was guilty of a serious crime against the ruler of the land. He therefore ordered Rabbi Shimon to bring his wife and young child before the emperor in Rome.

On the way Rabbi Shimon ben Gamaliel's wife stayed in an inn. It so happened that the innkeeper's wife had given birth to a son about the same time as Rabbi Judah's mother, and called

him Antoninus. The two mothers became very friendly. Antoninus'
mother soon discovered that the Jewish woman was very sad
and worried. She asked what was the cause of the trouble, and
was told about the purpose of this dangerous journey, which
undoubtedly would end in the death of the child, perhaps also
of his parents. The woman was very kindhearted and hated to
think of such a frightful end for the beautiful child. She therefore offered to give her son Antoninus, who was not circumcised,
to the Jewish mother so that she could prove her innocence before
the Roman emperor, while the Jewish baby would stay with her
until she returned.

Happy over this solution, Rabbi Judah's mother continued her
journey with the young Antoninus in her arms. When she arrived before the emperor and the Roman ruler saw that the
child was not circumcised, he became very angry at his governor
who apparently tried to make a fool of him. Without further investigation he sent a detachment of soldiers to seize him. Rabbi
Judah's mother, however, was given presents and sent back to
her husband, Rabbi Shimon ben Gamaliel.

The happy mother went back to the inn of the kind woman
and, full of gratitude, restored Antoninus to his mother. Antoninus' mother was happy to have helped her Jewish friend cheat
death and save her baby. Said the good woman: "Since G-D
saved your child through mine, the two boys shall be friends
forever."

Rabbi Judah grew up to be the leader of Israel, while Antoninus became one of the great liberals of the Roman Empire,
and for many years governor of the land of Israel.

All through their lives the two remained close personal friends.
Antoninus eventually accepted the Jewish faith and Rabbi Judah
Hanassi personally introduced him into the world of the Torah
and Judaism.

SOME INTERESTING AND IMPORTANT TORAH LAWS

THE TORAH WITH REGARD TO ANIMALS. If you studied your Bible history well, you will probably recall an interesting statement concerning the last of the ten plagues cast upon the Egyptians. Nothing and no one will stop the Israelites from leaving Egypt, the Bible tells us. All will be quiet and respectful. Not even the barking of a dog will be heard. Our Sages tell us that as reward for the respect shown by even the smallest dog, the dog was to have a part in Jewish life. If certain foods are considered unfit for human consumption, the Bible specifically tells us that they should be given to the dog as a reward throughout the generations for his restraint at the time of the exodus.

It is forbidden, according to the Torah, to hurt any living creature. On the contrary, it is one's duty to save living creatures from pain.

A typical example of the attitude in the Torah toward all G-D's creatures is a law concerning birds. The Torah tells us that if we see a bird's nest in a tree or on the ground with young ones or eggs in it and the mother sitting on them we may not take the mother and her young together; we must send the mother away. This law also applies to the slaughter of animals. The Torah tells us that the mother and her young should not be slaughtered on the same day.

40

If an animal has caused injury and damage and endangers the lives or the well-being of the people of the community, however, it is one's duty to kill it.

Animals may be used for medical research purposes, however, even though such practices may endanger their lives.

LAWS CONCERNING PHYSICAL INJURY. One is forbidden to cause injury to his fellow man by striking him directly or by any other means. Even raising one's hand against a friend or neighbor is considered wrong.

One is forbidden to do anything even on one's own premises that may cause harm or annoyance to one's neighbor.

The one who injures his neighbor, even though he gives money as compensation for the injury done, cannot be fully forgiven until he asks pardon from him.

THEFTS. It is forbidden to steal even a trifle from a Jew or non-Jew. Giving short change, short weight or short measure is considered stealing if it is done on purpose.

Cheating of any kind, even though it does not involve any loss of money to the other person, is forbidden.

It is forbidden to buy from the thief an article known to have been stolen. If we know that the seller is not a trustworthy person, we should not purchase anything from him.

It is forbidden to accept any charity from a known thief unless we know that he has repented of his ways.

It is forbidden to derive benefit from anything belonging to our neighbor without his knowledge even if we know that our neighbor will not mind. The "Tallis" is the only exception to this rule.

CHUKIM: THE LAWS OF SHATNEZ, TATTOOING AND SHAVING. As you know from reading the chapter on the dietary laws, there are certain laws in the Torah that were not explained and, therefore, we do not know the reasons for them. We are told by G-D through Moses that such laws are to be obeyed even though we do not know why we must obey them. These laws go under the general classification of "Chukim."

"But, why should we obey laws when we don't know the reason for them?"

How often does this question come up in class? Although it may be asked by only one member of the class, it is probably in the minds of most, just as surely as it is in the minds of most of you reading this chapter. Perhaps this question can be answered for you in the following pages.

Have you ever asked yourself why we need reasons? Well, let us tell you. When Columbus said that the world was round nobody believed him. His theory had to be investigated and proved correct before it was accepted. After all, Columbus was only a human being, he could have been wrong.

It took a long time before the world accepted the theory that the earth was round. But, why do we look for reasons in the Torah? Is it to find out whether the laws in the Torah are right? To find out whether G-D's laws are justifiable? Surely we know that G-D is right in everything that He wills. Can we question the ways of G-D? Can we question any law He has given us in His Holy Torah? Surely we do not need reasons for that purpose.

There is another purpose, however, in looking for reasons, which is applicable to our Torah. We look for reasons so that we can understand things. In classrooms all over the world, subjects like science, mathematics, geography, psychology and astronomy are studied to learn the laws of G-D in nature. We are always trying to learn more and more about the world we live in by understanding the reasons for things. When our rabbis studied the Torah, they found many deep meanings to the laws given by G-D. They taught these meanings to their students and studied them among themselves. Logical reasons were even given for some of the "Chukim." To this day, rabbis are finding new ideas in the Torah. This is the beauty of Torah. We never know everything about it. The more we study it, the more we learn about it.

So you see, we don't have to know the reason for a certain law in order to obey it. We obey these laws because they are given to us by G-D. Since He gave them to us, we know that they are right. Who knows, perhaps the "Chukim" were purposely given without reasons, just to test our faith in G-D.

SHATNEZ. One of the "Chukim" given to us in the Torah is the law of "Shatnez." We are commanded not to wear any garment that contains a mixture of wool and linen. This mixture is called "Shatnez." As these two materials are sometimes used in the manufacture of clothing, it is proper to have one's clothing checked in a "non-Shatnez" laboratory and have them remove the "Shatnez" if there is any.

TATTOOING. Another "Chok" (singular for Chukim) given to us by G-D is the prohibition of any kind of tattooing. By tattoos we mean permanent tattoos that are etched into the skin and cannot be erased. Many of our Sages felt that the reason for this prohibition can be found in the fact that tattooing was a common practice among the idol worshipers. In order to keep the Jewish people pure in their belief in one G-D, they were forbidden to imitate idol worshipers in any way.

SHAVING THE TEMPLES AND FACE. If you have ever traveled through some particularly Jewish sections of New York City, you may have seen many Jews wearing beards. Some of you may have grandfathers who wear beards. If you asked your parents why some people wear beards, they may have answered that they do so for religious reasons. Perhaps you felt that this answer was not sufficient. Let us find the full reason why some Jews wear beards.

The idea of wearing a beard does not come to us directly from the Torah. It is a custom accepted by some pious Jews. There is a law in the Torah, a "chok," that prohibits the shaving of the face with a razor. Another prohibition also includes the sideburns. Again, we do not know the reason for this prohibition, but the theory given by many of our Sages is that this custom was also practiced by idol worshipers. If the beard can be removed by another means rather than a razor, it is permissible.

Years ago, it was found that a certain powder, mixed with water could be used on the face to remove the beard. Since this was sometimes painful and irritating to the face, it was not used by many people. The only other alternative was to let the beard grow.

With the invention of the electric shaver, which operates like a scissor, a method was finally found for the removal of the beard without a razor. It was widely accepted by religious Jews as a permissible method of shaving and it is used by them to this day. There are some Jews, however, who would rather wear a beard to preserve the ancient tradition, and so they do not shave in any way.

THE LITTLE TYRANT

This true story was taken from the "Memoirs" of Rabbi Joseph I. Schneersohn (of blessed memory).

Once upon a time there lived in a little town in Russia called Harki, a melamed (teacher) whose name was Rabbi Nissan. He taught many Jewish children in Cheder (Hebrew school), and loved them dearly. He loved them no less than his own little son Yitzchak Saul. He also loved animals and birds and all G-D's creatures, for he was a very kindly man indeed.

Rabbi Nissan's favorite pet was a rooster. He treasured it so much because very early every morning it used to crow loudly and wake him up to go to Shul. He therefore personally looked after it, making sure it had enough to eat, and kept it in good condition, so that nothing should affect its excellent, clear crowing.

Every evening he used to bring it into the house, and put it in a warm, dry place, underneath the oven. Thus he would be sure to hear its crowing and wake in time to go to "davven."

The louder the rooster crowed, the more pleased was Rabbi Nissan. But not so his little son Yitzchak Saul. As much as his father loved the rooster, so did his young son hate it, and he delighted in persecuting the bird at every opportunity. Whenever his father was out of the way, little Yitzchak Saul used to chase the poor rooster all over the yard! He treated animals in no kindlier manner.

They had a "broody" hen which eventually hatched her eggs, and fluffy little chickens emerged, which were a joy to behold.

But the little tyrant used to pick up small stones and aim them at the birds, making them "run for their lives" all over the yard!

He thought nothing of catching flies and placing them inside a spider's web, so that he could have the pleasure of watching the struggle between the flies and the spider, until the latter finally captured its victims and killed them.

And if he could get a dog to chase a cat, why that was one of his special delights.

But one day, unnoticed by him, his father had come into the yard and observed his son's cruel behavior. Suddenly, Yitzchak Saul felt a heavy hand on his shoulder and, looking up, beheld his father's angry face.

"So this is the way you spend your time! Ill-treating helpless creatures!" his father rebuked him sternly. "I could never imagine that a child of mine could be so cruel!"

The frightened little boy thought his father would surely give him a beating, he looked so angry. He was a "melamed" and everybody knows that boys can drive any teacher to losing his temper, with blows to follow.

But Rabbi Nissan had never in all his experience laid a hand upon a pupil. His "Strap" was on the wall of the classroom, it is true. But if a pupil deserved a punishment, Rabbi Nissan had only to indicate the strap on the wall, and tell him what he deserved, and it was always enough for the culprit. He felt he had "had it" and resolved to make amends.

Rabbi Nissan's pupils, in fact, respected their teacher and were more afraid of him than the pupils of other teachers, who used the strap and enforced discipline and order by this means.

Entering the house with his son, Rabbi Nissan asked him to bring the book of the Talmud-"Shabbos" and open it at page 125 and loudly repeat the "Mishnah" relating the injunction to look after chickens with gentle care, lowering the basket for them to go out or to come in, until they were big enough and strong enough to manage it for themselves.

"See how the Torah thinks of everything and allows us to do

something on "Shabbos" which otherwise we are not allowed to touch, so that the tender little chickens should not have to hurt themselves by jumping a distance beyond their capacity!" Rabbi Nissan patiently explained this to his little son. "Then in 'Berachoth' we find on page 40 that we must never sit down to a meal before first looking after the dumb creatures. For first we find the saying: "I shall give grass in thy field for thy animals," and later, "And thou shalt eat and be satisfied."

"Thus we see that we must first of all care for the other of G-D's creatures before we look after our own needs. Yet you, my son, have not only ignored this teaching, but have, moreover, shown a cruelty towards the poor creatures which I could hardly have believed possible in a child of mine! You have acted murderously, and in a bloodthirsty manner!"

Yitzchak Saul trembled before the reproof and reproach in his father's cutting tones. He thought his father had finished with him when instead he heard his father saying in a very serious tone:

"You know that it is not in my nature to hit anyone, and I have never beaten you, but this time I am going to ask you to take down that 'cat-o'-nine-tails' which you see hanging on the wall, and I am going to whip you. I want you to feel the taste of real pain such as you have inflicted upon the creatures you have so thoughtlessly persecuted."

Yitzchak Saul, paling, took a chair and reached up for the strap which he had never before seen his father use. This in itself impressed upon him the enormity of his crime in his father's eyes.

His father very gravely took it from him and told him to stretch out on the bench, face downwards.

"Before I whip you," he said, "I want you to know quite clearly that the only reason I am doing this is that you will the better remember the pain you have inflicted upon the birds and other living creatures."

These were the first and last blows that Yitzchak Saul ever

received at the hand of his father, and he accepted them without
a murmur.

After the whipping, Rabbi Nissan quickly went into another
room without a backward glance, and a moment later Yitzchak
Saul heard his father crying, deep and painful sobs escaping
him, which he seemed unable to suppress.

When Yitzchak Saul heard his father's sobbing, he realized it
was all his fault for having made his father do something so
contrary to his nature, that is, to use the "cat-o'-nine-tails" which
had always seemed part of the furniture until now, and never
an instrument of "physical" punishment.

This gave the little boy more pain than the actual whipping,
and he determined from that moment, never again to hurt
anything or anyone.

He felt the pain for a couple of days, and walked about full of
regret and shame for his misdeeds. On the third day, he suddenly
went up to his father, kissed his hand, and asked him with tears
in his eyes, if he would forgive him.

Rabbi Nissan's eyes also filled with tears as he said to his son
tenderly: "My son, you are still a little boy and I, your father,
have to bear all your sins, which are not quite so serious. But it
would be dreadful if you grew up to be an unfeeling, bloodthirsty creature!"

Yitzchak Saul became a changed boy. So elevated was he since
his father's "lesson," that he could almost believe it was someone
else who had perpetrated the sinful cruelties which had earned
him such a just punishment.

During the following days and nights, he was haunted by
visions of himself, chasing and persecuting the birds, dogs,
cats, goats, and flies. But gone was his previous pleasure in such
pastimes. Instead these visions filled him with fear and pain, and
he knew he could never again inflict pain and be cruel.

LAWS CONCERNING MAN AND HIS FELLOW MAN

THE JEW AND HIS MORALS. One of the purposes of the Jewish religion is to teach morality to the world. The moral laws are the basis of our religion. The Ten Commandments that we received on Mount Sinai were divided into two parts. The first five commandments are laws between man and G-D. The other five commandments are laws between man and his fellow man. Just as the two sides of the Tablets are united so must we remember to follow both the laws of man and his G-D and the laws of man and his fellow man. A righteous man is considered righteous only if he accepts and follows all the laws.

PRIDE. What are morals and vices? How can we improve our morals and our virtues? Too much pride is a serious vice. Sometimes we refuse to do the right thing because we are afraid it will hurt our pride. Pride can also keep us from helping ourselves. We may need some help in our school-work, but we are too proud to ask for it. Often we insult a friend and we are too proud to apologize. Pride may satisfy us for the moment, but we will regret it later. We must learn to be humble and not to shy away from a little discomfort if it will help us or others in the long run.

ANGER. Did you ever hear the expression, "Always count to ten before you get angry?" What does it mean? It really teaches us an important lesson. It teaches us the importance of being calm at all costs. Anger seldom accomplishes anything good. When we are angry, we often say things that we regret later. We often insult our dearest friends for a silly reason. When we are angry, we have very little control over our actions or over our words. We may strike someone and harm him seriously for no reason at all. Let's always remember to think twice before getting angry—count to ten.

A GOOD FRIEND. Do you remember the saying, "You can tell a man by the company he keeps"? How true this is. Good people have good friends. One of the greatest blessings we can have is a good friend. Friends can help us enjoy ourselves. They can join us in work and in study. They can often help us in time of trouble or sorrow, for, as the saying goes, " a friend in need is a friend indeed." We must choose our friends very carefully so that they will not only be good companions, but good influences upon us.

LOVE YOUR NEIGHBOR. The famous words "love your neighbor as yourself" are taken from the Bible. It is a phrase used as a proverb by many people and many religions. With us it is more than a proverb; it is a law. A Jew is commanded by law to love all people, for we were all created in the image of G-D. We must show our love by always being ready to help others. If one sees his fellow man about to commit a crime, he should try to stop him. He should make his friend aware of the punishment for the crime and show him how wrong it would be to go against the laws of G-D. He should try his best to show his friends and acquaintances the right way of life by being a good example himself.

Ever since our father Abraham, the Jew has been the teacher of "good" to the people of the world. This has been our mission upon the earth as was decided for us by G-D. We must try our best to fulfill our mission, for it is only with our mission completed that the world will achieve everlasting peace. It is only when we have taught the world to live by the word of G-D that we will have accomplished our goal.

THE BEAUTY OF CHARITY. Do you know the Hebrew word for charity? What does it really mean? We do not believe that when we give money to the poor we are being generous. To the Jew it is the duty of everyone to give to the poor. Help should be given with a joyful feeling. We should feel proud that we have the privilege of helping our fellow man. Giving to the poor is our way of sharing the wealth that G-D has so generously given to some of us.

But this is not the only form of charity. A beautiful Jewish custom is to invite guests to our house on Friday evening to share the Sabbath meal with us. In some Eastern European communities it was customary for the poor to wait in the synagogue at the end of the Friday evening service. As the congregants were leaving the synagogue they would take with them a guest for the Sabbath.

Another beautiful custom in Eastern Europe, as well as in some of our communities here in the United States, is collecting money for a poor bride and groom. It is one of the greatest "Mitzvos" for it means contributing to the building of a new Jewish family. Both the contributor and the collector earn a reward for this "Mitzvah."

Charity can be given in a great many ways. We can help others by giving a needy person a job. We help our brothers and sisters in Israel by giving money to the various organizations collecting for them.

One of the nicest ways to give charity is giving it secretly. In this way we are sure that the person who needs it is not embarrassed. The best way of giving charity is for the giver not to know to whom it goes and for the receiver not to know from whom it comes.

The most important thing in giving charity is the giving. The amount is only secondary. Our Sages tell us that even a poor man who receives charity from others should give a certain amount, no matter how small it may be, so that he too may gain the "Mitzvah" of charity.

In the days of the Temple in Jerusalem, there stood a large chest near the Temple entrance. It had a hole at the top. The people of means who passed this chest would drop some coins into it; those who were poor and needed the money would take as much as they needed.

In most Jewish homes there is some kind of charity fund. In many homes there is a special box on the wall or the shelf called the "Tzedoko Box," that is used for charity collecting. It is a beautiful Jewish custom for the mother of the household to drop in a few coins just before she lights the Sabbath candles on Friday night.

We must always remember that the Hebrew word for charity is "Tzedoko." It des not mean generosity or pity. It means "right." When we give "Tzedoko," we are giving what our duty demands; we are doing what is right. Every time we drop a few pennies in the "Tzedoko Box" or give a donation to a needy person, let us remember that it is only through the grace of G-D that we are givers and not recipients.

HONOR DUE TO PARENTS. Long ago, in the days of the Temple, it happened that some precious jewels were needed for the robe of the High Priest. The jewels could be found nowhere and the robe could not be finished. After searching for many weeks, it was discovered that an obscure merchant, who dealt in precious stones, had just the right stones needed. Representatives of the Sages of Israel were immediately sent to purchase them. When they reached the merchant's house, they were greeted by his son.

"We have come to buy some precious stones needed for the High Priest's robe," they said.

"I would like very much to help you," he replied, "but you will have to come back a bit later."

"What?" they exclaimed. "Do you not realize that to help make the High Priest's robe is a great honor?"

"I do realize the importance of this great deed," replied the boy, "but you see, the precious stones are in a box. Father is the only one who has the key. He keeps it under his pillow so that it cannot be stolen or lost. He is sleeping now, and if I were to try to get it, he would surely awaken. Would I not be violating the commandment, 'Honor your father and your mother,' if I were to do such a thing?"

The Sages were amazed by the boy's reply. They waited for the father to awaken and they praised the boy for his righteousness.

Would you say that this story illustrates honor to parents? "Honor," you say, "why this story illustrates true saintliness."

Yes, that is what is expected of Jewish children, and adults. Honor to parents was considered so important that it was included in the Ten Commandments. How can we honor our parents according to Jewish law? Let's find out.

Our Sages tell us that honoring parents is equivalent to honoring G-D, for when we honor our parents, we are following one of G-D's commandments and we are, thereby, honoring Him.

One must fear and obey his parents just as one fears and obeys G-D. Parents are G-D's representatives. It is they who are our first teachers in the way of life. It is they who make us aware of G-D, and it is their behavior and concern for our health and happiness that teaches us to walk in the ways of G-D. By obeying them, we obey G-D.

One must not contradict his father or correct him in the presence of others, even if we know that he is wrong. If we are sure that he has made a mistake, we should wait until he is alone and then offer our opinion. If it is a matter that is urgent, we should call him aside and tell him our views. Embarrassing him in front of others would be a great dishonor.

If one's parent is ill and cannot care for himself it is the duty of the children to do their utmost for him. It must be done as an obligation and not as an act of charity. It must be done with love and with the greatest respect so as not to hurt his feelings.

It is the duty of every Jew to honor his parents even after their death. The best honor we can give them is to walk in the ways of G-D. We should also honor them by honoring their name. Giving to charitable institutions and organizations is one way. Another way is to commemorate their names in the form of memorial plaques in the synagogue, by attending services regularly, and by helping others to learn about G-D and how to worship Him.

Let us always remember that the greatest honor we can give our parents is to do good deeds and respect the rights of others, for the greatest pleasure a parent has is when he hears people say, "Happy are the parents who raised such a child."

HONOR TO TEACHERS, SCHOLARS AND THE AGED. If medals were awarded to the nations in the world who preached and practiced good conduct, respect to others, and honor to the worthy, the choice would have to include the Jewish people. It is the Torah which preaches these ideals. It has kept the Jews together through the many years of suffering and persecution. The Torah has been our weapon against any army that we have ever encountered. It has won every war against every nation that has tried to destroy us. It was our teachers and scholars who taught us how to use this spiritual weapon and it is our elders who can tell us from experience how useful this weapon has been. For this reason we always were and always will be respectful and reverent towards our rabbis and teachers.

What is a Jewish scholar and teacher?

A scholar must not only be a man who preaches good deeds; he must be a man who practices what he preaches. He must love his fellow man and do his utmost for him at all times. He must devote his time to the study of Torah and to the practice of its ideals. A man who has spent his time learning Torah and does not follow it is worthless. He has not gained anything from his study. In Judaism, it is the deed and not the words that are most important.

When a man has earned the name of "scholar" according to the Jewish concept of the term, he is given the greatest respect and honor. We are commanded to rise when a scholar enters the room. (This custom is practiced in our courtrooms today when the judge walks up to his bench).

A teacher, according to Jewish law, deserves the same respect as a parent. It is the teacher who becomes our guide to the ways of G-D when we reach school age. He fills the position of the parent and should for this reason be given equal respect.

In our religion old age is a great blessing, for when one reaches old age, he has much knowledge and experience. He can advise us in time of need. We are commanded, therefore, also to rise when an old man enters the room.

VISITING THE SICK. How many of us can remember the lonely feeling of having to stay in bed because of some illness? Our mothers certainly remember those days in bed, when we had nothing to do but annoy and pester them. How mother and you both wished that a friend would come in to talk with you and take you out of your boredom for at least a little while. And then one day a friend did come. What a pleasure it was to talk to someone your own age, to find out about things at school and the news around the block. When it was time for him to go home, didn't you wish that he could stay just a little while longer?

When a person takes ill with a disease that is not contagious, it is the duty of his friends and relatives to visit him and relieve him of his boredom and discomfort. This custom is known as "Bikur Cholim." They must try to cater to his needs. They must offer what help they can, especially if financial help is necessary.

When our Sages told us that it was our duty to visit the sick, they knew quite well the importance of this "Mitzvah," for there is nothing greater than helping a friend when he needs it most. Our Sages tell us that a visit to a sick person takes away one sixtieth of his illness.

There is one type of help that we can offer to the sick that involves a minimum of effort on our part; it is a prayer to G-D to help the sick. This prayer is recited in the synagogue at the Torah reading service on Mondays, Thursdays, on the Sabbath and at any other time when the Torah is read. The name of the sick person is submitted to the rabbi or sexton, who recites the prayer. Upon the passing of one's father, mother, brother, sister, husband, wife, or child, it is a Jewish law to have seven days of mourning. This seven-day mourning period is called "Shiva" which means "Seven." It is a very important "Mitzvah" at this time, for friends and relatives to visit the mourners to comfort them in their sorrow. This "Mitzvah" is called "Nichum Aveilim" which means "Comforting the Mourners."

YOHRTZEIT: ITS MEANING AND PRACTICE. When a flower withers it is soon forgotten, and when an animal dies it leaves no lasting memories behind. But, when a human being passes away, he leaves a great many memories and thoughts in the hearts of all those who knew him. To his family, he leaves the memory of the happy years they shared together. To his friends, perhaps the memory of the helping hand he offered them in time of need. And to the world, he leaves the memory of his devotion to G-D, to country and to his fellow men.

Our religion teaches us that these memories should never die; they must remain forever in the minds and hearts of the living.

Yohrtzeit is the Yiddish word for anniversary. We use this particular term only in reference to the anniversary of a death. Our Sages tell us that the day of the death of a parent or other close relatives should be marked and remembered throughout our lives. We should remind ourselves of the love and devotion they showed us during their lifetime. We should rededicate ourselves each year at the time of the Yohrtzeit to put into daily practice the good teachings and morals that they taught us when they were living.

On the evening of the Yohrtzeit, it is customary to light a candle. This candle is a symbol of the soul which lives on although the body has died. The Yohrtzeit candle should burn until the following evening. The day of the Yohrtzeit is determined according to the Jewish calendar. If the Hebrew date of the Yohrtzeit is not known and cannot possibly be ascertained, a rabbi should be consulted.

"Kaddish" is a prayer of praise to G-D; it is not a memorial prayer. It is recited by the Cantor during the services. It is also recited by mourners during services for a period of eleven months during the first year, and every following year upon the "Yohrtzeit." The "Kaddish" is recited when one mourns because it shows that although G-D has taken away a person beloved by us, we nevertheless praise Him for His just acts.

In addition to the Yohrtzeit day, there are four other days during the year when we recall our departed ones. These days are Yom Kippur, "Shmini Atseres," which is the last day of "Succos," "Achron Shel Pesach," the last day of Passover, and the second day of "Shavuos." On these days a special memorial prayer is recited in the synagogue after the Torah reading. It is called "Yizkor." It is customary to pledge a donation to charity on this day in honor of the departed. It is proper for all who have parents that are living to leave the synagogue until the prayer is over since they do not recite it.

THE CASE OF THE HARSH LAWYER

Rabbi Nahum of Horodne, affectionately called Rabbi No-hum'ke Horodner, was a great friend of the poor. Every day he used to go out to make a door-to-door collection for the poor and needy. No one ever refused him a donation, although, heaven knows, they were all none too rich.

One day Rabbi Nohum'ke called at the house of a well-to-do lawyer. This lawyer kept aloof from the Jewish community. He never went to the synagogue, nor had anything to do with communal matters. The man had the reputation of being a good lawyer, but he was a hard man who had little sympathy and no love for the poor.

When Rabbi Nohum'ke asked the lawyer to contribute something to a good cause, the lawyer became annoyed:

"This is a hold-up!" the lawyer said arrogantly. "I shan't give you a kopek! Good day, sir!"

Rabbi Nohum'ke did not expect such an outburst, but he did not say anything. He walked out quietly. He felt a pain in his heart thinking of the starving poor children; but it was even more painful to him to think that there were such harsh and inconsiderate Jews like that lawyer.

A few days later, the lawyer found himself involved with the law. He spared no money to clear himself and gradually spent his entire fortune. But he failed withal, and was sentenced to a prison term of two years.

When Rabbi Nohum'ke heard of this news, however, he hastened to the house of the lawyer, and found the lawyer's wife in deep grief. Her husband had now been "Buried alive" for two years, and had left her like a widow without means, as the courts had eaten up everything that had been saved. How could she keep up her home and feed the children?

Rabbi Nohum'ke asked her how much she needed for her household expenses.

"Twenty-five rubles a week," she said.

That was a considerable sum, but Rabbi Nohum'ke produced the money and said: "Here is a loan of 25 rubles. Now, don't you change your mode of living. Don't sell anything of the household, and don't worry. Just carry on your home as you did when your husband was with you."

Thereafter, Rabbi Nohum'ke would drop into the house once a week, leave twenty-five rubles on the table, and walk out.

Two years passed, and the lawyer returned home. He came in and could not believe his own eyes! Everything was just as he had left it. He was sure his wife had sold everything to feed the family during his absence. Who took care of them? Who supported them during the two years of his absence?

"That wonderful old man!" she said gratefully. "You know the man who goes from door-to-door to collect for the poor? Well, he supplied me every week with 25 rubles! Never missed once during the two long years! Were it not for him, we might have starved to death"

Tears appeared in the lawyer's eyes as he listened to his wife, and then he hastened out to find Rabbi Nohum'ke. The lawyer begged Rabbi Nohum'ke's forgiveness for the way he treated him when Rabbi Nohum'ke first came into their house two years before. He also expressed his deep gratitude to the Rabbi for his great kindness. He promised Rabbi Nohum'ke that he would repay him the full amount of the loan from his first earnings.

From that day on, the lawyer was a changed man. He repaid the debt in full, and continued to give Rabbi Nohum'ke a generous contribution for the poor every week.

CAST THY BREAD UPON THE WATERS

On Succoth we read the Book of "Koheleth" which was written by the wisest of all men, King Solomon.

One of his wise sayings is:

"CAST THY BREAD UPON THE WATERS, FOR YOU SHALL FIND IT AFTER MANY DAYS." Which means: Always be ready to do a good turn even if you don't expect a reward for it. For, some day, you will surely find your reward waiting for you.

The following story is a good illustration of this saying.

Bar Kappara, one of the scholars who lived at the time of Rabbi Judah Hanassi, was once walking along the seashore of Caesaria, when he noticed a shipwreck in the distance. As he stood and looked, he saw a man swimming from the wreck towards the shore. The man was obviously a good swimmer. But as soon as he reached land, he almost collapsed with weariness. Bar Kappara went forward and gave him a helping hand. The man staggered ashore and begged him to assist him. Bar Kappara took him home, clothed him, fed him and offered him some money so that the man went away refreshed and encouraged.

Some years later, the Jews of Caesaria found themselves in difficulty with the local authorities and decided to send a petition to the Governor. They chose Bar Kappara to go and intercede on their behalf.

Bar Kappara prayed to G-D to guide him aright and help him succeed in his mission.

When Bar Kappara reached the Governor's palace, he asked

for permission to see the Governor. When his request was granted, he was ushered into the presence of the Governor. To his great astonishment, Bar Kappara recognized him as the same man whom he had once saved and helped on the shores of Caesaria.

"What can I do for you, my friend?" The Governor greeted him warmly, recognizing Bar Kappara as his one-time "friend in need."

Bar Kappara begged the Governor to use his authority in helping the Jews, on whose behalf he had now come to intercede.

The Governor listened carefully to the story Bar Kappara unfolded before him and then said:

"I will gladly do this favor for you, my friend, because when I was in such a desperate position you helped me to the maximum of your ability without asking for or expecting any reward. Because of your unselfishness and kindness to me, I shall now help your suffering brethren at your request."

Bar Kappara had brought a large sum of money as a gift to the Governor from his fellow-Jews. The Governor, however, gave the money back to Bar Kappara, saying:

"Take this money back as a gift from me. Although the sum of money you gave me was not as great as this, to me it meant everything at the time of my need. You may return to your brethren and tell them that I am helping them out of gratitude to you, and take my blessing with you."

Bar Kappara joyfully hurried back with the good news to his fellow-Jews who were anxiously awaiting his return.

Great was the rejoicing among them at Bar Kappara's good tidings, and they all acknowledged how true was the saying of King Solomon:

"CAST THY BREAD UPON THE WATERS, FOR YOU SHALL FIND IT AFTER MANY DAYS."

THE JEWISH CALENDAR

THE MOON AND THE JEWISH MONTH. Do you know the difference between a solar and a lunar calendar? Sol means sun, and luna means moon. The calendar used by the Western civilization is based upon the revolutions of the earth around the sun. This is the calendar used here, in the United States. A solar year is 365 and one-quarter days. Each calendar year is a quarter of a day less than a true solar year, therefore, at the end of four calendar years, one day is added to make up for the one-day loss. The Jewish people calculate their calendar according to the revolutions of the moon around the earth. A lunar year is 354 days, which is 11 days less than a solar year.

Now we have a problem. The Bible tells us that the pilgrimage holidays, "Succos," "Pesach" and "Shavuos" are seasonal holidays. They must occur during specific seasons of the year. Let us suppose that the holiday of Passover, which occurs on the 15th day of the Hebrew month of "Nissan," correspondingly occurs on the 15th day of April of that year. The following year, since the lunar year is 11 days shorter than the solar year, the holiday of Passover would occur 11 days earlier—the 4th of April. After a number of years Passover, instead of being a Spring holiday, would be a winter holiday because it might occur in the middle of January.

To avoid such an occurrence the wise men of Israel added

63

an extra month every second or third year. When the leap year occurs, the extra month is added right after the month of "Adar," and it is called "Adar Sheini," which means the second "Adar."

Have you ever wondered why the Jewish people use a lunar, rather than a solar, calendar? Well, this may help to explain it.

THE MOON AND THE JEWISH PEOPLE. The moon has always been likened to the Jewish people by our Sages. It is symbolic of the history of the Jews throughout the ages. Just as the moon, at the beginning of the month, is small and insignificant-looking, so the Jewish people are at present small and their influence upon the world is seemingly insignificant. But, just as the moon, day after day, reveals more of itself to us, so that at the middle of the month we see it in its fullness and its beauty, so the Jewish religion from day to day reveals more of itself and is being better understood by the nations of the world. And one day, perhaps not too far in the future, the Jewish people will succeed in teaching the world the full significance of the Jewish way of life. That day the Jewish religion will shine among the religions of the world as the moon among the stars.

The wise men of the Talmud put it this way. Just as the moon is sometimes eclipsed and cannot be seen, so the Jewish people are sometimes hidden from the events of history. But, just as the moon shines brightly the following night, so the Jewish people consistently reappear, and they can never be destroyed.

So you see, the moon has served as a reminder to the Jewish people of their mission among the nations of the world. It has given them courage to continue in their teachings of the Torah and service to G-D. For this reason the new moon has always been greeted by Jews all over the world with song and praise to Almighty G-D.

"ROSH CHODESH" SABBATH. On the Sabbath before the New Moon, a special prayer is recited asking G-D to bless us with a happy and healthy new month; one devoted to Torah and good deeds. It is customary at this time to announce from the pulpit the day and the hour on which the new month begins. This day (sometimes two days) is called in Hebrew "Rosh Chodesh," "Rosh" meaning head or beginning, and "Chodesh" meaning month.

SANCTIFICATION. At the beginning of the month when the new moon appears in the heavens, it is an obligation upon every Jew to sanctify the name of G-D and praise Him for His creations that illuminate the heavens. This sanctification is usually recited outside the synagogue after the evening service. It is called "Kiddush L'Vonoh." It is always recited in the open air in order to be able to see the moon shining in the heavens.

"ROSH CHODESH." On the day (or days) of "Rosh Chodesh" the prayer "Ya'aleh V'yovo" is added to the "Shmoneh Esrei" and a special service of praise and thanksgiving is recited. This service is called in Hebrew, "Hallel," which means "praises." You will learn as you read through the chapters of this book that this service is recited on many other holidays. The "Hallel" is recited after the "Shacharis" service. Following the "Hallel," the Torah scroll is taken from the Ark and read. Unlike the Sabbath or the weekdays, four people are given the honor to recite the Torah blessing. After the Torah reading, the "Musaf" service is recited as on all holidays with a special "Shmoneh Esrei" for "Rosh Chodesh."

"Blessed art Thou, Lord our G-D, King of the Universe, who created the heavens by Thy command, and all their host by Thy word. Thou hast subjected them to fixed laws and time so that they will not deviate from their set function. They

are glad and happy to do the will of their Creator, the true worker, whose achievement is truth. He ordered the moon to renew itself as a glorious crown over those He sustained from birth, who likewise will be regenerated in the future, and will worship their Creator for His glorious kingdom. Blessed art Thou, O Lord, who renews the months."

(*Taken from the Sanctification*
of the New Moon)

THE RIDE THAT MIGHT HAVE BEEN

It was dawn. Jerusalem was beginning to awaken after the night's sleep. Here and there one could see the fluttering lights of candles as the people prepared for a new day. Shlomo ben Avrohom had been up for hours. He had watched the night at its blackest turn gradually into the silvery gray of the beginning of day. His heart beat rapidly. Today is the day. No doubt this time.

"I'd better dress quickly and run to Reb Meir," he thought, "and remind him of the job I have to do today."

He washed and dressed rapidly trying desperately to avoid his usual clumsiness of dropping his wash basin or his sandals. But to no avail. One brown sandal fell from his hand and awakened his father.

"Shlomo, is that you?" his father called.

"Yes, father," the fourteen-year-old boy answered.

"Draw the water for me, Shlomo. It is time for us to go into the field."

Shlomo drew the water into the bucket from the well outside their home. He poured some into the wash basin and handed it to his father. "I cannot go with you into the fields today, father," he said. "Surely you have not forgotten what day this is."

"And what is that, my son?"

"Today is the day the new moon is expected to rise in the heavens. Reb Meir of the Sanhedrin has promised that I shall have the honor of being one of the Sanhedrin's messengers to tell the people outside of Jerusalem the news," he said in one breath. Shlomo's father laughed.

"I have not forgotten, my son. However, that honor and responsibility will not be yours for hours. There is plenty of work that can be accomplished in the big long day ahead of us."

"But I want to feel fresh so that I can ride faster than the wind. The people must know the news in time."

"We will stop our work earlier today so you will have time to wash and refresh yourself. But come quickly now, and quietly. I don't want your mother and sister awakened before it is necessary."

Shlomo sighed. He realized that there would be no use in arguing with his father whose mind obviously was made up. "He just doesn't understand," Shlomo thought resentfully, as he picked up his plow and followed his father out of the tent.

All day long as Shlomo plowed in the furrow beside his father he kept glancing upward at the sky as though the bright sun could give him a sign that the new moon would rise this night. He pictured himself already on his horse riding so quickly that an onlooker might think that he was almost flying, and he thrilled to the thought. "I'll bet that I'm the youngest person ever to be given the honor of being messenger," he thought to himself.

At twilight he put down his plow and approached his father.

"May I go now, father," he pleaded.

"Yes, my son. Your mother has prepared food for you to eat on the way. Go, and G-D be with you."

Shlomo fairly flew home, said his farewells to his mother and sister and ran to Reb Meir's house. The other messengers were already there waiting for the official notice of the new moon.

"Reb Meir, Reb Meir, I'm here!" Shlomo burst out.

"Rest yourself, my boy. It's still too light to tell," Reb Meir said.

Shlomo sat down and waited. When it was dark he searched for Reb Meir and found him surrounded by the other messengers. "The two witnesses have just proclaimed the new moon," Reb

Meir was saying. "I will assign each of you to ride to one of the provinces outside of Jerusalem so that our brother Israelites will be aware of it too."

Shlomo received his assignment with joy. He mounted his horse proudly, said goodbye to Reb Meir and the other messengers and rode off. As he rode he thought of the importance of his job.

"The people of Elan are depending on me, for when I tell them that the new moon has risen in Jerusalem, they will know how many days to count until Yom Tov."

He rode quickly, scarcely feeling the horse's hoofs striking the ground. His assigned province was far from Jerusalem. He rode and rode and rode. Faster! Faster! He must reach there in time or the people of Elan would miscalculate the days until Yom Tov. He rode for an hour—two, then stopped to rest his horse and refresh himself. He drank from the gourd of water he carried and since there was no one else about with whom to speak, he addressed himself to his horse.

"Do you know, my four-legged friend, that I'm probably the youngest person ever to be given such a responsibility? It will be something wonderful to tell my children some day. But come, we have rested enough. We must ride quickly so that we will reach the province of Elan before nightfall."

He mounted his horse again and galloped steadily, this time not stopping for hours. Each time he passed someone on the road he would call out, "Is this the right way to the province of Elan?" And each time the answer was the same. "Yes, my son. Just keep riding straight along this road until it forks in three directions. Take the middle fork and it is just a few hours away from there." But no one told him how many hours it would take till he reached the Fork.

Dawn came. He rested his horse again and munched some of the food his mother had prepared. "How much longer?" Shlomo wondered. He tied his horse to a tree and lay down to rest for a while. His two-hour nap seemed but a moment. He awoke with a start. How long had he been asleep? The sun was now hot and strong and directly above him.

"It must be the noon hour," he thought in horror. I have fallen asleep for too long and now I will not get to Elan before nightfall."

He ate again, then untied his horse. He mounted and dug his heels mercilessly into the horse's side.

"Giddyap! We must ride quickly to make up for the lost hours."

He rode faster than he had ever ridden in his young life. But still he was nowhere near the fork in the road when night fell again.

"Oh, what shall I do? Reb Meir has entrusted me with this great responsibility and the people of Elan are waiting for my arrival."

Weary and exhausted, Shlomo again stopped at an inn for travelers to rest. It was impossible to continue riding without doing so. The proprietor spoke kindly to the boy.

"Where are you from, my son, and where might you be bound?"

"I have come from Jerusalem and I'm riding to Elan to tell the people there that the new moon has been seen. I must have lost the way, however."

"You have not lost the way, my boy. It is only that Elan is a long distance from Jerusalem."

The proprietor sighed.

"It is unfortunate that the people in the provinces a long way from Jerusalem can never know such news in time. I cannot imagine how they calculate the Yomim Tovim correctly."

Shlomo rested a while longer, then rode again. It took him till the next nightfall when he finally reached the province of Elan. He gave the message to the elders of the town and fell into an exhausted sleep.

It took him two more days to return to Jerusalem. He was ashamed that the ride to and from Elan had taken so long. He returned to Reb Meir with a sense of failure rather than pride.

"I'm sorry, Reb Meir, but the province of Elan is so very far.

I rode as quickly as I could but still it took two nightfalls to reach it. If only I hadn't napped as long as I did," Shlomo said, his head lowered in shame.

"Do not blame yourself, my son. You have done your job well. Many messengers have, as yet, not returned. It has become apparent that many of the provinces are too distant to be reached quickly. The people of Judea are having difficulty knowing when to celebrate the Yomim Tovim. Tomorrow the Sanhedrin will meet to discuss what shall be done about it."

Shlomo was relieved. He went home to tell his parents that his mission was accomplished.

THE "SIDDUR"

A NEW BOOK. Sometime about the middle of the first year of your Hebrew school career, after you had learned the Hebrew alphabet, you were given a book written entirely in Hebrew. It had long complicated words, most of which you had never even seen in your first reader. The first thought that came to you was, "How am I ever going to learn this; I can hardly read it?" That was your first experience with a prayer book.

"We call it a 'Siddur,' in Hebrew," your teacher said. "You must give it the utmost respect. Keep it covered and make sure that it doesn't get dirty. When you get home, put it in a respectful place. Don't just throw it on the table and run out to play. As a sign of respect keep this book on top of all your others except for your 'Chumosh.'" How proud you were that first day when you went home with your new Siddur tucked under your arm.

Just what did you have tucked under your arm that day? It was much more than a Hebrew textbook.

The "Siddur" is really a combination of a number of things. It is a book of Jewish law, for it contains selections from the Bible and the Talmud concerning certain rules and regulations. It is a book of Jewish history, for it contains many memorable events that happened to our people in the past. Lastly, it is a book of general quotations, for it contains from cover to cover the ideas, beliefs and traditions of our religion as they were expressed in poetic prayers by our prophets, and later by our Sages.

The "Siddur" is universal among Jews. Wherever you may travel throughout the world, in any synagogue you enter, you will find that the "Siddur" used is essentially the same as your own "Siddur." The prayers that compose each service have not been changed since the "Siddur" was first compiled in the year 850 C. E.

TYPES OF PRAYER. The "Siddur" is composed of many different types of prayer. Let us discuss three of them.

1. PRAISES. We praise G-D as the creator of heaven and earth. We declare His holiness and His presence in all parts of the universe. We declare the power of G-D to do whatever He wills. We testify to His lovingkindness and ask all the nations to praise Him for it. We express the thought that all G-D's creatures praise His name, which will live forever.

2. THANKSGIVING. Prayers of thanksgiving are recited every day by Jews all over the world. We thank G-D for the blessings of life. We thank Him for the blessings He granted to our forefathers years ago and for the many blessings He has granted to us personally. We thank Him for giving us the Torah and providing us with food, clothing and shelter.

3. REQUESTS. Most people think that all prayers are requests. They think that the only time it is necessary to pray to G-D is when they want something. We know that this atttude is wrong. Requests are only one of many types of prayer. In these requests we ask G-D for peace throughout the world. We ask Him to teach us to care for our fellow men and to bless us with a happy and healthy

life devoted to Torah and Jewish ideals. We ask for the
privilege of witnessing the restoration of Israel to its land,
and the rebuilding of the Temple in the spirit of our
Torah, as it was predicted by our prophets centuries ago.

These are three of the basic types of prayer found in the
"Siddur." As you study this holy book, you will find other
types of prayer among which are prayers of history, con-
fessions, and prayers concerning the study of the Law. All
prayers of every type are recited to express our deepest
feelings to G-D concerning the ideals and necessities of life.

Let us examine our "Siddur" more closely. In the table of
contents you will find a long list of prayers for every occasion.
As you will notice, the prayers recited most often, like the
morning, afternoon and evening services, are found at the
beginning of the "Siddur." They are followed by the services
for "Shabbos." The rest of the "Siddur" is devoted to prayers
that are recited on special occasions: the "Hallel," which is a
service of praises and thanksgiving to G-D recited on holidays, Grace After Meals, prayers before going to bed, and
part of the services recited on festivals and the High Holidays.

The very word "Siddur" is similar to the word "Seder,"
which means "order." For the "Siddur" has all the prayers
arranged in a special order.

One of the most essential parts of all services is the section
called "Shmoneh Esrei." As you probably know from your
Hebrew language study, these two words mean "eighteen"
in Hebrew. The "Shmoneh Esrei" is called by this name because it is composed of eighteen blessings. (An additional
blessing was later added to the "Shmoneh Esrei" for weekdays.) Because of the importance of the "Shmoneh Esrei,"
we stand while reciting it, so that we can concentrate better
upon the ideas of the words we are reciting. Many people
sway back and forth and keep their eyes closed so that they

may not be distracted for even a second. Prayers to Almighty G-D must be recited with respect, dignity and above all, sincerity. The "Shmoneh Esrei" contains prayers of praise, thanksgiving and request. It expresses our hope and desire for the return of the Jewish people to the land of Israel in the true spirit of Torah. The "Shmoneh Esrei" is an all-inclusive prayer and for this reason it is part of every service.

THE SERVICES. There are three services recited every day: (1) "Shacharis," (2) "Mincha," (3) "Ma'ariv."

SHACHARIS. This is the first service of the day. It is recited in the morning. "Shacharis" may be recited at any time from sunrise until noon. If you examine your "Siddur," you will find that this prayer is the longest of the three services recited during the day. The two most important parts of the "Shacharis" service are the "Shema" and the "Shmoneh Esrei." On Mondays and Thursdays in addition to the regular service, the Torah is read. This dates back to the time of Ezra, when the Torah was read in the market-place on these days. The Torah selection is read after the "Shmoneh Esrei" has been recited by the congregation and the cantor.

MINCHA. This is the afternoon service, recited from about 1 P.M. until sunset. As you will notice it is the shortest of the services for weekdays. "Mincha" is divided into three parts; the opening prayer, "Ashrei," the "Shmoneh Esrei," and the closing prayer "Oleinu." "Oleinu" is the closing prayer of every service. Our Sages tell us that "Mincha" is the most rewarding of the three services recited during the day. When a person takes time out from his business in the middle of the day to recite a service to G-D, he truly deserves reward. Perhaps this is one of the reasons why the "Mincha" service was made so short.

MA'ARIV. This is the last of the three services of the week-days. It may be recited from nightfall until dawn. It begins with a beautiful opening prayer to G-D, the Creator of light and darkness, day and night. The "Shema" and the "Shmoneh Esrei" are also included in the "Ma'ariv" service. The concluding prayer is "Oleinu."

SHABBOS services are basically the same as the weekday services except for a few additions and changes.

KABOLAS SHABBOS and MA'ARIV. As you know, "Shabbos" begins on Friday night. The "Ma'ariv" service begins with a welcoming hymn to the Sabbath. It pictures the Sabbath as a beautiful queen and greets her with song and praise. Several Psalms are recited in praise of G-D showing the greatness of His power. This special service is called in Hebrew, "Kabolas Shabbos." The rest of the "Ma'ariv" is recited immediately afterward; it is the same as the weekday "Ma'ariv" except for a few changes. The "Shmoneh Esrei," however, is one compiled especially for "Shabbos."

SHACHARIS. "Shabbos" morning the service is pretty much the same as the weekday "Shacharis" except for the addition of several Psalms. The "Shmoneh Esrei" is a special one for "Shabbos" morning.

TORAH READING. On "Shabbos," as on Monday and Thursday, a special selection is read from the Torah. This is called the "Sidrah" of the week. While on Monday and Thursday only three people are called upon to recite a blessing before the Torah, on Shabbos eight people are given this honor. The first Torah Honor, or as it is called in Hebrew, "Aliyah," is given to a descendant of Aaron, the priest, of the tribe of Levi. (Those descended from Aaron are called in Hebrew "Kohanim.") The second "Aliyah" is given to a "Levi," (other descendants of the tribe of Levi). The rest of the "Aliyos" can be given to any member of the congregation above the age of thirteen, who is not of the tribe of Levi. They are called Israelites. The last of the "Aliyos" is called "Maftir." It is usually given to a Bar mitzvah boy. "Maftir" may also be given to a "Kohein" or "Levi."

MUSAF. This service is an additional one recited only on "Shabbos," holidays and "Rosh Chodesh." It begins with an opening prayer, asking G-D to bestow His blessing upon the entire congregation and their dear ones. It is followed by the "Shmoneh Esrei" compiled especially for the "Musaf." The concluding prayer is the "Oleinu." The "Mincha" for "Shabbos" is essentially the same as the one for weekdays. It contains the same three basic prayers, plus an additional prayer after "Ashrei." A "Shmoneh Esrei" was composed especially for this service. At this service the Torah is read again. Three people are called to recite the blessing: a "Kohein," a "Levi" and any other male who is neither a "Kohein" nor a "Levi."

MA'ARIV. The "Shabbos" evening service may not be recited until "Shabbos" is over. This service is the same as the weekday "Ma'ariv" with the addition of a special paragraph in the "Shmoneh Esrei" that officially proclaims the end of the Sabbath. Before the "Oleinu" another version of this prayer is recited aloud to proclaim to all that the Sabbath is over. This ceremonial prayer is called the "Havdolah."

You now have a general idea as to the contents of the "Siddur." Surely you will agree that it is a priceless treasure. Like the Torah, the more we read and study the "Siddur," the more we learn about it. The "Siddur" has served the Jewish people for more than a thousand years in times of sorrow and in times of joy. The next time you attend a service stop and think of how many people all over the world are reciting these same prayers in the same language at that very moment. Millions of people raise their voices to G-D in solemn prayer. You are part of this great spiritual army of Judaism.

THE SIDDUR'S PRAYER

This was Friday and mother was cleaning the house to make it spic and span for the Sabbath. Her dust rag whisked across the bookcase when bang, down tumbled a dusty old prayer book.

"My, how old this Siddur is," said mother. "Its pages are yellow and dirty and the binding is falling apart. I do believe I'll have to throw it away."

"Oh, please don't hurt me," said a strange little voice. "Please, please, I pray you, save me."

Mother looked bewildered. "I save only useful things," she replied. "I cannot see of what further use you can be."

"Ever since I was created I prayed for others, now for the first time I pray for myself. Would you refuse to grant me my prayer?" cried the Siddur.

"Well, I don't want to refuse, but I see no purpose in keeping you around."

"I'll tell you what," bargained the Siddur. "If you promise not to hurt me I'll tell you what I have done in the past and what I can do for you."

"Now it's Friday," said mother hesitantly, "and I have a great deal of cleaning to get done. I don't believe I have time to listen to stories."

"Oh, that's all right. You can go on with your cleaning. If there is a heart to listen I can be heard over any amount of noise."

"Fine," said mother lightly, "you tell your story and I promise no one will hurt you."

The "Siddur" gave a polite "ahem," straightened its cover, and
began.

As you see me now I'm old, dirty and worn, but such was not
always the case. Once I was bright and shiny with gold lettering
on my cover and gold at the top of my pages. I stood on a pedes-
tal in the middle of the bookseller's window with a sign under
me reading, "Daily and Holiday Prayer Book." Every day a young
man with a pointed black beard and a derby hat would stop
and gaze at me longingly. Then one day he walked swiftly past
my window and straight into the shop.

"Mazel Tov, Mr. Ruben," said the proprietor. "I understand it's
a boy."

"Thank you, thank you," replied Mr. Ruben hastily. "I have
come to buy the Siddur in the window. My wife and I thought
it would be nice to have a new Siddur for the 'Pidyon Habein,'
the redemption of our firstborn son.

"Certainly," agreed the proprietor. "Now just which prayer book
did you have in mind?"

"The one in the window with the black covers and gold lettering."

I arrived in the Ruben household in time for the party prepared in honor of little David who was just one month old. It
was a grand party with all the uncles, aunts, nieces and
cousins adding to the merriment. The table had so much food
on it that it looked as if it might collapse from the strain. There
were all sorts of sweets and goodies and in the middle stood a
beautiful birthday cake with pink and white icing and one candle
stuck in the middle. Baby David gurgled peacefully while Mr.
Ruben gave Mr. Cohen five silver dollars so that David might be
redeemed from the priesthood's claim on him. Then everyone
kissed the baby while his mother cut the cake with the pink and
white icing. I remember very well that the icing was pink and
white because some of it fell on my shining new page. If you

open me to the service for the "Pidyon Habein" you will see the stain it made.

At first I was very much annoyed with the stain and felt rather sad about it. But I soon got used to such trifles. Only books which are never used remain new. It wasn't long before the first stain was joined by many others. Each and every Friday night Mr. Ruben would hold the goblet of wine over me as he said the "Kiddush" and each and every time a drop of wine would fall. Before long the entire page was filled with wine stains, and if it weren't for the fact that Mr. Ruben knew the "Kiddush" by heart I am sure he would have had great difficulty reading it. As a matter of fact Mr. Ruben knew almost all of the prayers by heart, but he nevertheless always read them because he believed that in that way he could concentrate better and pray with more devotion.

My pages soon became wrinkled and earmarked as they were constantly being turned, morning, afternoon and evening. You must not imagine that I was uncomfortable. On the contrary, everything was most pleasant. The Ruben household was filled with music and laughter in those days. It seemed to ripple across my pages and tickled my binding.

One Saturday night, as I lay open to the "Havdolah" service and Mrs. Ruben held the braided candle aloft and the sweet smell from the spice box mingled with the smoke, there came the sound of a terrible groan from little David's room. Mrs. Ruben shook and the melted wax came down in a great big blob smack in the middle of the page! From that moment on it seemed as if laughter had been outlawed. Everything was hushed and quiet and I heard only the patter of feet hurrying to and fro and the stifled sobs of Mr. and Mrs. Ruben. I lay constantly opened to the prayers for those dangerously ill and with each succeeding day those pages became more wrinkled from the stains that were on them from the bitter tears. Finally, when the hushes of the house became almost unbearable, a trembling hand turned my page and read: "With the permission of Almighty God, the name of our sick child David shall be changed to Chaim and by that name shall he be called and by that name may he live." From that moment on the hush began to lift until at last one bright day the note of a child's laugh broke the grip of sorrow.

The years tripped by and I did not realize that I had been with Mr. Ruben for over twelve years until one day I felt a pair of strange boyish hands opening me. The hands are slightly dirty and smell from the basketball court but day after day they open me to the prayers before reading the Torah and hour after hour they trace a smudge under the holy words while a clear, sweet, young voice chants over and over again the sacred melodies. At last the great day arrives. The air is thick with "Mazel-Tovs." David Chaim, spotlessly clean in honor of the occasion, with a white "Yarmelke" and a new "Tallis," stands before the Holy Ark chanting his portion from the Torah and Prophets. I didn't remember having seen so many relatives and friends since that time thirteen years before when the baby David was redeemed by his daddy. The joy that could be read in Mr. Ruben's eyes on that day was great, but the joy of this day was greater still because he now had the heart-warming knowledge that he had brought up his boy to be a true son of Israel.

The seasons passed with the years. Once, on Purim, David Chaim and his friends twirled their groggers so hard when the wicked Haman's name was mentioned that they caused my pages to fly up, so that they got caught in the noisemakers and ripped. That is why you will notice all the mending on my pages relating the Esther story. My gold edging was turned brown on Chanukah when the "Shammash" candle was dropped and I nearly burned to death. My binding was broken the night of "Hoshana Rabbah." Mr. Ruben was attempting to sit up all night to study but sleep overcame him, and as he dozed off he accidentally knocked me off the table.

Bruised and scarred though I was, nevertheless I was quite happy. I was Mr. Ruben's constant companion and friend. Wherever he went, I went. On business trips, on vacations, and even the time the family went to the big city for David Chaim's marriage, I, too, was brought along.

The years following David Chaim's marriage were dull and routine. For some time Mr. Ruben needed glasses to counteract his increasing nearsightedness, but he did nothing about it until one day he held me so close that he bumped his nose. The years had taken their toll and his step was no longer light and quick. But it was Mrs. Ruben who was ailing. All winter the house smelled of medicine. "Pesach" came and the family held their last "Seder" together. Shortly before "Shavuos" Mrs. Ruben died.

His wife's death seemed to take the spark out of Mr. Ruben. "Blessed be the True Judge," he continually murmured to himself. In scarcely a year the True Judge demanded that Mr. Ruben's soul should join his wife's, and he died. A few weeks later I found myself, along with a number of other well-used volumes, packed in a crate. After a time I was removed and put on the back shelf of this bookcase, where I remained until you pushed me down today.

Now I admit I'm not much to look at anymore, but I served Mr. Ruben faithfully for many years and I believe that I could also be a true companion to you.

At that moment the door creaked.

"Hush," said mother, "I think I hear my husband coming."

"Judith, where are you," shouts a husky male voice.

"In the library dear, cleaning."

"Judith, I want to show you a copy of the set of prayer books I am presenting the synagogue in memory of my parents."

"Why they're just lovely, dear. Incidentally, are you going back to the bookbinder's this afternoon?"

"Yes."

"Then David, darling, I wonder if you would mind taking this old prayer book with you to have it rebound?"

"Of course not. Wouldn't it be better to buy a new one?"

"I don't know. David, were you ever renamed Chaim?"

"Goodness, yes. How did you know?"

"And doesn't Chaim mean life?"

"Yes but . . ."

"Well, I have decided to rename this 'Siddur' Chaim and give it another chance at life. And besides, I don't see the point in discarding something that still has use. In thumbing through it, I noticed that the pages containing the prayers for naming a daughter have never been touched. Now we have two boys, but I think our third is going to be a girl."

THE SYNAGOGUE

THE THREE NAMES. When the Temple in Jerusalem was destroyed and the Jews were exiled to Babylonia, the new type of house of worship, the synagogue, increased in importance. The synagogue was known as the "Mikdosh M'at," the "small temple." It served three purposes. It was a "Beis Tefillah," a "House of Worship," where the community gathered daily for services. It was a "Beis Midrash," a "House of Study," where children and adults received instruction in Jewish living. It was a "Beis Kneses," a "Community Center," where problems and affairs of the community were discussed.

The synagogue became a second home to the Jew. When Jews moved to a new town or community the synagogue was the first institution they built. It was the synagogue that served the Jew in times of happiness and in times of sorrow. In the synagogue, the rich and the poor, the teacher and the student, the young and the old, all found an opportunity to associate with one another and work together for the benefit of the community.

Throughout the generations, to the present day, the synagogue has served to unite in spirit the Jews all over the world. The synagogue speaks the language of the Jew. Within its walls no Jew is a stranger.

LAWS OF THE SERVICE

Minyan. In order to conduct a public service whether in the synagogue or at home, there must be at least ten male adults present. To be counted in this quorum, one must be at least thirteen years old. The quorum of ten males is called a "Minyan." The special memorial prayer "Kaddish" can be recited only when there is at least a "Minyan." Also the reading of the Torah scroll may take place only when there is at least a "Minyan."

When conducting a service it is necessary that the "Minyan" be present in the room where the service is taking place. If some of the men are in a nearby room they may not be counted in the "Minyan."

The Cantor. The "Chazan," the reader of the service, is considered a man of importance. Our Sages tell us that a "Chazan" should be chosen wisely. He should be G-D fearing. He should understand the prayers he recites in the service. Above all, he should realize his responsibility as a representative of his people before G-D.

Our Sages teach us that there must be friendship and cooperation in the synagogue. Without friendship and cooperation a synagogue cannot function properly. For this reason the "Chazan" should be the choice of the entire congregation. If the synagogue does not have a regular cantor, the reader for each service should be appointed by the rabbi or the sexton. Anyone who goes to the reader's desk to lead a service without the consent of the congregation is not considered a true representative, and his prayers are not accepted.

THE SYNAGOGUE OBJECTS

The Ark. The most treasured object in the synagogue is the Torah. In every synagogue a special cabinet is built to house the Torah scrolls. This cabinet is called the "Aron Hakodesh," the "Holy Ark." Whenever possible the "Aron Hakodesh" is built on the eastern wall of the synagogue so that the congregation faces eastward toward Jerusalem during the services.

The Poroches. The "Aron Hakodesh" is usually nicely decorated. On the outside of it is a "Poroches" or "Ark Curtain." The "Poroches" is usually made of plush, velvet or satin. It comes in different colors. For the High Holidays a white "Poroches" is selected, and is embroidered with a variety of Jewish symbols and sayings.

The Torah Mantle. The Torah scroll is treated with great reverence. When it is not being read it is kept covered with a decorated and embroidered cover called a Torah mantle. A Torah scroll may be uncovered only when it is read or being fixed.

Klei Kodesh. In many synagogues the Torah scroll is decorated with valuable silver ornaments. These ornaments are called "Klei Kodesh," or "holy vessels." Among the silver ornaments are the "Rimonim," two tall silver pieces that are placed on top of the wooden rollers of the Torah scroll, also, the "Keser Torah," a silver crown placed over both rollers of the Torah scroll.

The breastplate is another Torah ornament. It is attached by a chain to the rollers and hangs down over the front of the Torah mantle. Many synagogues have several sets of the "Klei Kodesh" and use them on holidays or on other occasions when more than one Torah scroll is read. As a sign of respect the Torah parchment must not be touched with one's hands while it is being read. Many synagogues have a silver pointer used by the Torah reader. As he reads from the Torah scroll he points to the words with the pointer, or "Yod," as it is called in Hebrew. When one is given an "Aliyah" the reader points to the verse where he will begin reading so that the former might follow him.

The Neir Tomid. Above the "Aron Hakodesh" hangs the "Neir Tomid," the "Eternal Light." It is kept burning day and night to commemorate the Menorah that stood in the Temple in Jerusalem. The light of the "Neir Tomid" nowadays, as the light of the Menorah in the days of the Temple, symbolizes the life of the Jewish people. Just as this light is always kept burning, so the Jewish people will have everlasting life as a nation. But, just as the light in the Menorah or the "Neir Tomid" could be extinguished if it were not nourished with fuel, so the life of the Jewish people as a nation could be extinguished if it is not nourished with the learning and practice of Torah and good deeds.

A TENTH TO MINYAN

A brilliant sun hung in a cloudless sky above Hebron. Its strong rays shone down on the "Meoras Ha-machpeilo," the double-cave burial place of Abraham and Sarah and the other Patriarchs.

A hot wind blew from the south and brought with it sands of the desert and clouds of dust. These darkened the air a bit and gave the town a mournful look.

Here and there a bird wheeled in lazy flight. To one side one could see an Arab peasant picking his black grapes, his wife helping him, while their small child was playing on the ground. Around them stretched miles of golden grain fields.

The Jews of Hebron were plunged in sorrow. Every so often they would climb up to the high roof of the synagogue, shield their eyes from the sun and stare out into the distance. Two young men had gone to the outskirts of the city to search. Perhaps G-D would grant them their request. All eyes looked toward the north; toward Jerusalem. Perhaps help would come from there. They strained their eyes in all directions searching the horizon. Ah, that group of moving shadows! They look like Jews. But alas, all hope comes dashing down, for as the dark shapes come nearer they see that they are Arab peasants.

Now their gaze becomes fixed upon the cemetery. All the gravestones are smooth—no inscriptions. This is an old custom in Hebron. The names of the dead are not put on the stones. Suddenly they see a fresh grave, recently dug. All those on the roof stare at it. It is the grave of Rabbi Yitschok the Elder, who died yesterday and left the Jews in a very sad predicament. You see, Rabbi Yitschok was the man who completed the "Minyan" of ten men. Without him there were only nine men in the community and so they could not conduct services. It was the night of Yom Kippur and there wasn't a Jew to complete the "Minyan." Under other circumstances the Jews of Hebron would have taken their families and traveled to Jerusalem to pray there during the holy day. But Rabbi Yitschok's passing had been very sudden and there was no time to travel to the holy city.

But still the Jews of Hebron waited for some miracle from Heaven. They waited for G-D to supply them with a tenth man for the required "Minyan."

The silence thickens. One can almost hear the sun pushing through the clouds bringing the holy day closer and closer. No one speaks. It almost seems as if with Rabbi Yitschok's death all life died in Hebron. Even the street of the Jews looks lifeless.

Rabbi Shmarya who was "Chacham" or head of the Jewish community, was also caretaker or "Shammash" of the synagogue. For in his great humility he wished to serve in the House of G-D. Rabbi Shmarya was in the synagogue preparing the candles for Yom Kippur. He also prepared ten chairs for ten worshipers. But in his heart he gave up the hope of any Jew coming other than the nine who lived in the community. For what Jew travels on erev Yom Kippur? The sun was already dipping into the west. Where should a Jew come from?

Yet a faint hope would not leave him that G-D, somehow, would not forsake his children in this hour of need. He put a new white covering on the Holy Ark and swept out the synagogue.

One old Jew still remained on the roof of the synagogue. His hand over his eyes, he searched the horizon. Below, an old woman wandered through the street of the Jews. She gave a deep sigh. The Jews of Hebron would not have a "Minyan" this holy day.

The old man on the roof of the synagogue narrowed his eyes at every dot that moved on the horizon. He focused his sharp sight out into the haze of the far distance; into the long shadows that the sun left behind her. One moment his heart would leap with joy and anticipation as he thought he saw a Jew in the distance but the joy turned to sadness as he recognized the approaching figure to be an Arab returning home from the fields.

❊   ❊   ❊

The two courageous young men were still patrolling the outskirts of the city. They climbed one hill after another, their eyes stabbing and searching. A hot wind blew, tossing their beards and earlocks in all directions. But they felt nothing. One thought beat in their minds: "Jew, where are you!" They had already come a third of the way to Jerusalem.

A band of peasants passed on their way home. They stopped to start at the young men and one called out, "What are you looking for?"

"Have you seen a Jew along the road?" asked one of the young men.

"No, we haven't," answered the Arabs.

"A Jew must be lost," said one Arab to the other. They picked up their song and disappeared down the road.

It was a half hour to Kol Nidre. Another thirty minutes and all would be over. The "Chacham," Rabbi Shmarya, and two other Jews were already in the synagogue. They were wearing their "Taliyos" and preparing themselves for the holy day. All hope was abandoned. They were troubled and pained only by the realization that they would not have a "Minyan" on this holy occasion.

Only the old man on the roof did not lose hope. He was still up there looking and searching. He could not bear the thought of praying without a "Minyan" on this holy day.

The old man looked toward the side of the "Meoras Hamachpeilo." There on the balcony of the mosque stood a Mohammedan crier, preparing to call the Arab faithful to pray. Suddenly the face of the old man darkened. A shining pillar of light seemed to appear on the "Double Cave" and opposite it a thick shadow which immediately disappeared. It looked as if a giant door had opened on its side.

The Arab crier fell on his face from fear and a great panic broke out among the Arabs near the cave. But the old man on the roof just turned away. His interest was only to find another Jew for the Yom Kippur services. Suddenly the old man stiffened. His eyes reported something but he couldn't believe what they told him. A Jew had appeared behind the "Meoras Ha-machpeilo." The old man was astonished that he had not seen this Jew before. It seemed as if this Jew had hid behind the cave to torment the Jews of Hebron until now.

The Jew was coming closer. He was a strange looking man, armed with a staff, his bag on his shoulders, and his clothes ragged and patched. But his face! His face was radiant, his eyes a deep black. He walked along slowly, using his staff, not realizing the great joy his presence was causing among the Jews of this little community.

The old man on the roof of the synagogue almost fainted from sheer joy. In a voice that he didn't recognize as his own, he shouted, "Here is a Jew—A Jew has come. A tenth to a 'Minyan!' "

When Rabbi Shmarya and the others, who were already in the synagogue, heard the old man's cries, they thought he had gone mad. From where could a Jew come now, almost after sunset? But still they ran out. Their eyes bulged and their hearts pounded, for sure enough there was a Jew, walking calmly along and approaching the synagogue. They all noticed that the city of Hebron did not seem strange to him. He recognized the synagogue, and needed no directions. They all grouped around him and shook his hand bidding him "Shalom." "Where do you come from?" they asked. The stranger did not reply.

Meanwhile the two young men returned from their search discouraged and disappointed. How happily surprised they were when they saw the tenth Jew. They danced for joy.

Everyone entered the synagogue. The guest was given the seat of honor, on the east wall near the Holy Ark. But the stranger didn't prefer that seat and he spent most of his time near a window which looked out upon the "Meoras Ha-machpeilo."

Rabbi Shmarya the "Chacham" began the service. The stranger stood for the entire Yom Kippur holiday with his face turned toward the wall. He didn't move his body. There he stood like a pillar of marble. His lips moved but no sound came from his mouth.

✻   ✻   ✻

The time for the "Neilah" service approached. The sun was sinking below the horizon and the gray light of dusk filled the synagogue. The "Eternal light" threw weird, dancing shadows on the wall. The window that faced the cave suddenly grew bright, as if it had caught fire. A thick shadow appeared in the distance.

The Jews turned toward the stranger. He wasn't there. He has probably gone out for a moment, they thought.

It was now time for the final blast of the shofar to end the holy day. They waited for the stranger but he did not return. The two young men scouted the outskirts of the city but they returned disappointed for there was no trace of the stranger. And so the shofar was sounded, the "Maariv" service was recited individually and all returned to their homes.

The Jews of Hebron felt very sad. In fact they felt worse now than they felt on erev Yom Kippur. For after G-D had sent them a Jew for the "Minyan" the Jew got lost. Perhaps he had an accident or was very ill and died. With heavy hearts and even heavier sighs the Jews of Hebron broke their fast that Yom Kippur night.

✻   ✻   ✻

A pale moon floated across the heavens of Hebron. It made its way among the silvery clouds like a sailing ship on a calm sea. A silent wind scattered the clouds sending their shadows dancing across the hills of Hebron.

One of the young men was staring out the window thinking about the stranger. Suddenly his wife called to him. "You know, dear, I was in the synagogue today and I didn't see any stranger. You were all talking about him but I didn't see anybody."

The young man stared at his wife open-mouthed. Did she really mean what she said?

✿   ✿   ✿

Rabbi Shmarya the "Chacham" awoke from his sleep early the next morning with a happy glow on his face. It seemed as if he had a wonderful dream. When Rabbi Shmarya arrived at the synagogue that morning he found all the Jews gathered there to ask his opinion of what had happened the previous day. Rabbi Shmarya told them that the stranger appeared to him in a dream that night and told him that he was our father Abraham who saw the pain of the Jews of Hebron and came to complete the "Minyan."

And now everything became clear. The stranger preferred to stand by the window because his soul longed to return to its eternal resting place. The flashes of light were caused by the opening of the "Meoras Ha-machpeilo."

On the spot where Abraham stood, the Jews of Hebron built an Ark and to this day the synagogue in Hebron has two Arks. To one of the young men who searched so diligently for a tenth Jew to "Minyan," was born a son whom he named Abraham. To the other was born a daughter whom he named Sarah. When the children grew up they married and were loyal, faithful Jews all their lives.

THE ROLE OF THE JEWISH WOMAN

BAS MITZVAH. This term is a fairly new one in Jewish life but the idea is not new at all. Many girls feel that all the Jewish laws are for the men, and that women have very little to do with their religion. This notion is quite untrue. In Judaism, everyone has his or her job. Would you say that a woman is inferior because she doesn't go out and earn a living? Of course not! Her job is taking care of the house and raising the family. It is certainly as important as earning the money, perhaps even more so.

SARAH AND REBECCA. Throughout Jewish history women have played important roles. The mother of the Jewish people, Sarah, is a perfect example. She was given great respect by her husband, Abraham. When he made his first journey from his birthplace to the new land that G-D was going to show him, he camped at a place called Beth-El, where he pitched his tent. Our Sages tell us that the first tent he pitched was Sarah's. Her role was the most important ever given to a woman. She was to be the mother of the Jewish nation. She was to raise a child for Abraham. This child was to be the second leader of the Hebrews. But she was not the only great woman in Israel. Her son's wife, Rebecca, was perhaps equally as great. Our rabbis tell us that as long as Sarah lived, a cloud rested over Abraham's tent showing the presence of G-D. It vanished when Sarah died, and returned when Rebecca came. As long as Sarah lived the doors of hospitality were always open. When Sarah died this hospitality ceased; it returned when Rebecca came.

Generation after generation saw Jewish women mold the character of leaders in Jewry, and when there was no man to fill a position, the woman took over. Who does not know the story of Deborah, the judge, who led Israel to victory?

But let us answer our first question. What are the duties of the Jewish woman? Does she have any specific commandments? Yes, she has many of the commandments of the man and three additional commandments of her own. We will discuss each one of these three separately.

CANDLE LIGHTING. It is an obligation upon every married woman to light candles on Friday eve. The woman has first priority, but if she is not in the house, then the man lights the candles. Children do not light the candles unless there is no adult present. The candle lighting is an important and sacred ceremony; it should be performed only by someone who understands its meaning. The two candles that are lit represent the two versions in the Torah dealing with the Sabbath, which are part of the Ten Commandments:

"Remember the Sabbath day to keep it Holy." (Shmos. 20:8)

"Observe the Sabbath day to keep it Holy." (D'vorim 5:12)

Our Sages tell us that when these commandments were given to Moses on Mount Sinai, the words "Remember" and "Observe" were uttered at the same time. Since the Ten Commandments were recorded twice in the Bible, one contains the word "Remember" and the other the word "Observe."

By lighting the Sabbath candles, the woman brings the Sabbath to her home and her family. It is her responsibility to prepare her family and household for this occasion all during the week.

It is also the obligation of the woman of the house to light candles on all holiday eves.

FAMILY PURITY. One of the most important obligations of a mother is taking care of and raising her children. It is her obligation to see that the home is run properly. She has jobs that often keep her busy day and night. This is probably one of the reasons why the Torah did not put so many obligations upon her. She must, however, exert her influence and encourage her husband and children to perform the "Mitzvos" which apply to them. She is what you might call the conscience of the family. Many times it is the mother's influence that decides whether the children will be brought up in a religious way. Perhaps some of you are going to Hebrew school because your mother wanted it very much. In many families it is the mother's influence that changes the attitude of the whole family from a nonreligious to a religious one. A woman must realize this responsibility, however, long before she is married. She must learn of her duties while she is still in Hebrew school and must try to gain as much information and knowledge as possible.

When a girl is ready to be married, she and her husband-to-be should consult with the rabbi of the community. He will explain the special marriage laws that apply to Jewish couples.

TAKING THE CHALLA. The third "Mitzvah," which was perhaps more applicable to the average woman many years ago than it is today, is the law of "challa." Whenever a woman baked bread for her household, she would take off a piece of dough and burn it in the oven. In the time of the Temple this piece of dough was given to the "Kohein," the priest. Since the "Kohein" had no land to work in order to grow his food, the Israelites were commanded in different ways to take care of his needs. It was a form of tax. Later when the Temple was destroyed, the custom remained, but the piece of dough was no longer given to the "Kohein"; it was burned. Nowadays, since the woman of the household rarely bakes her own bread, she cannot "take the challa." In kosher bakeries, however, this "Mitzvah" is always carried out.

This is what Bas Mitzvah should really mean to a girl when she reaches the age of twelve. She should be old enough to realize her obligation as a future mother in Israel. She should know that her duties in Judaism are as important as the duties of the man. She should dedicate herself to acquiring as much knowledge as she can about her religion and learn to observe Jewish law. Above all she should remember that not too far in the future, she herself will be a mother in Israel, and as a mother she will have to teach all she had learned to her children. Lastly, she should be able to answer the question raised at the beginning of this chapter. Why are the Mitzvos given to the men whereas the Jewish women are absolved from observing most of them?

THE LOST SISTER

I. *The Dike Is Broken.* It was a cool morning in the early Spring. From their window, Gittchen and Ellen looked out upon the blue sea. The sun shone bright and golden upon the water. "Hurry," called Ellen, "or we'll be late for school." Gittchen and Ellen were two Jewish girls whom their mother called, Gittele and Leah'le. They lived in a small town in Holland, not far from the sea.

A little later the two girls were off! Hand in hand, they wended their way towards the little schoolhouse. Ellen, the elder of the two, was a kind and quiet child with deep blue eyes. But seven-year-old Gittchen was quite the opposite. Her merry black eyes twinkled mischievously as though she were always contemplating some new prank, or laughing at some mischief she had already done. Although the two little girls were so different, they never quarreled. They were rather greatly attached to each other.

That winter, when Gittchen had slipped on the ice and injured her foot, Ellen did not go to school for many days. She sat at her sister's bedside all the time. When Gittchen grew tired of one game, Ellen would play another, and when Gittchen grew tired of play, Ellen would tell her stories or read to her. Although Ellen could see the boys and girls frolicking on the ice, and could hear their merry shouts, she never left Gittchen's bedside, until Gittchen could walk again.

Finally they reached the school. This was everyone's favorite hour. The classroom was quiet. There was no sound except that of the teacher's voice telling the exciting tale of Samson, while the class listened spellbound. Suddenly, the door flung open. An excited and terrified-looking youth stood in the doorway. In a voice hoarse with terror, he cried, "Flee, flee for your lives. The dike has broken! The water is coming up. Run to the plain!"

A wild panic gripped the children. Everyone stampeded to the door. In the street were hundreds of people, pushing, running, fleeing for their lives!

The mob surged forward at breakneck speed, racing with the water. When the plain was sighted, a cry of relief broke from the panting people. At last they were safe. Everybody was there but little Gittchen. She was not able to keep up with the mob. Her old wound had reopened and she fell behind. Exhausted, she threw herself on the ground, and in a few minutes she was fast asleep. She was blissfully unaware that the surging water was coming closer and closer, and in another minute she would be swallowed by the foaming sea.

II. *The Peasant's Hut.* The next morning Gittchen awoke and rubbed her eyes sleepily. "Oh," she cried looking about her. "Where am I?" Gittchen lay upon a bed in a little room. "How did I ever get here?" she thought to herself.

The door opened, and in walked an old woman with hard and cruel eyes. "Well, little girl," she said in a harsh voice, "you have me to thank for this. If I hadn't found you and carried you up to my cottage on the hill, you might have drowned."

Gittchen looked about her in bewilderment. At last she was beginning to understand what had occurred. But it was difficult indeed to thank the ferocious-looking old hag for saving her life. "Five long miles I carried you," the woman muttered. "You will repay me for my kindness, though."

"But where are my mother and my father?" cried Gittchen. "Where is my sister Ellen?"

"I want to go home," cried Gittchen again.

"You have no home any more except this home here!" replied the woman. "You have no one left in the world but me. You might as well get used to the idea." The old woman forbade Gittchen to mention her parents or her sister, and besides, she made Gittchen work so hard that she had no time to think of them at all.

As the days passed Gittchen began to forget her parents, and her home, and her dear sister Ellen. Saddest of all, Gittchen began to forget that she was a Jewish girl. For the old woman never lit the Sabbath candles, or recited a blessing, or kept the Sabbath. So, Gittchen, too, forgot how to do these things.

The old woman's appearance did not belie her character. She was as mean and cruel as she looked. For the three years that she kept Gittchen with her, Gittchen never had a moment of rest from morn till night. With the first light of day, she would rise to milk the cows. Then she would lead the cows to the pasture and bring them home again. She had to fetch water from the well, and keep the house tidy and clean. Her cheeks lost their rosy look, and her eyes no longer twinkled. Her little hands were red and rough. At night her little bones ached because of the long hours of drudgery and back-breaking toil. Never was a little girl so unhappy as Gittchen.

III. *The Sabbath Candles.* It was Thursday evening. Gittchen was sitting in the kitchen mending some clothes. "Gittchen," called the old woman, "come here."

Obediently, Gittchen went into the next room and the old woman said to her: "Tomorrow, there will be a fair near the village of Yondam. You will take the butter and cheese that you have prepared this afternoon, to the fair. Be sure that you get a high price, and don't let anyone fool you. You will start at dawn, but you must be back before nightfall, if you don't want a beating. Now get back to your sewing."

As she sewed, Gittchen mused about the task that she had to perform the following day for the first time. "I hope there will be other people from the neighborhood going to the fair. I will surely be afraid to go home all by myself, and Yondam is so far away."

The next day, at dawn, Gittchen started for the fair. She had plodded a good many miles along the dirt road before she came to Yondam. But she soon forgot her fatigue. She had never seen such a gay and exciting event. Vendors calling their wares, farmers and merchants bargaining and talking together. After Gittchen had sold the dairy and made some purchases for the old woman, it was nearly dusk, and she started on her way back. Wearily she trudged through streets that were deserted and dark.

Suddenly, through the shutters of a little window she saw the gleam of candles. They struck a chord in her memory that had long lain forgotten. Somewhere, long ago, she had seen these same candles. They held her like a magic spell. She stopped in front of the little house, and was watching the candles flicker and play on the shutters. Suddenly familiar scenes of her childhood came back to her. She remembered her mother lighting the candles on Sabbath eve. She remembered the table on Friday night, laden with delicious food, everyone sitting about with shining eyes and smiling faces, and she could not resist an impulse to enter the little house where the candles shone in the window. "At least, once again I will see the Sabbath table as it was in my own home many years ago," thought Gittchen, and she knocked timidly at the door. The next moment, the door opened.

"Gittchen!" cried Ellen. "Is it really you, Gittchen?" she cried again, embracing her long-lost sister.

"Oh, Ellen!" Gittchen cried, and fainted.

A little while later, Gittchen was sitting by the table surrounded by her parents and sister. "At last, Gittchen, you have come home again! We thought you had drowned on that fateful day when the dike broke. Where have you been? What brought you back to us?"

Gittchen told them what had happened to her, and with tears of joy gleaming in her eyes, she concluded: "The candles, mother! The Sabbath candles, burning in the window, brought me back home!"

ROSH HASHONAH: THE HEAD OF THE YEAR

THE STORY OF A PRAYER. In the city of Mayence early in the fourteenth century there lived a wealthy Jewish scholar. He was highly respected in the community and was always consulted on important Jewish problems. His name was Rabbi Amnon. Because of his brilliance and his great influence upon the community the local Bishop tried his utmost to convert him to Christianity. In this way the Bishop hoped that he might be able to convert the entire community, for all the Jews would follow Rabbi Amnon's example. Rabbi Amnon, of course, would not consider such an idea and he refused even to talk with the Bishop about it.

One day, after constant and persistent urging by the Bishop, Rabbi Amnon said that he would need three days to think the matter over. When the Bishop left, Rabbi Amnon deeply regretted what he had said and decided to forget the whole matter. The Bishop, however, did not forget the matter at all.

After three days, he sent for Rabbi Amnon to appear before him and give an answer. Rabbi Amnon refused to come and was brought before the Bishop by force. When the Bishop asked him what his punishment should be, Rabbi Amnon replied: "Let my tongue be cut out for daring to deny our G-D and our religion by saying that I needed three days to think the matter over."

The Bishop burned with anger. "I will not cut out your tongue, but I will cut off your legs," he replied, "for not coming to me as I commanded." Rabbi Amnon's legs were cut off. He was promised, however, that his life would be spared if he would convert.

When the Bishop saw that his efforts were useless, he had Rabbi Amnon thrown out into the street, more dead than alive. Several days later, on Rosh Hashonah, Rabbi Amnon, severely crippled and aching with unbearable pain, asked to be brought to the synagogue. He was carried to the front and was placed near the cantor. The cantor was about to begin the "Kedusha" prayer. "Give me just a few moments," said Rabbi Amnon, "to sanctify the name of our G-D and atone for my great sin." Rabbi Amnon lifted his eyes to heaven and from the depths of his heart came one of the most stirring and beautiful prayers ever written, the "Unesaneh Tokef." After his confession he closed his eyes and died.

This prayer was considered so expressive of the true spirit of Rosh Hashonah that it was permanently included in the Rosh Hashonah and Yom Kippur services. It is titled by the two words with which it begins, "Unesaneh Tokef."

WHAT IS THE SIGNIFICANCE OF ROSH HASHONAH? To the Jewish people Rosh Hashonah, the beginning of the year, is a time for taking inventory. If your father is in business, you probably know this term well. At certain periods during the year, the businessman or storekeeper checks his stock in order to find out how his business is doing. At the end of the year he again takes inventory, to determine whether he has had a good or bad year. As part of his inventory, he tries to detect the mistakes he made in order to better his business in the coming year.

To the Jewish people the new year means exactly this. When Rosh Hashonah comes we look back through the entire year and try to determine how well we have lived up to the Torah way of life. We take an inventory. How many "Mitzvos" have we fulfilled? How much charity have we given? How often have we acted wrongly toward our fellow men? We must make a thorough self-examination.

But, just as the businessman does, we must detect our mistakes. Where have we fallen short of what the Torah expects of us? How can we improve ourselves as Jews, as men? Again we can find the answer by studying the process of inventory. Just as the businessman plans his coming year so that he would not make the same mistakes that he made in the past, so the Jew makes a resolution to improve his ways in accordance with the ideals of Torah.

According to Jewish tradition, Rosh Hashonah is the day of judgment. On this day all of humanity must give account of its deeds in the past year, to G-D. If they have been good to their fellow men and have lived a life of honesty and kindness, they are more certain of being inscribed for a good year.

But, the Bible tells us, ". . . no man is so righteous upon earth, that he should always do good and not sin" (Koheles 7:20). So, on Rosh Hashonah, Jews all over the world assemble in synagogues to ask forgiveness from G-D. They repent for their sins and honestly resolve to improve their conduct in the coming year.

But to insure a good year, there must be three actions on our part: repentance, prayer and charity. We must repent of our sins in sincere prayer to G-D and promise that in the coming year we will improve in our fulfillment of "Mitzvos." We must show our sincerity by acting justly toward our fellow men for we are all children of G-D and we all deserve to share in the blessings He has granted.

LAWS AND CUSTOMS. *"Elul."* The Hebrew month of "Elul" is one of the most important months of the year. It is in this month that Jews the world over begin to make spiritual preparation for the forthcoming High Holidays, Rosh Hashonah and Yom Kippur. It is customary to sound the shofar during the month of "Elul" every morning after "Shacharis" to remind and stir the people to repentance. Special prayers are added to the morning and evening services during this month for the same reason.

SLICHOS. On the Saturday night before Rosh Hashonah we begin to recite special prayers of penitence; they are called in Hebrew, "Slichos." The first "Slichos" service begins after midnight. It is recited every morning thereafter until Rosh Hashonah. If Rosh Rashonah occurs on a Monday or Tuesday, the "Slichos" services begin on Saturday night a week earlier. The reader who leads the "Slichos" service should be a G-D fearing man and learned in the Torah.

THREE OTHER NAMES FOR ROSH HASHONAH. Rosh Hashonah occurs on the first and second days of the Hebrew month of "Tishrei." As its name implies, it is considered the beginning of the year. Although Rosh Rashonah lasts for two days, it is considered like one long day. Rosh Hashonah is also known by three other names; "Yom Hazikoron," "The Day of Remembrance"; "Yom Truoh," "The Day of Sounding," and "Yom Ha'din," "The Day of Judgment."

YOM HAZIKORON. On this day G-D remembers the deeds performed by every human being during the past year. In turn, every Jew asks G-D to have mercy upon him and to consider his good deeds and the good deeds of his forefathers.

YOM TRUOH. This name refers to the sounding of the shofar.

When we hear the shofar we become aware that it is time for repentance. The sound of the shofar recalls to us the courage of Abraham when he was told to sacrifice his son, Isaac. It brings to mind the revelation of the Torah to Moses and the Israelites at Mount Sinai. Just as the trumpet and the bugle are a call to arms in time of war, so the shofar is a call to duty for every man and woman and every boy and girl to fulfill their obligations to G-D, to Torah and to Israel.

YOM HA'DIN. Rosh Hashonah is the day of judgment; the day upon which the future of every human being is decided. The judgment by G-D is based upon two things: the individual's action during the past year and his resolution to improve his ways in the coming year.

THE SERVICES. Rosh Hashonah, as all Jewish holidays, begins in the evening with the "Ma'ariv" service. The services on Rosh Hashonah are read from a special prayer book. It is called a "Machzor" which means "cycle." The service is essentially the same as the daily "Ma'ariv" service except for the addition of a special sentence about the shofar before the "Shmoneh Esrei," and a special "Shmoneh Esrei."

After the "Ma'ariv" service it is customary for the people in the congregation to wish each other the traditional greeting, "L'shono Tovo Tikosaivu," "May you be inscribed (in the book of life) for a good year."

Upon returning from the synagogue, the "Kiddush" for Rosh Hashonah is recited and the holiday meal begins. It is customary to dip a piece of "challa" in honey and eat it at the beginning of the meal to symbolize a good and sweet year.

The following morning the entire family attends services. The "Shacharis" service is longer than a regular holiday "Shacharis" for it contains many added prayers of repentance.

After the "Shacharis" service, two scrolls are taken from

the Ark and six people are honored to recite the Torah blessings. If Rosh Hashonah falls on a Sabbath, seven people are called to the Torah (not counting "Maftir").

SOUNDING OF THE SHOFAR. After the Biblical portion had been read, we are ready to sound the shofar. The "Baal Tokaya," the man who sounds the shofar, recites two blessings. The first blesses the name of G-D, who commanded us to hear the sound of the shofar. The second, the "Shehecheyonu," thanks G-D for enabling us to reach this holiday season in health and happiness. The "Baal Tokaya" now sounds the shofar.

There are three series of notes sounded by the "Baal Tokaya": the "Tekiah," one long blast on the shofar, the "Shevorim," three shorter blasts, and the "Truoh," nine short sharp blasts.

If Rosh Hashonah occurs on a Sabbath the shofar is not sounded.

THE CANTOR'S PRAYER. Following the sounding of the shofar is the lengthy and impressive "Musaf" service. It begins with the recitation of a very humble prayer by the cantor. The prayer is titled by the three words with which it begins, "Hinini Heoni Mimaas." In this prayer the cantor appeals to G-D for himself and for the people of Israel, as a son appeals to his father. He asks for G-D's help to succeed in securing through his prayers a happy and healthy year for all Israel. The Torah scroll is then returned to the Ark and the special "Shmoneh Esrei" is recited by the congregation and repeated by the cantor.

ANOTHER BEAUTIFUL PRAYER. In the "Shmoneh Esrei" is found the very famous "Unesaneh Tokef" prayer that we mentioned at the beginning of this chapter. It describes Rosh Hashonah in G-D's Kingdom in heaven. G-D is seated upon

His throne surrounded by all the angels. The "Book of Remembrance" is opened and the deeds of every human being announce themselves. Just as the shepherd musters his sheep and causes them to pass beneath his staff, so G-D, the Shepherd of all living things, causes His creatures to pass before Him to face judgment.

THE THREE SECTIONS. The remaining portion of the "Shmoneh Esrei" is divided into three sections.

MALCHIYOS. This section is composed of prayers describing the glory of G-D's Kingdom and declaring His dominion over the universe.

ZICHRONOS. This section brings to mind the miracles G-D performed in the time of our forefathers and their devotion to His Glorious Name.

SHOFROS. The prayers in this section describe revelation of the Torah at Mount Sinai. They recall the thundering, the lightning and the loud blast of the shofar that was heard. Portions of the prophetic writings are read that predict the sounding of the shofar to summon the Jews scattered all over the world to return to the land of their fathers, under the leadership of the Messiah, a descendant of David.

THE CUSTOM OF TASHLICH. On the first day of Rosh Hashonah, in the late afternoon, it is customary to stand near a flowing river or stream and recite a special prayer to G-D asking forgiveness. We ask G-D to cleanse us of our sins and cast them into the river, for we regret that we have committed them and resolve not to sin in the future. This prayer is called, in Hebrew, "Tashlich" which means "casting away." At the end of the prayer we shake our garments as a symbol that we are resolved to shake off our sins.

TSOM GEDALIAH. The third day of the Hebrew month "Tishrei," the day after Rosh Hashonah, is a fast day. It is called "Tsom Gedaliah," the "Fast of Gedaliah." It is fully explained in the chapter on Fast Days.

THE TEN DAYS OF PENITENCE. The ten days beginning with Rosh Hashonah and ending with Yom Kippur are called "Aseres Y'mai T'shuvoh," the "Ten Days of Penitence." These days are designated by G-D as a trial period to find out whether we have truly turned over a new leaf for the coming year as we promised on Rosh Hashonah. Special prayers of penitence are added to the daily services during this period.

Our Sages tell us that our penitence on Rosh Hashonah and Yom Kippur can bring forgiveness only for the sins that we have committed against G-D. In order to be forgiven for the sins we have committed against our fellow men, however, we must ask forgiveness from the man whom we have wronged. This must be done before Yom Kippur.

SHABBOS SHUVO. The Sabbath between Rosh Hashonah and Yom Kippur is called "Shabbos Shuvoh," the Sabbath of Returning." It was given this name for two reasons. First, it occurs during the "Aseres Y'mai T'shuvoh" the days during which we return to G-D with all our hearts. Second, the "Haftorah" that is read on this "Shabbos" begins with the words, "Shuvoh Yisroel," "Return O Israel."

> *"Return O Israel to the Lord thy G-d; for thou hast stumbled through thy sins. Take with you words, and return to the Lord; say to Him, 'Pardon all our sins and accept our return to good; and let us render for steers the offering of our lips."*
> (*Hosea 14:2–3*)

ROSH HASHONAH IN BERDITCHEV

It was the first day of Rosh Hashonah in the synagogue of Rabbi Levi Yitzchok, the Rabbi of Berditchev. The synagogue was crowded. The Rabbi himself was at the "Amud" (reader's desk) leading the congregation in prayer.

"All declare Thy majesty, O G-D, who sittest in judgment . . ."

The Rabbi's soft voice touched the hearts of every worshiper. Hardly anybody's eyes were dry. From the women's gallery many a heartbreaking sob was heard.

"To Him, who searches the hearts on the Day of Judgment . . ."

As the Rabbi pronounced the words, his voice broke and everyone's heart was filled with sadness. Everybody pictured himself standing before the Seat of Glory, where the Judge of the whole universe presided, to dispense justice and pronounce the verdict. "Be merciful and gracious to us," was the silent plea coming from the hearts of every member of the congregation.

The Rabbi recited every line of the solemn prayer, which the congregants repeated, until he came to the line, "To Him, who acquires His servants in judgment . . ."

Here the Rabbi suddenly paused, his words dying on his lips. His "Tallis" slid from his head to his shoulders, revealing his pale face; his eyes were shut and he seemed to be in a trance.

A shudder passed through the worshipers. Something was wrong. A critical situation must have arisen in the Heavenly Court. The Prosecution was apparently on the verge of triumph, . . . Only increased prayer and repentance could change the probable verdict. . . . The congregation of worshipers held its breath, and waited with anxious hearts.

A few minutes later, the Rabbi seemed to come out of his trance. The color returned to his face, which now became radiant with joy. His voice shook with ecstasy and triumph as he recited:

"To Him, who acquires His servants in judgment!"

After the services, when the Rabbi was sitting at his festive table, surrounded by his ardent followers, one of the elders worked up enough courage to ask the Rabbi what had caused the interruption in his prayer and why precisely at those words.

The Rabbi began to relate:

—I felt myself lifted up to the gates of heaven, and then I saw Satan carrying a heavy load. The sight filled me with anxiety, for I knew that the "unholy one" was carrying a bagful of sins to put on the Scale of Justice before the Heavenly Court. Suddenly Satan put the bag down and hastened in a downward swoop—no doubt to pick up other sins committed by some Jew on this very solemn day. The bag having been left unattended, I went up to it and began to examine its contents. It was crammed with all kinds of sins; evil gossip, hatred without reason, jealousies, wasted time which should have been spent in the study of Torah, thoughtless prayers, and so on—ugly creatures of sin, big and small. And while I was wondering what to do, I knew that at that very moment the "One with a Thousand Eyes" had spied yet other sins and would soon bring them and put them into the bag.

"Things don't look so good," I thought. I pushed my hand into the bag and began pulling out one sin after another, to look at them more closely. I saw that almost all the sins were committed unwittingly or in sheer ignorance. No Jew was really bad, but the circumstances of exile, poverty and hardships, sometimes harden his heart, set his nerves on edge, bring about petty jealousies, and the like.

And strangely enough, as I was examining these sins and

thinking what was really behind them, they seemed to melt away, one by one, until hardly anything was left in the bag. The bag dropped back, limp and empty.

The next moment I heard a terrible cry. Satan was back. Discovering what I had done, he was filled with anger. "You thief! What did you do to my sins?" He grabbed at my beard yelling, "Thief! Robber! All year I labored to gather these precious sins and now you have stolen them. You shall pay double!"

"How can I pay you," I pleaded. "My sins may be many, but not so many."

"Well, you know the law," Satan answered. "He who steals must pay double, and if he is unable to pay, he shall be sold into servitude. You are my slave now! Come!"

The thought of being Satan's slave chilled my blood, and I almost collapsed. Finally my captor brought me before the Seat of Glory, and pleaded his case before the Judge of the Universe.

After listening to Satan's complaint, the Holy One, blessed is He, said: "I will buy him, for so I promised through my prophet Isaiah (46:4): 'Even to his old age, I will be the same, and when he is gray-haired, still will I sustain him. I have made him, I will bear him, I will sustain and save him.'"

At this point I came to—concluded the Rabbi of Berditchev. Now I understand the meaning of the words, "To Him, who acquires His servants in judgment."

YOM KIPPUR: THE DAY OF ATONEMENT

PURITY. The color of Yom Kippur is white. When you enter the synagogue on Yom Kippur eve you will see that the Holy Ark is covered with a white curtain and the cloth on the pulpit desk is white. The Torah scrolls, too, have white mantles. The congregants are wrapped in white "Taliyos" and are wearing white skullcaps. Some congregants are wearing the traditional white robe, the "Kittel."

What is the significance of white on Yom Kippur?

White is a symbol of purity. Doctors and nurses wear white uniforms as a sign of cleanliness. People who handle medicines and certain foods wear white aprons and white masks.

When we appear before G-D on Yom Kippur we are impure. We have sinned during the year and have blackened our record with bad deeds. The white we see in the synagogue is an expression of our desire for G-D to purify us by forgiving our wrongs. By devoting ourselves to prayer during the entire day of Yom Kippur, we show our sincerity when we ask for forgiveness. And this is the great power of Yom Kippur. Our Sages tell us that all those who honestly repent on Yom Kippur and promise to improve themselves during the coming year are forgiven; they are purified. They become as white and clean as a new-born child. They begin the new year with a fresh start.

But we must remember that white has another quality. It shows dirt very easily. So it is with us on Yom Kippur. We must remember to keep ourselves pure by living up to the promises we made.

We must seek only good and keep away from all evil. We must devote our lives to the study and practice of the Torah.

LAWS AND CUSTOMS. The holiday of Yom Kippur occurs on the tenth day of the Hebrew month of "Tishrei." It concludes the "Ten Days of Penitence."

A COLORFUL CEREMONY. On "Erev" Yom Kippur an interesting symbolic ceremony is performed; it is called "Kaporos," which means forgiveness. In the days of the Temple a special sacrifice was offered on Yom Kippur. It was called the "Offering of the Scapegoat."

Nowadays, although we no longer have our Temple in Jerusalem, we perform a ritual resembling the Yom Kippur sacrifice. We circle a fowl over our head and recite the prayer, "This is offered for us; this is our ransom; this is our atonement. This fowl shall meet death, but we shall find a long and pleasant life of peace." The fowl is then slaughtered and given to the poor. Money may be substituted for the fowl, in this ceremony, after which the money is given to charity. In this ritual we symbolically transfer our sins to the fowl and offer its death as our atonement. True forgiveness for our sins, however, can only come through repentance, prayer and deeds of righteousness.

"EREV" YOM KIPPUR. To show the sincerity of our repentance, it is a "Mitzvah" on Yom Kippur to remain in the synagogue for the entire day to devote ourselves to prayer. If we were too hungry and weak on Yom Kippur, however, we would not be able to concentrate properly on our prayers. For this reason, it is a great "Mitzvah" to eat a hearty meal on "Erev"

Yom Kippur, the day before Yom Kippur, in preparation for the fast.

On "Erev" Yom Kippur, in the late afternoon, it is proper to attend "Mincha" services at the synagogue. A special prayer of confession is added at the end of the "Shmoneh Esrei" of "Mincha." This prayer is called "Vidui" which means "confession." This is the first of nine confessionals that are recited on Yom Kippur. As a last gesture of righteousness before Yom Kippur, it is proper to give money to charity. In many syngagogues there are collection plates arranged on a table marked with the names of different institutions. These plates are called "K'aros Tsdokoh," which means "charity plates."

Towards evening the last meal before the fast takes place. This meal has its own special name. It is called "S'udah Hamafsekes" which means the "final meal." It is customary to eat a piece of bread in honey at this meal, as is done on Rosh Hashonah, as a symbol of our hope for a sweet year.

FASTING. The fast of Yom Kippur begins before sunset on "Erev" Yom Kippur and ends after dark the following day. Once the fast has begun, it is forbidden to have food or drink until it is over. It should be remembered that fasting applies only to males above the age of thirteen and females above the age of twelve. In case of sickness or inability to fast, a rabbi should be consulted. Although the other Fast Days of the year are postponed, should they fall on the Sabbath, this rule does not apply to Yom Kippur.

AN INTERESTING THOUGHT. On Yom Kippur it is customary to wear soft shoes or sandals that are not made of leather. Some people walk in the synagogue in their stockinged feet. Such practices are a sign of mourning; they express our sorrow on this solemn day for the sins we have committed during the year; also, it is one of the five pleasures forbidden on Yom Kippur.

There is another reason given to us by our Sages for this custom which is perhaps a bit more colorful. They tell us that when Adam, the first man, sinned by eating of the fruit of the Tree of Knowledge, the Earth that had brought forth this fruit became unholy. For this reason man was told to wear shoes to separate his feet from unholiness. When Moses approached the "burning bush" G-D told him to remove his shoes for the land that he was standing upon was holy; he had no need for shoes on holy land. Yom Kippur is the holiest day of the year; it brings holiness to the entire world and purifies it. And so, on Yom Kippur there is no need to wear shoes, for on this day even the ground becomes holy.

BLESSING THE CHILDREN. It is customary for the father to bless his children before the family leaves for the synagogue for the Kol Nidrei service. In this blessing the father asks that it be G-D's will that in these children be implanted the love and fear of G-D so that they will not sin. He prays that they will always desire to fulfil the "Mitzvos" and be inscribed for a good year among the righteous of Israel.

THE KITTEL. In many synagogues it is customary for the adult worshipers to wear white robes on Yom Kippur. This robe is called a "Kittel." The "Kittel" is a symbol of cleanliness; and it is cleansing from our sins that we wish to attain on this Day of Atonement. The curtain on the Ark, the cloths on the pulpits and the mantles on the Torahs are white for this same reason.

During the Kol Nidrei service all male worshipers wear "Taliyos." This is the only occasion during the year that the "Tallis" is worn by the congregation during an evening service.

THE SERVICES. Kol Nidrei is the opening prayer of the Yom Kippur services. The congregation assembles in the synagogue. Two Torah scrolls are removed from the Ark and are held by the leaders and elders of the congregation. The Kol Nidrei is chanted by the cantor three times in a tearful melody that reminds us of the centuries of suffering and torture endured by our people.

KOL NIDREI. Kol Nidrei is a petition presented to G-D asking Him to cancel those vows we may make to Him in the year to come which we might be unable to fulfil. This prayer is meant to include only the vows made between man and G-D. Any vows or promises made between one man and another must be kept unless they are canceled by both parties.

Though the author of the Kol Nidrei is unknown, it is held that it was written about the eighth century. In ancient times, as well as today, vows to G-D were often made without thinking and many times they were not fulfilled. To avoid such violations and use of the Name of G-D in vain the Kol Nidrei was composed to officially cancel such vows on Yom Kippur. In lands where the Jews were often forced to promise to accept another religion, it was this prayer that brought them peace of mind on Yom Kippur.

The "Ma'ariv" service for Yom Kippur is essentially the same as the one for Rosh Hashonah except for a special sentence about forgiveness that is recited before the "Shmoneh Esrei." At the end of the "Shmoneh Esrei," the second confessional is recited and the third at the completion of the "Ma'ariv" service.

SHACHARIS. The "Shacharis" service of Yom Kippur is similar to the one on Rosh Hashonah except for the addition of several prayers of repentance and declarations of the holiness of Yom Kippur. The fourth confessional is recited in the silent "Shmoneh Esrei," and the fifth at the close of the service.

After "Shacharis" the Torah scroll is read and is followed by the recitation of the memorial service called "Yizkor." This prayer recalls beloved parents and relatives who have departed. It helps us keep their pleasant memory fresh in our minds.

SEDER HOAVODAH. The "Musaf" of Yom Kippur is similar to the one recited on Rosh Hashonah except for a few additions and substitutions. The sections "Malchiyos," "Zichronos" and "Shofros" are not recited. Instead, a new section entitled "Seder Hoavodah" which means the "Order of the Temple Service," is substituted. "Seder Hoavodah" describes in detail the service performed by the High Priest in the Temple on Yom Kippur. When the cantor reaches the part that describes how the High Priest knelt and bowed down before G-D, he also kneels and bows down. In many synagogues it is customary for the men in the congregation to kneel and bow down with the cantor. By participating in this way, the service becomes more impressive.

OUR JEWISH MARTYRS. Another inspiring section in the "Musaf" on Yom Kippur is the "Aileh Ezherah," which means "These do I remember." This prayer is a description of the death of ten great Jewish scholars who were killed by Hadrian of Rome about the middle of the first century of the Common Era. These scholars defied the laws of Hadrian that prohibited the Jews from learning Torah and practicing Judaism. They met secretly to study and teach the religion that was so dear to them. When discovered they were subjected to severe torture and a painful death. Their memory has lived on through the ages as the martyrs who died for the sanctification of G-D's Name.

The sixth and seventh confessionals are recited during the "Musaf" service.

THE PRIESTLY BLESSING. The "Musaf" is concluded with the priestly blessing recited by the cantor, and the "Kohanim." This custom dates back to the time of Aaron, the first High

Priest of Israel. The "Kohanim" ascend the pulpit and recite in a chant the ancient blessing. They are led by the cantor.

"MINCHA." The afternoon service, "Mincha," begins with the Torah reading. The last person to receive a Torah honor chants the "Haftorah." The "Haftorah" is taken from the book of Jonah. It tells the colorful story of Jonah and the whale and teaches us the lesson that it is never too late to repent for our sins. The eighth and nine confessionals are recited at this service completing the confessionals for Yom Kippur.

NE'ELAH. The closing prayer of Yom Kippur is called "Ne'elah," which means "closing." There are two reasons for this name. The great Sage Rabbi Johanan held that "Ne'elah" referred to the closing of the Temple gates in Jerusalem, which took place after the priestly blessing. Another great Sage, Rav, held that "Ne'elah" referred to the gates of heaven, which are closed at the end of this service. As the day fades into the dusk with the recitation of prayers of repentance and quotations from the Bible, the gates of heaven are closed and our judgment is sealed. "Ne'elah" ends with the famous proclamation of our religion, "Hear, O Israel, the Lord our G-D, the Lord is One."

The shofar is sounded to announce the end of Yom Kippur, which is followed by the "Ma'ariv" service. The congregants return to their homes exhausted and hungry, but joyful and confident of a happy and healthy new year.

After the evening meal is over and everyone is rested, it is customary for the father and the children to go out into the yard and in some small way begin building the hut for the forthcoming holiday of "Succos." By this act we begin the new year and our clean page in G-D's "Book of Life" the best way possible: with a "Mitzvah."

THE OPEN MACHZOR

It was Yom Kippur eve. A breathless hush descended on the congregation as all eyes turned upon the figure of the "Baal Shem Tov." He stood there dressed in his white "Kittel" and wrapped in his "Tallis," which covered his bowed head. As everyone waited while the "Baal Shem Tov" prepared himself for the sacred "Kol Nidre," those nearer him saw a shadow pass over his face, but no one dared ask him what was wrong. His distress was reflected in the faces of all present, as they recited the moving prayer "Kol Nidre."

During the brief pause between "Kol Nidrei" and "Ma-ariv" the "Baal Shem Tov" again became sunk in thought. Suddenly a gentle smile lit up his face, and as he asked for the "Ma'ariv" service to be recited, everyone present felt relieved. They did not know the reason for their Rabbi's earlier distress, nor did they know the reason why he smiled. All they knew was that whatever affected their saintly leader, also affected each and every one of them.

At the conclusion of Yom Kippur the "Baal Shem Tov" told his followers this story:

My friends, I am going to tell you what affected me so deeply last night during the services. The story is connected with a Jewish innkeeper in a nearby village. The innkeeper was a fine, honest and G-d-fearing Jew whom the landlord, a Polish noble-man, greatly admired and treated as a personal friend. Suddenly, without any warning illness, the innkeeper died, leaving behind him a young widow and a baby boy. The poor young woman became deeply affected by her loss, and before long she, too, died.

The Polish nobleman was greatly upset by the passing of his tenant and friend, and when the widow also died he felt it his duty to take the baby into his care. He gave the baby the best care and brought him up as his own son.

Years passed, but the child did not know that he was not the son of the Christian nobleman. One day, however, the nobleman had invited some friends to visit him at his estate. While the children were playing in the garden, one of them, in the course of a quarrel called the nobleman's "son" a Jew. The boy quickly ran to the nobleman crying, and asked him if it was true that he was a Jew.

"My dear boy," he replied gently. "You know how much I love you and that I have treated you as if you were my very own son. When I die you will be my heir; I'll leave everything to you; my estate, my orchards and my forests. What more could I do for you?"

"So I'm not your real son! I'm a Jew, and you never told me," the boy burst out sobbing. "Who were my parents? I must know, please!"

The nobleman put his arms around the boy's shoulders trying to comfort him. "My boy, you can be proud of your parents. They were very fine people indeed; good, G-d-fearing Jews. Your father was my friend. It was for his sake that I felt it my duty to take you into my home and bring you up as I would my own son. You know I have no other children and I love you very dearly."

Bit by bit the boy got the story of his own poor Jewish parents. The nobleman told him that his parents had nothing at all to leave him excepting a small package which he had hidden away in a safe place, waiting for the right moment to give it to him. The moment now had come and so he went and brought the package and gave it to the boy. With trembling hands the boy opened the package and beheld an old black velvet bag with strange gold lettering on it. He opened the bag and took out a white woolen shawl, two small black boxes wound about with leather straps, and a book. Of course the boy did not know what the "Tallis" and "Tephillin" were, nor could he understand what was in the thick book, which was a "Machzor." But because these precious things had once belonged to his parents, his real parents, whom he had never known, he meant to treasure them as long as he lived.

Once the nobleman had to leave on a business trip, which gave the boy a chance to think in peace and quiet. He took long walks in the woods and spent hours thinking. He had loved the nobleman and was grateful to him, and yet a strange feeling took hold of him, which urged him to seek out his Jewish brethren. He knew there were some who lived on the nobleman's estates. He would go and see them; talk to them. Perhaps some of them remembered his parents.

That night he dreamt that his parents came to him. They told him he was no longer a child. He must realize that he is a Jew and go back to his people.

The next day, very early, he darted out of the house so that none of the servants should stop or question him. He walked until he reached the next village where he saw some Jews packing bundles and loading them on carts.

"Good day," he called to them. "Are you going to some fair?"

"No, not this time," they replied. "It will soon be our holy day Yom Kippur. We are taking our families to the next big town so that at least at this sacred time we can all pray in the synagogue with other Jews."

The boy returned home lost in thought. Why had he not taken his parents' gift with him to show to these Jews? They would have told him what these things were and how they were to be used. The thought gave him no rest.

A few days went by and the nobleman had not yet returned. The boy suddenly decided he was old enough to make up his own mind about this problem which affected his whole future. He was a Jew and he meant to go back to his people. So he packed some clothing, took some food, left a note telling his father where he had gone, and set off for the town to which the village Jews said they were going.

After several days of traveling, getting a hitch when he could, he finally reached his destination. He found out where the synagogue was and reached it just as the haunting notes of "Kol Nidre" were being sung. Quietly the boy slipped inside and took a place near the door. The scene which met his gaze filled him with awe. He looked around him and beheld Jews of all ages praying with all their hearts, some with tears in their eyes. He felt a lump in his own throat as he quietly took out his own white shawl and wrapped it around his shoulders. He took out his book and tried to hold it as he saw the others hold theirs. But when he opened it and could not read the words, sobs suddenly shook his young body.

With tears streaming down his cheeks the boy cried out: "O, G-D! You know I cannot read, nor do I know what to say or how to pray. I am just a lost Jewish boy. Here is the whole Prayer Book! Please, dear G-D, take out the right words to form the prayers for me."

The despair of this poor Jewish boy reached the Heavenly Court and the gates were flung open for his prayer. And together with his simple prayer, our prayers were accepted.

❖   ❖   ❖

When the "Baal Shem Tov" finished this moving story, tears stood in the eyes of all his listeners. And often, when praying, they thought about this strange story of the young Jewish boy who had been lost to his people for a time. And they thought of themselves, that they, too, were often like lost souls who did not really know how to pray as they should. They all earnestly hoped, like the boy, that the kind and merciful G-D on High would accept their prayers and grant each and every one of them a truly happy new year. For the important thing about prayer, after all, is the sincerity and devotion to G-D, which come from the heart.

SUCCOS: A LESSON IN HAPPINESS

WHAT IS HAPPINESS? If all the people in the world were asked what they wanted more than anything else, they would probably answer "happiness." But if you asked them how to achieve happiness, they would probably all give different answers.

Many people think that money can buy happiness. They spend a whole lifetime accumulating wealth. They work extra hours on their job; they save, they invest their money in different businesses and spend their free time thinking up new ideas on how to acquire more wealth. The more money they have, the more they think they need. As King Solomon so wisely said, "One who loves money can never have enough of it" (Koheles 5:9). They give so much time to their businesses that they have little time to use the money they earn. In later years, when they look back at their wasted life, they realize that money is no guarantee for happiness.

Some people think happiness means having a good time. These people spend most of their time at parties and other such social events and neglect their family life. Only when they lose the respect of their children do they realize that the way of life they have been leading is wrong.

How can we achieve true happiness?

The holiday of "Succos" gives us a wonderful lesson. On "Succos" the Torah tells us to leave our fine homes and live in small humble huts for seven days. Only in the small hut, the "Succah," can your holiday be a true "Zman Simcho-seinu," "The Time of Our Rejoicing," the Torah tells us.

Gather your family, relatives and friends into the "Succah" for they are your most precious possessions. Eat, drink, sing and dance with them for seven days and learn the lesson of "Succos."

You don't need material possessions to be happy. As the "Succah" has shown you, people can be happy in even a small hut. You do need love. Love your family, love your neighbor, love all of G-D's creations, and above all, love G-D. Remember that it is His kindness that has given you all the blessings of this world. Remember that it is His wisdom that has given you the world's greatest treasure, the Torah. And as you look up through the temporary roof of your "Succah" and see the soft white clouds upon the pale blue sky, learn the most important lesson of "Succos." All was created, all exists, and all is responsible to, the King of Kings, the Holy One blessed be His Name.

LAWS AND CUSTOMS. The holiday of "Succos" begins on the fifteenth day of the month of "Tishrei," the fifth day after Yom Kippur. It is a nine-day celebration. "Succos" commemorates the time the Israelites lived in temporary dwellings, in huts, during their wandering in the wilderness for forty years before they were permitted to enter the Promised land of Canaan.

"Succos" is one of the three pilgrimage festivals, the "Sholosh Regolim." It was on these three festivals: "Pesach," "Shavuos" and "Succos" that Jews from all parts of Israel made pilgrimages to the Temple in Jerusalem.

CHAG HO'OSIF. Another name for "Succos" is "Chag Ho'osif" which means "The Holiday of Gathering." It commemorates the harvest season in Israel. In the days of the Temple, having gathered the harvest, the people joyfully made their pilgrimage to Jerusalem where they expressed their gratitude to G-D. It was gratitude for the season's crop, part of which they brought as a gift to the Temple.

Z'MAN SIMCHOSEINU. "Succos" was always celebrated with great rejoicing. In the days of the Temple, the joyous processions and the throngs of pilgrims in Jerusalem were anxiously awaited by all Israel. Nowadays it is a time for family and friends to rejoice in the "Succah" and in the synagogue. It was aptly given the name "Z'man Simchoseinu," "The Time of Our Rejoicing."

THE PARTS OF THE HOLIDAY. The holiday of "Succos" is divided in the following way: The first two days are called days of "Yom Tov"; they are full holidays to which all the laws of holidays apply. The following four days are called "Chol Hamoed"; they are half holidays and are, from the standpoint of holiday laws, almost like weekdays. (The holiday laws are the same as those for Shabbos" except that cooking and carrying are permitted.)

The seventh day of "Succos" is called "Hoshanah Rabboh." The eighth and ninth days are days of "Yom Tov" where again all the holiday laws apply. The eighth day is "Shmini Atseres" and the ninth day is "Simchas Torah." These two days are added to the seven-day holiday of "Succos" and are celebrated as part of it.

SUCCAH. It is a commandment in the Torah that the Jews should live in huts at this season for seven days. These huts are called "Succos." Many people construct their own "Succos." In this way they are participating more fully in the "Mitzvah." The "Succah" has a temporary roof of bamboo sticks or pine branches loosely arranged so that the sky can be seen through them. The roof covering is called "S'chach."

When we sit and eat in the "Succah" we can truly picture the lives of our ancestors as they wandered through the wilderness.

OOSHPIZIN. Each time we enter the "Succah" to have a meal we recite a prayer known as "Ooshpizin." This prayer refers to our forefathers Abraham, Isaac, Jacob, Joseph, Moses, Aaron and David who are invited to our "Succah" as welcome guests. They were the builders of Jewish life in the past and we look to their spirits to inspire Israel to build Jewish life in the future.

KIDDUSH. During the days of "Yom Tov" we recite the traditional holiday "Kiddush'" in the "Succah." Whenever we enter the "Succah" it is proper to recite the blessing honoring the Name of G-D, who commanded us to dwell in the "Succah." On the first two nights of "Succos," and on "Shmini Atseres" and "Simchas Torah," the "Shehecheyonu" is also recited. We thank G-D for granting us the blessing of reaching this holiday season in health and happiness.

THE FOUR SPECIES. "And you shall take for yourselves on the first day the fruits of goodly trees, branches of palm trees, boughs of thick trees and willows of the brook, and you shall rejoice before the Lord for seven days." (Vayikro 23:40). From this sentence in the Torah our Sages learned that there are four species of plant that are to be used as symbols on the holiday of "Succos." They learned through tradition that these four species are the "Esrog"—the citron; the "Lulov"—the palm branch; the "Hodos"—the myrtle branch, and the "Arovoh"—the willow branch.

Three of the "Hodos" branches and two of the "Arovoh" branches are tied to the "Lulov." Whenever ceremonies are performed with these species the "Lulov" is held in the right hand and the "Esrog" in the left.

Many people make a special effort to secure an "Esrog" that was grown in Israel, for Israel specializes in the growing of citrus fruits. Thus in addition to the "Mitzvah" of "Esrog" we also establish closer contact with the Holy Land.

Every morning from the first through the seventh day of "Succos" (except on the Sabbath) we hold the "Esrog" and "Lulov" and recite the blessing honoring the Name of G-D who commanded us to fulfil this "Mitzvah." On the first day of "Succos" also the "Shehecheyonu" is recited. Should the first day of "Succos" fall on "Shabbos" when the "Esrog" and "Lulov" are not used, the "Shehecheyonu" is recited on the second day.

MEANING OF THE FOUR SPECIES. A colorful interpretation of the four species is given in the "Talmud." The four species represent four categories into which the Jews fall.

1. ESROG. This fruit has both good taste and pleasant aroma. It represents the Jew who has knowledge of the Torah and also good deeds.
2. LULOV. This branch comes from a tree, whose fruit has a good taste but no aroma. It represents the Jew who has knowledge of the Torah, but is lacking in good deeds.
3. HODOS. These branches have no taste but have a pleasant aroma. They represent the Jew who has little or no knowledge of the Torah but yet performs good deeds.
4. AROVOH. These branches have neither taste nor aroma. They represent the Jew who has neither knowledge of the Torah nor performs good deeds.

The binding and holding of the four species together carries with it the message of national unity. Although Jews are different from each other in many ways, every Jew is necessary to the People of Israel. We must all realize this. Only in this way can all Israel benefit from one another.

HOSHANOS. On the first six days of "Succos," following the "Musaf" service, special prayers asking for G-D's help are recited. These prayers are called "Hoshanos," the plural form of the word "Hoshano," which means "O Help Us." As these "Hoshanos" are recited all males in the congregation who have an "Esrog" and "Lulov" follow the reader around the pulpit in a single procession. On the seventh day of "Succos," which is called "Hoshano Rabboh," "Great Hoshano," all the "Hoshanos" that were recited during the past six days are recited again. On this day the procession goes around the pulpit seven times. This ceremony is in commemoration of a similar ceremony that took place in Jerusalem, at this time, in the days of the Temple.

SIMCHAS BEIS HASHOEIVOH. In the days of the Temple, on the eve of the second day of "Succos" a beautiful ceremony took place. It was called "Simchas Beis Hashoeivoh," "The Celebration of the Water Drawing." The "Kohanim" together with the "Leviyim" and the rest of the people in Jerusalem formed a procession to the well outside the city. The procession was led by the "Kohanim," also by the "Leviyim," who played musical instruments and sang songs of praise to G-D. The streets were lit with torches carried by the people to light up the way. When they arrived at the water well they drew water and brought it to the Temple. There it was poured on the altar by the "Kohanim."

"Simchas Beis Hashoeivoh" was a celebration looked forward to by all Israel. The event was considered so spectacular that it led one of our Sages to declare: "He who has not seen the Celebration of the Water Drawing has not seen a real celebration in his life."

Nowadays, in commemoration of this ceremony, a joyous celebration is held on the second night of "Succos." Congregations have parties in their "Succos" where they eat, drink and sing songs.

LAWS OF THE SERVICES. During the entire holiday of "Succos" the "Hallel" is recited after the "Shacharis" service.

Every day of "Succos" the Torah is read and the "Musaf," the additional service for holidays, is recited.

"SHMINI ATSERES." The eighth day of the "Succos" holiday celebration is called "Shmini Atseres." This day is a holiday in itself. Our Sages interpret this extra day as if it were a plea from G-D to tarry with Him an additional day.

On "Shmini Atseres," as on all holidays, the morning service, "Shacharis," is essentially the same as the Sabbath "Shacharis." The "Musaf" includes a holiday "Shmoneh Esrei." After the "Shacharis" service, the Torah scroll is read and is followed by the "Yizkor" prayer, a memorial service for the dead.

In the "Musaf" "Shmoneh Esrei" the cantor recites a prayer called "T'filas Geshem." As its name implies, it is a prayer asking G-D for ample rain during the season so that we will have abundant crops.

"SIMCHAS TORAH." The day after "Shmini Atseres" is perhaps the most joyous and most widely celebrated Jewish holiday. This holiday is called "Simchas Torah," which means "The Rejoicing with the Law." On this day we complete our weekly Torah readings. The readings are arranged to complete the entire Torah in a year cycle. The completion of the Torah is celebrated with song, dance and much merriment.

HAKOFOS. On the eve of "Simchas Torah" after the "Ma'ariv" service, there is held a beautiful and joyous Torah procession called "Hakofos," which means "Circling." First, a prayer called "Atah Horeiso" is recited, each verse by different members of the congregation. The Torah scrolls are then taken out of the Ark and carried around the synagogue seven times. The processions are conducted with much singing and dancing by the Torah bearers and the congregation. It is customary for the children to follow the Torah bearers, during each procession, carrying flags with various inscriptions. After each procession the Torah scrolls change hands, so that every member of the congregation is given a chance to carry the Torah around the synagogue. The "Hakofos" are repeated the following morning after the "Shacharis."

EVENING TORAH READING. After the "Hokofos" the Torahs are put back into the Ark with the exception of one, which is placed on the reading table. Three persons receive Torah honors, "Aliyos." The eve of "Simchas Torah" is the only time the Torah is read at night.

MORNING TORAH READING. After the "Shacharis" service and the "Hakofos" which follow it, the Torah scroll is read. Three Torahs are used on this day. In the first scroll we read the last portion of the Torah entitled "V'zos Habrochoh," the two words with which this portion begins. On "Simchas Torah" morning all the males in the synagogue are called to the Torah, even those who are not yet Bar mitzvah but can recite the blessings.

KOL HAN'ORIM. In order to give even the smallest male child the privilege of a Torah honor, a special ceremony is performed. This ceremony is called "Kol Han'orim," which means "All the Boys." An adult is chosen to recite the Torah blessings. He goes up to the reading table with a large "Tallis" spread over him like a canopy. All the children who are too young to recite the Torah blessings themselves are gathered under the "Tallis." The adult recites the blessings word by word and the children repeat after him.

CHASAN TORAH. After all the congregants have received their Torah honors one person is chosen to recite the final

Torah blessing for the concluding portion of the Torah. This special honor is called "Chasan Torah," which means "the Bridegroom of the Torah."

CHASAN BEREISHIS. With the completion of the first scroll the second scroll is put on the reading desk. On "Simchas Torah" we not only complete the Torah readings for the year, but we also begin them.

And so, a member of the congregation is given the special honor of reciting the Torah blessing upon the freshly begun Torah. This honor is called "Chasan Bereishis," which means "The Bridegroom of Bereishis." ("Bereishis" is the first portion of the Torah.)

The "Chasan Torah" and the "Chasan Bereishis" symbolize the everlasting quality of the Torah. As soon as it is finished it is begun once more. There is no end to the reading of the Torah, just as there is no end to the knowledge we can gain from studying it.

The third Torah scroll is now put on the reading desk and the "Maftir" is called. With the recitation of the "Haftorah" the lengthy Torah reading for "Simchas Torah" is brought to a close. The "Musaf" is recited, and is followed later in the afternoon by the "Mincha" service.

In the evening the "Ma'ariv" service is recited, which includes the "Havdolah" ceremony that divides holidays from the weekdays. This final ceremony officially ends the nine-day celebration of "Succos."

THE SECRET WEAPON

Corporal Irving Stolz was really angry when his furlough was cancelled. He had made all arrangements to spend "Succos" in Tokyo with some old friends. He had visions of sitting in a peaceful "Succah" away from the battle front, where the singing of "Zmiros" would not be drowned out by the drone of airplanes overhead and the bursting of shells too close for comfort.

Providence wanted it otherwise. Two days before "Succos" the orders came through: in three hours the division was to move forward. It had been held in reserve for the all-out attack on the Central Korean front which was to be launched immediately.

Well, that was that. This was war and there was nothing Irving could do about it. Hastily he gathered his few belongings together. He fingered tenderly for a moment the little velvet bag which held his most precious possession, the "Tephillin," before he packed them in. Pretty soon his pack was full and ready. Just then the mail carrier brought him a Special Delivery package. It was from his father. Irving was delighted to find in it a "Lulov" and a beautiful "Esrog," which was quite perfect, without a spot or flaw. "A jewel of an 'Esrog,'" Irving thought, inhaling the beautiful fragrance. "How thoughtful of Dad to have sent me this wonderful thing!" Irving thought gratefully but there was no time to put his thoughts down in a letter home. Who knows when he would be able to write again?

Irving looked at the "Lulov" with the willow and myrtle twigs tied to it, and the "Esrog" and wondered whether he would be able to use them. Finally, he put them back in their tin foil wrapping and carefully put them in his bag. The next moment the order came to move. Irving took his place on the jeep and off they went on the muddy and uneven road that led to the front lines. His nervousness which had filled his mind at the thought of going into enemy fire, gave way to a new feeling stirred up by the gift from home that he received a few moments ago. Somehow he felt a great spiritual comfort at the thought that in addition to the "Tephillin" he also had the "Four Kinds" (Lulov and Esrog, myrtle and willow) to protect him in time of danger.

During the next few days Irving's division was involved in bitter fighting. Irving had little opportunity to think of "Yom Tov." But twice he was able to unpack his "Lulov" and "Esrog" and recite the blessing over them. Although hardly able to stand on his feet from fatigue, and while his comrades dropped down to snatch a few minutes of sleep, Irving fervently made the prescribed motions moving the "Lulov" and "Esrog" back and forth in the direction of the four winds and toward heaven and earth and proclaiming G-D's rule over the universe and dispelling the forces of evil. He felt that there was more power in that symbolic act of Jewish faith than there might be in any weapon he might use against the Reds and he was filled with a peace he had never known before.

The attack of the U.N. forces carried them deep into enemy lines, and although the objectives were attained, a good many days were spent in consolidating positions.

"Succos" had thus long passed. The "Lulov" and "Esrog" had shriveled almost beyond recognition, but Irving could not make himself throw them away although they were of no further use to him.

One misty night the Reds began their counter offensive. The surprise of the counter attack gave the Reds the advantage. They overran the positions of the U.N. forces and forced them to retreat. In the hasty retreat Irving lost his belongings. Irving's company bore the brunt of the attack, for they held a strategic mountain and were ordered to hold the enemy as long as possible to enable the major forces to withdraw. It was there that Irving was seriously wounded.

When he next opened his eyes, he found himself in the military hospital in Tokyo, where he had been flown by airplane. He was now out of danger and on the road to recovery.

One day Irving was called into the main office. He was greeted by a smartly dressed captain of the Army Special Service. "How do you feel, Sergeant Stolz?" the captain asked him with special emphasis on his rank.

"Corporal Stolz, sir, at your service," Irving replied. "I feel very well, thank you, sir."

"You have been promoted, Sergeant Stolz. Furthermore, you have received a citation for bravery beyond the call of duty and are a candidate for the Purple Heart."

Irving was quite surprised. "What did I do?" he said in a shaky voice.

"You saved many lives and nearly lost your own. I am proud to shake your hand," the captain said.

Allowing Irving to recover somewhat, the captain then took out a large file from his suitcase and unfolded quite a story.

"We would like to clear up a few things, Sergeant Stolz," he said, and went on:

"When our forces captured the field headquarters of the Red Intelligence, we found a file marked 'Secret and Confidential.' It contained a report of a new weapon captured from the U.S. troops. The Red Intelligence worked very hard to determine the nature of the new weapon but could not solve the mystery. The new weapon was described as a suspicious looking thing, about the size of a hand grenade, camouflaged by something like the branch of a palm. The report went on to say that after having taken all necessary precautions, the objects were dispatched to Moscow for special examination and determination, and the matter awaited further results. The file contained a special film I will throw it on the screen."

The captain turned to the projector and set the motor in motion. Irving soon recognized his bag which he saw opened by a Red Korean Intelligence officer. The next moment he saw the Red bring out a tin can in which he kept the "Esrog," and the tin-foiled "Lulov." The Reds handled these objects very carefully, showing them from all sides and angles, and then put them in a special steel safe with a special label. Here the film ended, and Irving's laughter began. He laughed and laughed and the captain joined him. Their laughter roared like thunder until a couple of orderlies anxiously peered in to see what had happened.

Finally, the captain became serious, and said, "It so happens that several of these 'secret weapons' passed through our office to the Jewish chaplains for the Feast of Tabernacles. Were you an Acting Chaplain, sergeant?"

"No, sir. My father sent me the 'Lulov' and 'Esrog' as every Jew must observe a special precept involving them on the holiday of 'Succos.'"

"But surely you could have put in a few extra rations if you had not taken them to the battle front. Was it so important to take the 'Lulov' and 'Esrog' into battle?"

"You see, captain, the 'Succah,' which is the booth that is built for this festival, and the 'Lulov' and 'Esrog,' assure us of Divine protection. I cannot tell you how much those sacred objects meant to me. They gave me courage and faith. That's why I took them with me to the front."

"Do you think you would have been able to do the things you did without them?"

"I don't know, sir, but I am sure they helped.

"Good Heavens! I wish all the Jewish servicemen had taken a 'Lulov' and 'Esrog' along with them to the front. Maybe the war would have been won by now. Anyway, my heartiest congratulations, Sergeant Stolz, and my best wishes for a 'Refuah Shlemah!'"

"Are you Jewish, captain?"

"Yes, my friend, but till now I did not know how Jewish I was. 'Shalom!'"

The two soldiers parted smiling.

CHANUKAH: A SPIRITUAL VICTORY

It is interesting to note that of all the holidays in the year, Chanukah is the only one that we are told to publicize. We are told that the "menorah," which is the symbol of Chanukah, should be put on a window sill or near the window so that all who pass will see it. What makes this holiday so important that we want everyone, Jew and non-Jew alike, to take notice of it?

To answer this question, we must understand the reason why we celebrate Chanukah. Chanukah is celebrated for two reasons. The first is the victory of the Maccabees over the Greeks and the second is the miracle of the cruse of oil that burned for eight days when it only had the natural capacity to burn for one. Let us take the first reason and analyze it more carefully.

UNDER THE RULE OF ANTIOCHUS. Antiochus, the Greek ruler, did not want to destroy the Jewish people; he wanted to destroy the Jewish religion. If the Jews were to become pagans, idol worshipers, Antiochus would have granted them full citizenship in his domain. What was the situation among the Jews that made Antiochus think that he could influence them to convert to paganism?

In those days there were Jews who rebelled against the laws of Judaism. They circulated among the people and tried to persuade them to become like the Greeks, under whose rule they lived. They argued that separating themselves from the Greek culture had caused the Jews much trouble. Some of the people were influenced by these rebels and they went to the king to get permission to introduce pagan customs among themselves. The king granted them permission and they erected a gymnasium in Jerusalem, where Greek games and idol worship were practiced, and abandoned themselves completely to the practice of the pagans.

Some years later, Jason, who was the High Priest of Israel at that time, promised the king much money if he were granted permission to build a college and an institution for physical exercise, and the inhabitants of Jerusalem were granted citizenship of Antioch. The king conceded and Jason began leading his countrymen astray, persuading them to adopt the customs of the Greeks. He discarded the customs of the Jewish religion and substituted for them Greek customs. Jason and his followers had so great an influence upon the Jews that even the priests neglected their duties in the Temple and instead ran to participate in the Greek games.

Antiochus would never have tried to convert the Jews had he not been reassured by the priests of Israel that Judaism no longer held first place in their hearts. The priests told him that the Jews were only waiting for him to place a Greek idol in the Temple.

THE REBELLION. There was one priestly family that did not think as the ungodly priests; it was the family of the Hasmoneans, or Maccabees, as they were later called. Mattathias and his five sons knew that it was wrong to forsake their religion. They knew that the Jews had sinned greatly in adopting the customs of the Greeks, which were so contrary to Jewish beliefs. When an altar was put in the market place of the town of Modin for sacrifice to the Greek god, Mattathias was the first to be approached.

"Though all the nations that are under the king's dominion obey him, and all fall away from the religion of their fathers," he said, "yet will I and my sons walk according to the ways of our fathers." And when one of the Jews stepped out from among the crowd that had gathered in the market place, to sacrifice to the Greek god, Mattathias killed him, together with the king's officers who stood there.

"Whoever is for G-D follow me," he shouted, and he and his sons fled to the mountains.

In a short time Mattathias raised a small army and planned to free the Jews from the Greek influence and the rule of Antiochus. As you remember, the Jews won great victories under the leadership of Judah Maccabee, who had replaced his aged father, and they returned to Jerusalem.

When the Maccabees saw the Temple desecrated by the Greek idols, their hearts bled, but they did not lose courage. They threw the Greek idols out of the Temple, cleaned it, and replaced the old vessels with new ones. As a final touch, they had to light the "Menorah."

By law the "Menorah" was to be kept burning in the Temple continuously. Specially prepared oil was used for this purpose to insure its purity. The oil was put into containers that were marked with the seal of the High Priest. When the Maccabees looked for the oil, they found a small cruse which contained only enough oil for one day. They put it into the Menorah and hoped for the best. In the meantime they began to prepare new oil. The process took eight days. To their surprise, the oil in the Menorah, which was enough for only one day, lasted miraculously for eight days. The rededication of the Temple occurred on the twenty-fifth day of the month of Kisleiv in the year 165 B. C. E.

Not only did the Jews win a victory over Antiochus, but even more important, they won a victory over themselves. It took a Mattathias to teach them that the right way is the way of the Torah. Only the Torah can preserve the Jewish people. It was the example set by one family that influenced all the people. This is the lesson taught by Chanukah. Our Sages tell us to display the Chanukah "menorah" at the window so that all who see it will remind themselves of the Chanukah story. As Mattathias in his day, we in our day must set an example for all the people. By displaying the "menorah," we show all who pass our window that we are proud of our heritage.

LAWS AND CUSTOMS. The Chanukah festival, which is observed for eight days, begins on the twenty-fifth day of the Hebrew month "Kisleiv." The word Chanukah is composed of two parts, "Chanu" and "Kah." "Chanu" means "they camped" referring to the victory, and "kah" are the Hebrew letters "kaf" and "hei," which together mean twenty-five. And so we have the name Chanukah, which means "They camped on the twenty-fifth day." This holiday is also known as the "Feast of Lights" and the "Feast of Dedication."

THE MENORAH. As a symbol and a reminder of the miracle of the oil, we light and display a model "menorah" each night of the holiday. We begin with one candle and add one candle each night, bringing it to a total of eight candles on the eighth night of Chanukah. The "menorah" is lit by a special lighting candle called a "shamash." It is placed a little higher in the "menorah" to show that it is not part of the Chanukah candles. The candles are put into the "menorah" from right to left, the candle on the extreme right is put in on the first night. Each night a new candle is added on that side. In lighting the "menorah," however, we go from left to right. The newest candle is lit first, and followed by the second newest and so on.

The "menorah" should be lit in the evening after the "Ma'ariv" service. The candles should burn for at least half an hour. When lighting the "menorah" the entire family should be present to fulfil the "Mitzvah." On the first night of Chanukah, three blessings are recited before lighting the candles. They follow the same general pattern as the "Megillah" blessings on Purim. The first blessing indicates the fulfillment of the "Mitzvah"; the second thanks G-D for the miracle, and the third, the "Shehecheyonu," thanks G-D for enabling us to reach this holiday season in health and happiness. After the first night, only the first two blessings are recited. Each household must light its own "menorah."

On Friday eve, the Chanukah "menorah" must be lit before the Sabbath candles. Had the Sabbath candles been lit first, it would not have been permissible to light the Chanukah candles, since the Sabbath would have already been officially accepted. On Sabbath night the "Havdolah" is recited to officially end the Sabbath and then the "menorah" is lit.

ADDITIONAL PRAYERS. On Chanukah a special prayer is added to the "Shmoneh Esrei," thanking G-D for the miracles he performed for our ancestors at that time. It is also included in the "Grace After Meals." It is similar to the prayer added on Purim and is called by the same name "Al Hanissim." In addition to this prayer, the "Hallel" is recited during the "Shacharis" service every day of Chanukah. Each day of Chanukah the Torah is read in the synagogue after the "Shacharis" service.

MIRIAM'S FIRST CHANUKAH

Miriam drew the collar of her coat close about her neck, and hastened to join her friends Judith and Naomi. They had been waiting for her at the foot of the school steps before she finally appeared.

"Hi, there," called Naomi.

"What kept you so long?" called Judith.

"Teacher was telling us a Chanukah story, and we wanted to hear the end so badly, she allowed us to remain a few minutes after class," Miriam replied breathlessly.

"Oh, I know all about Chanukah," announced Judith proudly. "At our house we have a Chanukah party every year. Mother lets me invite some of my friends along with the other guests, and she makes delicious 'Latkes.' My mouth is watering already, just at the thought of them."

"My mother and Dad give 'Chanukah Gelt' every Chanukah, and at night, after Dad lights the candles, he plays 'Dreidle' with us," said Naomi.

Miriam was silent as she walked along with her two friends, whose eager voices betrayed their great impatience for Chanukah's coming. She, alas, had nothing to say. Her face flushed with shame as she listened enviously to the bright picture of Chanukah her friends painted to her.

When the children reached Miriam's door, they paused a moment to chat, and then went on their way. Miriam walked up the path to her house, her imagination kindled by the wonderful Chanukah story she had heard, and her mind full of plans.

"If only I, too, could have a real Chanukah," thought the little girl sadly.

II

It was dinnertime. The whole family was seated at the dinner table, when suddenly Miriam, who seemed to have been brooding about something all the afternoon, asked,

"Father, when Chanukah comes, may we have a Chanukah menorah and candles to celebrate it?"

Miriam's father did not reply at once. He pretended to be busy with his food for a little while, and then asked, "Why do you want to light Chanukah candles?"

"Well, our teacher told us the story of Chanukah, all about the little cruse of oil that lasted, through a miracle of G-D, for eight days. It was right after the Jews defeated the Syrians. She said it was important for every Jew to celebrate the victory and the miracle. All my friends are . . ."

"You see," said her father, turning to her mother, "I warned you against sending her to that school where they teach such nonsense.'"

"Oh, father, it's no nonsense. Every word is true. May I, please, light the candles?"

Miriam's father regarded her in silence, and did not reply. Her brother's eyes were scornful and mocking. Only her mother's eyes were kind and gentle, full of encouragement, as they met the little girl's. Miriam's words evoked before her the image of the day when she herself was a young girl in her father's house. Oh, what a festive time Chanukah was then! The door was open to all. Young and old came to join her father, the Rabbi, in the Chanukah festivities. Piping hot "Latkes" were piled high on the plates. Song and joy filled the air, and the Chanukah candles shed their kindly light and blessing over the whole gathering. "Oh, what fun to receive your 'Chanukah Gelt,' and how happy everyone was. And what of my little girl? No such wonderful heartwarming memories will be hers to cherish and look back on fondly when she has grown up and left us," Miriam's mother said to herself.

"Miriam, this Chanukah you may light the candles. I will help you, and we will have a real Chanukah!"

Miriam beamed with joy.

"Do you really mean it, Mother?"

"Of course, my dear."

"Thank you, Mother," Miriam cried, leaping for joy. "Thank you a thousand times."

III

At last the first night of Chanukah had arrived. Miriam had brought from school that day a plain, tin Chanukah menorah, which she had bought for ten cents. She had also received a package of colored Chanukah candles. Full of pride and joy she displayed her priceless possessions to her mother. Now they were all set to light the first Chanukah candle.

"What a pity the boys are not here," Mother said sadly.

The door flung open and in burst Maurice. "Good evening, mother; hi, Miriam. I see, you are going to light the Chanukah candles. Mind if I look on?"

"Happy Chanukah, Maurice," both Mother and Miriam replied.

The door flung open again, and in rushed Bennie. "Hello, everybody. Felt rather hungry, so I came home early. Why, Miriam is going to light the candles after all! What a girl!"

They all crowded around Miriam as she slowly and thoughtfully stuck a little candle in the Chanukah menorah, and prepared the "Shamash" and matches. Miriam took her time, and now and again glanced at her wrist watch. "If only father were here, too, we'd have a real family reunion!" Miriam thought, and when she looked into her mother's eyes she knew that her mother thought the same thing.

Someone was hastily approaching the door, then hesitated. The door opened slowly, and in walked Father with measured steps. Though he had tried to hide it, nobody was deceived. He had been rushing home, and the beads of perspiration on his forehead, which he had mopped before entering the house, had come out again.

"Good evening, everybody. Quite a full house! Nice. Glad there was not much to do at the office today, so I came home early. Don't mind me. Go right ahead with your little celebration. Perhaps you will invite your old Dad to join, too?"

"Of course, Father," Miriam said. "We are so happy you are here in time."

With a smile on her lips, and with her eyes glistening with happiness, Miriam recited the three blessings over the First Chanukah Candle in a clear voice.

The following night, the boys, strangely enough were at home; they had not gone out all evening. Father came in early. Once again the whole family was there when Miriam lit the Chanukah candles. There was a little surprise as father produced a "dreidle" and a handful of coins. "Here, try your luck, and play fair," he said, as he handed it all to Miriam to divide the money among themselves and play "dreidle" while the Chanukah candles shed their modest lights in the room.

But the biggest surprise came when the following night Miriam's father brought a little package and gave it to Miriam. "A little Chanukah gift for you," he said with a smile.

Miriam unwrapped the package, and her little hands shook as she saw the beautiful silver Chanukah menorah which lay snug in the box. The inscription on the lamp, read:

"TO MIRIAM—A REAL HASMONEAN, FROM DAD, CHANUKAH, 5719"

"TU BISHVAT": THE HOLIDAY OF TREES

"Tu Bishvat" is considered one of the minor Jewish holidays. Our Sages tell us that "Tu Bishvat" is called "Rosh Hashonah Lo-ilonos," the "New Year for Trees." Hence fruit grown after the fifteenth of Shvat cannot be given as tithe (tenth part to a Levite) to redeem fruit grown before the fifteenth.

Trees were always considered important by man. They serve as food, lumber, raw material for paper and as a source of many medicines, to name just a few things. The Bible taught man the importance of fruit trees and, therefore, prohibited him from uprooting them. Even when the Israelites were about to enter Canaan, they were told not to cut down any fruit trees. Ordinarily this would have been a good military tactic. By destroying the trees they could cut off part of the food supply and also prevent the enemy from hiding among them.

So you see, the importance of trees was taught to us thousands of years ago by our Torah. It was recognized by our Sages who established a holiday for its sake. This holiday takes place on the fifteenth day in the Hebrew month of "Shevat," which marks the beginning of the Spring season in the land of Israel. "Tu," the Hebrew letters "Tes" and "Vov" are the ninth and sixth letters of the alphabet. Together they form the number fifteen, giving us "Tu Bishvat," the "fifteenth of Shevat."

CELEBRATING THE HOLIDAY. In the land of Israel this holiday is celebrated with song and dance. The children leave their schools, go out into the fields and plant little saplings. The rest of the afternoon is spent in picnicking, singing and dancing.

Here, in the United States, on "Tu b'shevat" we are still in the midst of our Winter season. We celebrate the holiday by learning about it, hearing stories about it, and by eating fruit imported from the land of Israel. In this way we honor both our holiday and our religious homeland, Israel.

TREES

Normally I do not think of trees and flowers during the winter. Who does? It's different in the spring or summer. Then you cannot help thinking of nature's beautiful gifts. Your eye is caught and held by the deep green of nature's cloak; you are tempted to snatch a walk in the park, or you are driven to the country by the sheer heat of the sun. There you find yourself in the bosom of nature, and it would be the height of ingratitude if you did not give thought to the surrounding trees and flowers. So it is quite natural to think of trees in the spring or summer. But in the winter? Truthfully, I never give them a thought.

The other day, however, I found myself thinking of trees, and on a cold winter day at that! Very strange, you will say. But if I tell you the reason, you will not think it strange at all. It was Chamisho-ossor b'Shevat—the fifteenth day of Shevat—New Year for Trees!

I was returning from the Yeshivah, a little earlier than usual, because of the special occasion. I was walking along the parkway, and out of curiosity began counting the trees on each block. This shows you that trees were in my mind. Small wonder, for at the Yeshivah each one of us had received a bagful of fruit in honor of the day. Every one of us had brought some fruit from home also, and for a moment our classroom looked very much like a fruit market. Some of our business-minded boys began a lively trade. Bananas changed for oranges, dates for figs, and of course carobs were at a premium. The spirit of "Rosh Hashonah Lo'-Ilonos" was very much in evidence.

So now walking home along the parkway, the events of the

day were still quite alive in my mind, and, as I told you before, I was counting the trees on the block. I discovered that there were fifteen trees on the block, on each side of the alley. Not a terribly important discovery, I admit, though it did occur to me that the figure was quite a coincidence.

The trees looked bare, dry and lifeless. But, of course, I knew they were not dead. Deep in the ground the roots were at that very moment busy supplying the trunk and branches with the vital elements which are the food and drink of trees. I knew that with the first warm smile of the sun, the trees would bloom forth and change their attire from a lifeless gray into a rich deep green. The branches and twigs would be buried under a heap of leaves, so that they could not be counted, as they could be at this very moment—if I had time to do it. No, I was not sorry for the trees.

I decided to be sociable, and entered into an imaginary conversation with the tree directly overhanging the bench upon which I settled down for a few moments.

Said I: "Hello, Tree. Are you asleep?"

Tree: "I was until today. I'm wide awake now."

I: "You look so bare; no coat, no gloves, no ear-muffs. Aren't you cold?"

Tree: "Oh, no! I keep my feet deep in the ground. The frost does not reach there. So long as my roots are warm, I am not afraid of Uncle Frost."

I: "For a moment I almost felt sorry for you."

Tree: "There is nothing to be sorry for, as far as I am concerned. But my neighbor here . . ."

The tree waved a dry branch in the direction of a fairly young tree on my right.

I: "What's the matter with it? Is it sick?"

Tree: "Worse. It's dead!"

I gasped. The tree continued: "Its roots were bad. You see, a tree must be firmly rooted in the ground. The very life of the tree depends upon this. Now, this tree was unfortunate. It was not to blame; it had been badly planted. It struggled for a while, but I knew that unless it were replanted it had no chance. You cannot tell by looking at it now. But when spring comes and all the trees will be wrapped in green, this poor tree will remain lifeless, and then the people from the Department of Parks will dig it out and cart it way. . . ."

I felt very sorry indeed for that poor tree. Presently the conversation continued.

Tree: "You feel sorry for this poor tree, and for other trees like it. Let me tell you, my boy, I feel just as sorry for some of your friends. . . ."

I: "My friends?"

Tree: "Let me explain. Many boys pass along this parkway every morning, to and from school. I am talking of Jewish boys. Some of them, like you, go to the nearest Yeshivah or Talmud Torah. For these boys I am happy. But others do not go to the Yeshivah or Talmud Torah. See what I mean?"

I: "You mean that those who go to the Yeshivah are like trees firmly rooted in the ground, but those that don't, are like . . . like this tree here?"

Tree: "Precisely. The Torah, the Mitzvos, Jewish tradition and all that that implies, 'Shabbos,' Festivals, and so forth, are to the Jews what the soil is to us trees, or what the water is to fish. This is how G-D created us, and there is nothing we can do about it. There is one difference, however. Take a tree away from its soil, or take a fish from its water, and it dies. Once they are dead, you cannot revive them. If you put a dead fish back into the water, the poor fish will not come back to life. But it's different with you. Your roots never wither completely. G-D is very kind to you."

❖   ❖   ❖

Normally I do not think of trees during the winter. But as I left the "talking" tree on the parkway. I was glad we have at least one day during the winter when we are reminded of the trees and what they teach us. They give us plenty of food for thought, don't you think?

PURIM: A LESSON IN HISTORY

There is no doubt that by this time in your Hebrew school career you have learned the Purim story many times and are quite familiar with it. But it is not just a story. It is an event in Jewish history that teaches an important lesson. Let us try to understand this lesson by reviewing the main parts of the Purim story and comparing it to Jewish history throughout the ages.

THE STORY. After the banishment of queen Vashti, king Ahasuerus, the ruler of Persia and Media ordered a contest to select for himself a new queen. Esther was forced by the king's officers to enter this contest. As instructed by Mordecai, she did not tell anyone that she was Jewish. It was an act of G-D that made king Ahasuerus choose Esther for his queen, and it was a choice that he never regretted, for Esther always served him as a trustworthy and devoted wife. This trustworthiness and devotion won much favor in the king's eyes and he granted her all that she desired.

It was not long before the love and admiration that Esther had earned was put to the supreme test. Haman, second to the king in command, requested the king's permission to kill all the Jews in his kingdom. He was enraged by the Jews, who refused to honor him as a god, and particularly by

Mordecai, who refused to bow down as Haman passed him every morning through the royal courtyard. Haman's plot reached the ears of Mordecai who reported it to queen Esther. When Esther heard of this terrible plan, she fasted for three days and ordered Mordecai and all the Jews of Persia to do the same. After spending three days in fasting and prayer she went to seek an audience with the king. With this act Esther took her life into her own hands for it was the law of the land that no one was to appear before the king except when summoned by him.

Queen Esther and Mordecai succeeded in defeating wicked Haman's plan, with the result that the Jews were saved and wicked Haman and his equally wicked sons were hanged.

THE LESSON OF PURIM. A tyrant arises to destroy the Jewish people. The situation seems hopeless, but the Jews are saved. How typical this story is of Jewish history throughout the ages. There is no better proof that "history repeats itself" than the history of the Jewish people. From the time the Israelites became a people, many nations have tried to destroy them. Nebuchadnezzar of Babylonia, Antiochus of Syria, and, during recent years, Hitler of Germany, all tried to annihilate the Jews. But despite their great power as leaders of powerful nations, they failed to accomplish their cruel objective. They did not want to learn the lesson taught to their predecessor Pharaoh Rameses of Egypt. G-D is with the Israelites and it is His will that they should never die, in order to fulfil their noble mission. And so, nation after nation, and tyrant after tyrant has learned this lesson through their own sad experience.

But lessons in history are not for tyrants alone. They should be learned by all the people of the world, this lesson in particular. And to us, as Jews, this story should give courage and assure us that no matter how hopeless a situation may seem and no matter how many Hamans arise in each generation, G-D will always remember the Jewish people and come to their aid in time of need if they turn to Him honestly and sincerely.

LAWS AND CUSTOMS OF PURIM. The thirteenth day of the Hebrew month of "Adar" is a fast day called in Hebrew "Taanis Esther," to commemorate the fasting period imposed upon themselves by queen Esther, Mordecai and the Jews of Persia. If Purim falls on a Sunday, the fast of Esther is observed on the preceding Thursday since fasting is prohibited on the Sabbath and "Erev Shabbos." Yom Kippur is the only exception when it falls on a Sabbath, when fasting is mandatory.

THE NAME. Purim is celebrated on the fourteenth of "Adar." Purim means "lots." (It is similar to a raffle.) The holiday was given this name to remind us of the lots Haman cast to determine the most favorable day upon which to kill all the Jews of Persia. As we know from the story, the thirteenth day of "Adar" was chosen. On that day the Jews battled and overpowered their enemies and celebrated their victory the next day.

THE MEGILLAH. On the eve of Purim and the following morning, the Purim story is read in the synagogue. To recall the period of the story in a realistic way, it is read from a parchment scroll, the way it was read in the days of Esther and Mordecai. The parchment is called "Megillah." The writing in this scroll is done by hand in Torah script.

Before the reading is begun, three blessings are recited by the reader. The first is to indicate the fulfillment of the "Mitzvah"; the second to thank G-D for the miracle; the third, the "Shehecheyonu," to thank G-D for enabling us to reach this holiday season in health and happiness. If one is ill or cannot attend the "Megillah" reading at the synagogue, it may be read to him at home.

When Haman's name is mentioned during the reading of the "Megillah," it is customary to make noise in contempt of the cruel tyrant.

AL HANISSIM. On Purim, beginning with the "Ma'ariv" service, a special prayer is added to the "Shmoneh Esrei." The prayer is called "Al Hanissim." It is a prayer giving thanks to G-D for the miracles He performed for our ancestors in the days of Mordecai and Esther. This prayer is also added in the Grace After Meals.

HALF A SHEKEL. Before the reading of the "Megillah," it is proper for each person to donate half a dollar to commemorate the custom started during Biblical times. In ancient times this money was used for the upkeep of the Temple and the purchase of sacrifices. It was collected during the month of "Adar." Today the money is given to some charitable cause.

HAMANTASCHEN. We are commanded to eat, drink and rejoice on Purim. For this reason a special Purim Feast is prepared for the whole family, and is marked by song and merriment. A favorite at the Purim Feast is a cake known to most people by its Yiddish name, "Hamantaschen." In Hebrew it is called "Oznei Homon," or "Haman's ears."

MISHLOACH MONOS. A beautiful custom typical of the joyous festival of Purim is the sending of gifts to one another. We call it "Mishloach Monos." Who could think of a better way of celebrating a holiday than giving gifts? For giving makes us feel even happier than when we receive. Purim should be made a joyous holiday for all, especially those who are less fortunate than we and cannot afford the luxury of a Purim Feast. By helping them, we will be bringing happiness not only to them, but to ourselves.

PURIM OF THE CURTAINS

Our present story takes us back over three hundred years to the ghetto of Prague, Bohemia. It was during the Thirty Years' War which was then raging between the Catholic and Protestant countries of Europe. As always, throughout history, the Jews suffered the most.

Emperor Ferdinand II of Hapsburg, becoming desperate at his ever-shrinking treasury due to the terrific expense of the war, turned to the Jewish bankers and merchants of his country to help him out of his financial difficulties. As a reward, he granted these Jews all kinds of privileges and rights. This aroused the jealousy of the lower nobility and clergymen who sought to make trouble for the Jews.

The new governor of Bohemia, Rudolph of Wenceslaw, was one of those who resented the friendliness of Ferdinand toward the Jews. The Jews of Prague at that time numbered about ten thousand. They had a good reputation. Jews and nonJews alike were still under the influence of the great Rabbi Judah Loew. The governor could not easily provoke any riots or pogroms against the Jews of the ghetto. Something happened in the winter of 1623, however, which gave the governor the opportunity for which he was waiting.

Governor Rudolph of Wenceslaw had the responsibility of caring for all the precious furnishings and draperies of the palace. Right through the spring, summer and fall, he had everything stored away to avoid their spoilage from sunlight. Only for the winter season were the precious carpets and hangings brought out for use in the palace.

Among these treasures were some heavy gold brocade curtains, artistically woven by a famous medieval master weaver. These draperies were considered priceless and the governor was personally responsible for them to the Crown. The governor in turn entrusted the keys of the treasure chest to Hradek, the chamberlain, who was next in importance to Rudolph.

December came and Hradek began to unpack all the precious carpets and hangings as the palace had to be prepared for the winter festival season. Each item was taken out of the storage and noted on the catalogue. But when the iron chest that should have contained the gold brocade curtains was opened, it was empty.

Word quickly spread that the priceless curtains were missing. The governor, upon hearing the shocking news, immediately gave orders that no one should be allowed to leave the palace until a thorough search and investigation was made.

Rudolph tore around like a raging lion, snarling at everyone whom he questioned.

"If those curtains are not back here by tonight, I shall have you all thrown into prison," he screamed at his servants.

"Might I respectfully suggest, your honor, that all pawnshops and warehouses in the city be thoroughly searched," ventured Hradek. "And a sharp eye should be kept on the Jews' stores," he added slyly.

"That's an excellent suggestion, Hradek," said the governor, cheered up by the prospect of making trouble for his enemies in the ghetto.

He immediately gave orders that a house-to-house search was to be made and every house and store in Prague was to be turned upside down until those priceless curtains be found. He had the ghetto gates locked without previously informing the Jews about the matter and had his men search every likely and unlikely place where the curtains might be.

The Jews, naturally enough, were terrified at the unexplained "search." When the governor's men reached the large house and store of the councillor of the ghetto, Enoch Altschul, they burst into the house and opened all the cupboards and closets, strewing the contents all over the floor. When they found nothing they approached Altschul with a pistol pointing at his heart.

"Show us where you keep your most precious merchandise or we shall shoot you without mercy," they shouted at him.

The poor old man, trembling with fear, led the men to the back of his store and opened a secret vault. There, in a plain wooden box, they discovered a glittering heap of material. Yes, here were those precious missing curtains. With triumphant cries, they pounced upon the poor old man and clamped him into heavy chains. Then they snatched up the curtains.

At the point of their guns the men led the Jewish merchant and scholar through the silent and shocked ghetto crowds, and then through the wild and screaming mob lining the streets of Prague.

Governor Rudolph of Wenceslaw was pacing the floor of his state-room as Enoch Altschul was brought in. A cry of relief escaped the lips of the governor as he beheld the precious curtains. And when he heard that they had been found hidden in the store of a Jew, a malicious gleam crept into his wicked eyes.

"And so, the honest Jew has been caught as a thief," he sneered. "Explain yourself if you can, Jew."

"I gave my word of honor to a most noble member of your court," replied Enoch Altschul quietly. "Unless he himself grants me permission to speak I cannot explain the presence of those curtains in my store."

"A very likely story, indeed," said the governor. "We shall see whether the lashes of my servant's whip will loosen your tongue."

Immediately the governor ordered his servant to give the Jew fifty lashes. This was the opportunity Rudolph had been waiting for since he had become governor. He hated the Jews and rejoiced at the thought that the emperor would now see how wrong he had been to show kindness to these ungrateful people.

In the evening Enoch Altschul was again brought before the

governor. He had been so badly beaten that he had to be carried in. But he persisted in keeping silent.

"You have until tomorrow morning at ten o'clock. If by then you still refuse to tell me how you obtained the curtains, not only shall you and your family he hanged but I shall order troops to storm the whole ghetto. Now take this man away," said the governor. "Perhaps he will find it wiser to speak tomorrow."

All that night poor Enoch Altschul tossed in pain. His body ached and his mind was tortured. What should he do? He prayed hard for heavenly guidance. Out of sheer weariness he fell into a deep sleep.

Suddenly, it seemed as if the room was flooded with light. His dearly beloved teacher and friend Rabbi Judah Loew appeared, assuring him that everything would be all right.

Greatly encouraged by his dream, Enoch Altschul awoke the next morning feeling full of hope. He immediately began his morning prayers and recited them until the guards came to take him before the governor. Despite the horrible whippings he had received the previous day, Enoch Altschul's face bore a calm and dignified look as he was again carried in. The whole court was assembled in the governor's state-room. The governor had Enoch carried to the window overlooking the huge plaza below.

"You see all those heavily armed men down there?" said the governor. "At a signal from me they are ready to break into the ghetto and destroy every house there."

Enoch Altschul winced hearing those terrible words and his face turned pale at the thought of this awful threat. Yet before he had a chance to say anything there was a stir and the chamberlain, Hradek, stepped forward.

"Your honor," he said to the astonished governor, "I am the guilty one in this case. This noble old man is keeping silent because he wishes to protect your personal honor."

The governor and the astonished assembly could hardly believe their eyes and ears. Hradek continued:

"Several months ago I was in dire need of twenty-five thousand ducats of gold which I had lost through heavy gambling. I hit upon the idea of taking these precious curtains to this Jew who had previously helped me out with a loan of money. I wrote a note in your name and sent it with your seal. In the note was a promise from you to treat the Jews kindly if Enoch Altschul would keep the pawning of these curtains a secret. On the other hand the note threatened the worst punishment for the whole ghetto if he so much as uttered a word about this incident."

The whole court listened spellbound. Why was Hradek confessing? They wondered, and soon they heard the answer from Hradek's own lips.

"I would have kept silent about this matter," Hradek continued, "but last night I had a terrifying dream. The famous late Rabbi of the Prague ghetto, Rabbi Judah Loew, appeared before me. I was filled with the same fear that was felt years ago by those who tried to plant guilt on innocent Jews. The Rabbi said, 'You must tell the truth tomorrow, Hradek. Be warned!'"

As he talked Hradek kept on clutching at his throat as if he were choking, and when he finished he fell to the floor in a dead faint. The governor and all those assembled rushed forward. There was no doubt about it that Hradek was dead, and by his own confession, the guilty one.

The governor had no choice but to free Enoch Altschul and give orders that the waiting mobs be dispersed. The Jews were to be left in peace.

Great was the jubilation among the Jews of Prague at the miraculous turn of events. It was on the twenty-second day of "Teveis" that this miracle happened in Prague. For many years this day was celebrated by the Altschul family and the Jews of Prague as the "Purim of the Curtains." For on that day their sadness had been turned to gladness, as in the Purim of old.

PESACH: THE TIME
OF OUR FREEDOM

One of the most beautiful and delightful holidays of the Jewish religion is Passover. Passover is our oldest holiday— it marks the anniversary of the birth of Israel as a people, and there is a great deal that we can learn today from its history. Let us examine the four names by which this holiday is known: "Chag Hamatzohs." "The Holiday of the Unleavened Bread"; "Chag Hapesach," "The Holiday of Passover"; "Z'man Cheiruseinu," "The Time of our Freedom"; and "Chag Ho'oviv," "The Holiday of Spring."

CHAG HAMATZOHS. What is matzoh? It is a replica of the bread that the Israelites ate after they hastily left Egypt. It is also called "lechem oni," or "bread of poverty." Matzoh is a symbol of the life the Israelites led in Egypt. They were slaves of Pharaoh. From day to day their work was made more difficult. Taskmasters were set over them to see that they did not idle even for a moment. Even in their wildest dreams, they did not hope to leave Egypt, for they knew that it was humanly impossible. Pharaoh was their ruler; he tried to be their god. But Pharaoh made a costly mistake, for it was the will of G-D that the Israelites leave Egypt and devote themselves to Him as His nation. No human being can set himself up as a god. History has taught us that the wicked perish in the end; justice will ultimately win out.

And so, with the help of G-D and under the leadership of Moses, the Israelites prepared to leave Egypt. They couldn't believe their eyes. After being enslaved for so long under so cruel a Pharaoh, they were to leave Egypt without even a battle. Truly this was the work of G-D. They couldn't wait to leave. There was not even enough time to bake bread in the proper way. Before the bread had time to rise, they had to go. They took their unleavened bread and started on the long journey.

When we eat matzoh on Passover, we relive the lives of our ancestors who were in Egypt. We remind ourselves that it is the will of G-D that no man serve another in such a way as the Israelites were forced to serve the Pharaohs. Man is to serve only G-D, the true ruler of the universe.

CHAG HAPESACH. Because the Israelites lived in Egypt for so many years, many of them adopted Egyptian customs. When they were to leave Egypt, they had to leave not only the country, but also the idolatrous practices that they had learned there. And so they were put to a test. The lamb was a sacred animal to the Egyptians and they worshiped it. In the evening of the fourteenth day of "Nissan," the night of the last plague, the Israelites were told to sacrifice a lamb to G-D. The blood of this lamb was to be sprinkled upon their doorposts as a sign. That night when the Angel of Death would pass through the land of Egypt to kill all the firstborn males of the Egyptians, he would *pass over* the houses of the Israelites; the blood would be his sign and that house would not be touched by the plague.

Let us try to understand the meaning of this test. The Israelites who believed in G-D knew that there was no reason for them to fear the Egyptians. Even though the fulfillment of G-D's command meant enraging the Egyptians, G-D would protect them. By sacrificing the lamb—a sacred god of Egypt—they would prove to the Egyptians that worship of the lamb was false.

The Israelites who believed in the sacredness of the lamb, along with the Egyptians, and did not trust in G-D, would never perform the sacrifice, for it would endanger their lives. First, they would be afraid to sacrifice the lamb since they believed that it was sacred. Second, even if they did sacrifice it, who would protect them from the anger of the Egyptians? They were not sure that G-D would protect them. Such people were not worthy of being freed by G-D, for they did not trust in Him.

The sacrifice of the "Paschal lamb" was carried on from generation to generation as a remembrance of the miracles in Egypt and the loyalty our ancestors showed to G-D.

Z'MAN CHEIRUSEINU. Perhaps this name expresses the meaning of the holiday of Passover better than any of the other names, for it brings to mind the point of the whole story. The Israelites were slaves to Pharaoh in Egypt and they were freed. But their slavery was not limited to physical labor; they also were enslaved spiritually. They no longer remembered the G-D of their forefathers Abraham, Isaac and Jacob. They were enslaved to the worship and practices of the Egyptians. Egyptian customs and their way of living became so much a part of the Israelites that they could not think freely and discover the true G-D. Even those who believed in G-D began to lose hope and trust in Him. Many of them addressed their prayers and sacrifices to the Egyptian idols. They thought that in this way they would win favor in the eyes of the Egyptians and their gods and be treated more kindly. In their fear and confusion they did not realize their foolishness, for the worship of false gods could not help them.

The time of freedom finally came. Out of Egypt, into the wilderness and on to the promised land of Canaan went six hundred thousand Israelite males and their families. They were to become a free people under G-D, devoted to His Torah and loyal to their mission.

CHAG HO'OVIV. The holiday of Passover ushers in the spring season. It brings with it the happiness and joy that we all experience when we see the rebirth of nature. Trees and flowers again begin to bloom and the air is once more filled with the sweet fragrance of new life. Spring is truly the symbol of the holiday of Passover, for just as spring symbolizes the rebirth of nature, so the holiday of Passover symbolizes the rebirth of the nation of Israel. Just as spring symbolizes a new start in life for trees and flowers, so the holiday of Passover should symbolize a fresh start in life for all the Jewish people; a life devoted to the fulfillment of Torah and good deeds.

THE STORY. The story of Passover begins with the story of Joseph, the son of Jacob. Joseph, as you remember, was sold into slavery by his jealous brothers, and was finally brought to the land of Egypt. Because of his wisdom and foresight, he became a great man in this land; second in command to the Pharaoh himself. When Joseph achieved this high position, he brought his father Jacob, his brothers and his entire family to the land of Egypt. In Egypt, Jacob and his family, which consisted of seventy people, settled in the land of Goshen. Joseph's brothers and their families lived together with their father for many happy years.

Time passed and eventually Jacob and his twelve sons died. His family, however, grew larger and larger as years went by. After many years a new Pharaoh arose on the throne of Egypt. He did not wish to remember the important contributions that Joseph had made to the welfare and the development of Egypt. This wicked Pharaoh imposed heavy taxes upon the Israelites and subjugated them. Because of their increasing number, Pharaoh was afraid that they might someday take over his kingdom. Eventually the Israelites became slave laborers. It was the Israelites who built the great fortresses of Pithom and Rameses. But despite the harsh treatment the Israelites received, they multiplied rapidly and became stronger. And so, Pharaoh issued an edict to kill all the newborn sons of the Israelites. This he felt would be the answer to his problem.

The plight of the Israelites grew steadily worse, until finally G-D in His kindness and mercy sent them the greatest of all prophets, Moses, the son of Amram. With his brother, Aaron, Moses appeared before Pharaoh, king of Egypt, and asked him, in the name of G-D, to free the Israelites and to allow them to go out into the wilderness to worship their G-D. Pharaoh refused. Moses then performed a miracle. He threw down his rod and it became a snake. He wanted to convince the king that he came in the name of G-D. Pharaoh was not impressed by this miracle and he refused to free the Israelites. G-D then began to punish the Egyptians with severe plagues. It was not until the tenth plague, the slaughter of the firstborn males of every Egyptian family, that the will of Pharaoh was broken; for he himself was a firstborn and he feared for his own life. In the middle of the night, Pharaoh, whose own son lay dead before him, called for Moses and Aaron and begged them to take the Israelites out of Egypt. Moses gathered the Israelites together and left Egypt in great haste.

LAWS OF PASSOVER. Passover is celebrated from the fifteenth through the twenty-second day of the Hebrew month "Nissan." The first two and the last two days are called "Yom Tov"; the middle four are called "Chol Hamoed."

It is customary to begin to study the laws of Passover thirty days before the holiday in order to become familiar with all the regulations connected with this holiday.

MAOS CHITTIM. In preparation for Passover, our first responsibility is to make sure that all our fellow Jews are provided with the means to properly celebrate the holiday. Immediately after Purim, the leaders of the community collect funds in order to provide the poor with matzoh, wine and all the other necessities for the celebration of Passover. This Passover fund is known in Hebrew as "Maos Chittim," "money for wheat" or "money for matzoh."

SHABBOS HAGODOL. The "Shabbos" before Passover is known as "Shabbos Hagodol," the "Great Sabbath." It was on this day that a minor revolution took place in the land of Egypt. The Egyptians were so terror-stricken that they revolted against their king for not letting the Israelites leave. This act began the redemption.

MATZOH. One of the most important symbols of Passover is matzoh. It is baked with water and wheat alone. It symbolizes the "poor man's bread" that our ancestors ate in Egypt, and the unleavened bread that they baked hurriedly after they left. The Torah states, "In the first month, on the fourteenth day of the month *in the evening,* you shall eat unleavened bread, until the twenty-first day of the month in the evening" (Shmos 12:18).

CHOMETZ. It is forbidden for any Jew to have leaven products in his possession during the Passover holiday. Such products are called in Hebrew, "chometz." This prohibition is based upon two verses in the Torah which state, "Seven days shall there be no leaven found in your houses" (Shmos 12:19), "And there shall be no leavened bread seen with you in all your borders . . ." (Shmos 13:7). Everything that has a mixture of leaven in it, even a very minute amount is forbidden on Passover. Dishes that were used for "chometz" may not be used on Passover. It is best to buy new utensils for Passover use. If this is not possible, certain utensils may be made permissible for Passover use by special cleansing processes. If such is the case, a rabbi must be consulted.

M'CHIRAS CHOMETZ. Since "chometz" products and utensils are forbidden to be in our possession on Passover even though we are not using them, they must be sold to a non-Jew. Nowadays this process, which is called in Hebrew, "M'chiras Chometz," is usually done by the rabbi of the community. He draws up a bill of sale stating that all the "chometz" products and utensils found in our house are being sold to him. Then the people who wish to sell their "chometz" sign the bill of sale, and he in turn sells the "chometz" to a nonJew. After Passover, it is bought back by the rabbi from the nonJew and returned to the Jews of the community. According to the agreement, the "chometz" may be kept in our house until after Passover. But it must be put away in a place where it will not be touched.

B'DIKAS CHOMETZ. On the night preceding the eve of Passover, when the house is clean and ready for the holiday, we make a last search for any "chometz" that we may have overlooked. This search is called in Hebrew, "B'dikas Chometz."

This picturesque ritual is performed in the following manner: First we put ten pieces of bread in different parts of the house to make sure that some "chometz" will be found during the search, for if no "chometz" is found the blessing will have been recited in vain. We now recite the blessing for the fulfillment of the law. It is customary to search for the "chometz" by the light of a candle. After the search is completed and the "chometz" is gathered, it is put away until the morning, when it is burned together with any bits of "chometz" that may have been left from the breakfast meal. This process is called, "Biur Chometz," the "burning of the chometz." After the "chometz" is burned, we officially disown any other "chometz" that may be found in our possession.

EREV PESACH. On "Erev Pesach," the day before Passover, it is customary not to eat matzoh so that our appetite will be fresh for the fulfillment of the "Mitzvah" at night. On this day it is also customary for the firstborn son of every family to fast to recall the kindness shown to the firstborn sons of the Israelites during the last plague, the death of the firstborn. Since it is difficult to fast on this day because there is much work to be done in preparation for Passover, our Sages allowed the firstborn to participate in a special service conducted in the morning called "Siyum B'chorim," when a tractate of the Talmud is completed and a feast made, of which the firstborn partakes.

If "Erev Pesach" is on "Shabbos," the searching ceremony is held on Thursday night. The morning service of "Erev Pesach" is then held at an early hour to permit the eating of a breakfast of "chometz" after services. This would be impossible if the "Shabbos" services were held as usual, for "chometz" is not permissible after the first third of the day on "Erev Pesach," about 9:30 A.M.

TAL. On the first day of Passover, in the "Musaf" service the prayer for dew is recited. In Hebrew it is called "Tal" which means dew. "Tal" is recited during the repetition of the "Shmoneh Esrei" by the cantor.

ACHRON SHEL PESACH. The last day of Passover is called "Achron Shel Pesach." On this day the special memorial service called "Yizkor" is recited.

THE ORDER OF THE NIGHT OF PASSOVER. The first two nights of Passover are called "Seder" nights. The word "seder" means "order." On these nights there is a special order that we follow at the table.

SEDER-PLATE. This is a special plate that holds the symbolic foods that we use during the "Seder" service to remind us of the lives of the Israelites in Egypt.

KITTEL. In many homes the person conducting the "Seder" service wears a white robe. It is called a "Kittel." White has always been a symbol of purity and holiness to the Jews. A white garment was worn by the priests in the Temple in Jerusalem when they offered sacrifices.

HAGGADAH. This Hebrew word means "telling." It is the title of the book used for the "Seder" service. It tells the story of our people's fight for life and liberty. It reveals the glory of true freedom. It tells us that it is every man's duty in every generation to look upon himself as though he personally had come out of Egypt. For if G-D had not taken our ancestors out of Egypt, our people might have still been enslaved there.

HASIBA. To accentuate the fact that we are a free people, it is customary for the leader of the "Seder" to sit in a reclining position on a comfortable couch or a thick pillow. In olden times this was something only kings and princes would do.

DROPS OF WINE. It is customary to spill drops of wine into a special dish when we recite the ten plagues during the "Seder" service. This is done to remind us that even Passover has its sad note. Although the Egyptians were our enemies, we should not rejoice at their suffering. Our cup of wine, which represents our happiness, cannot be full as long as there was any suffering even for our enemies.

THE "SEDER" SERVICE. The following is an outline of the

"Seder" service as it is performed on the first two nights of Passover:

1. *"Kadeish."* After the father returns from the synagogue and all are seated at the table, the first act that begins the "Seder" service is the recitation of the "Kiddush" by all the males. This is the first of the required four cups of wine during the "Seder" service.

2. *"Urchatz."* The hands are washed in preparation for the dipping of the "Karpas." No blessing is recited.

3. *"Karpas."* The next step is the distribution of the "Karpas" which is either a piece of parsley or cooked potato. It is dipped into salt water, the blessing is recited and it is eaten. The "Karpas" symbolizes the poor diet that our ancestors had in Egypt; the salt water reminds us of the tears they shed due to their suffering.

4. *"Yachatz."* At the beginning of the "Seder" a plate containing three matzohs is placed before the leader. The three matzohs represent the three classes into which the Israelites were divided. The first, the "Kohein," the priest, who was in charge of all offerings and services performed in the Temple. The second, the "Levi," who was an assistant to the "Kohein" and was also the singer and musician. During the services the "Leviyim" would sing and accompany themselves on a musical instrument. The third classification was that of the "Yisroel," the ordinary Israelite. At this point, the leader takes the middle matzoh, which is called the "Levi," and breaks it in half. One part is put away to be used later as the "Afikomon," and the other piece is left on the plate.

5. *"Magid."* The family now recite the "Haggadah." The opening passage, "Ho lochmo anyo," is an invitation to all who are hungry or needy and cannot have their own "Seder" to come and join our "Seder" and thereby fulfil the "Mitzvah." This paragraph is followed by the tradi-

tional "Four Questions." They are usually asked by the youngest child although they may be asked by any child at the "Seder." This is followed by the answer which explains the story, the miracles and the lesson of Passover. After reciting the "Haggadah," we drink the second cup of wine.

6. "*Rachatz.*" Again the participants in the "Seder" wash their hands, but this time they recite the blessing, since they are to eat the matzoh.

7. "*Motsee Matzoh.*" While holding the two whole matzohs and the middle piece, the blessings are recited by the leader. Pieces are given to each member of the family, and all recite the blessing and eat the matzoh.

8. "*Moror.*" The leader of the "Seder" now takes some bitter herb, usually horse-radish, dips it into the "Charoses," a mixture of shredded apple, nuts, cinnamon and wine, recites the blessing and eats the mixture. This is done by the entire family. The "Moror," or bitter herb, symbolizes the bitter times the Israelites had in Egypt. The "Charoses," which is a brown color, reminds us of the mortar that the Israelites used in building the cities of Pithom and Rameses. Our Sages tell us that the "Charoses," which has a pleasant taste, is also a symbol of G-D's pleasantness and kindness toward the Israelites, which made slavery a bit easier to bear.

9. "*Koreich.*" The leader of the "Seder" now takes two pieces of matzoh, puts some grated "Moror" between them, recites the passage: "This was Hillel's custom . . ." and eats the sandwich. This procedure is followed by all the people at the "Seder." In the time of the Temple in Jerusalem it was the custom of the great Sage, Hillel, to take some matzoh, "Moror," and part of the paschal lamb and eat them together in order to properly fulfil the commandment in the Torah, "It (the paschal lamb) shall be eaten on matzoh and bitters." Nowadays, when

we have no sacrifices, we have no paschal lamb. To carry on Hillel's custom, however, we make a sandwich of matzoh and "Moror" alone.

10. *"Shulchon Orech."* The customary festive meal is now served. We begin the meal with the roasted egg. The egg symbolizes the special holiday sacrifice that was offered in the Temple at this time by the pilgrims to Jerusalem. These pilgrimages were made by the Israelites three times a year: on "Succos," "Pesach," and "Shavuos." The roasted egg is also a symbol of mourning and sorrow for the destruction of our Temple. We pray that this act of remembrance will be accepted before G-D as the sacrifices of old.

11. *"Tsofun."* After the meal, the "Afikomon" is taken or redeemed from the children who "stole" it. The "Afikomon" is the dessert of the "Seder" service. It is an obligation for everyone participating in the "Seder" to eat a piece of it. It takes the place of the paschal lamb and is eaten last at the "Seder" so that its taste may linger in our mouth. The "Afikomon" must be eaten before midnight. On the right side of the "Seder" plate there is a roasted shankbone. It is another symbol of the paschal lamb.

12. *"Boreich."* The leader requests all the participants to recite the Grace After Meal as wine is poured into the cups for the third time. At this time the cup of Elijah, the prophet, is also filled. Elijah, who, according to our Sages, will come three days before the Messiah to announce his arrival, is anxiously awaited on the holiday of Passover. The Messiah, according to tradition, will establish a new world of peace and freedom for all. The reason for expecting him on Passover is based upon a statement in the Talmud, a book of Jewish law, that "In Nissan they were redeemed (the Israelites) and in "Nissan" they will, in the future, be redeemed again."

The Grace is recited by all and it is followed by the third cup of wine. The "Seder" night, according to our Sages, is a "Leil Shimurim," a "protected night." On these nights we are protected by G-D from all evil. To show that we have no fears on this night, we open our doors. At this point we recite a prayer to G-D to destroy the enemies of peace and freedom forever. The fourth cup of wine is then filled.

13. *"Hallel."* The spirit of praise to G-D is continued with the recitation of the remaining Psalms of thanksgiving. It is followed by the fourth cup of wine, which is the last for the "Seder."

14. *"Nirtsoh."* The closing songs and hymns joyfully bring the "Seder" service to an end. It is our hope at this time that our service to G-D will be accepted by Him.

ALILAS DAM—BLOOD ACCUSATION

It was the first "seder" night. In the synagogue they had just finished the "Ma'ariv" service and the sexton took a bottle from a compartment below the "Aron Hakodesh" and filled a cup with sparkling red wine. Just as the cantor was about to begin the "Kiddush" someone began to pound on the door of the synagogue. The sexton walked to the door and opened it.

"Welcome," he said to the two strangers who were standing outside the door. "Come right in. Is there anything we can do for you?"

Two stalwart, ferocious looking gendarmes strutted into the synagogue. Without turning their heads they walked over to the bottle of wine and pointing to the bottle shouted in a menacing voice: "In this bottle is the BLOOD OF A GENTILE BOY."

When he had uttered these fearsome words, every person in the synagogue trembled, except the sexton.

"Surely there must be some mistake," he said. "You see, I have already poured some of this wine into a cup. To prove your mistake, I will drink it," and he drank out the whole cup. "It is very good wine too," he said, refilling the cup. "Here, have some."

While this had been going on, the expression on the men's faces changed completely. Their grim air had given way to one of amazement and when the sexton offered them to drink, one of them slowly moved his arm to accept it, as though he had been hypnotized. First he took one careful sip and then another, but after that, he drained the cup with one gulp.

"You are right," he said, as his face turned crimson with embarrassment. "This is wine," and without another word the two men left the synagogue.

For a few seconds afterward no one spoke. They were too mystified to utter a word. Then they suddenly broke out in a multitude of questions: What did they want? Why did they leave after one of them had a cup of wine? When they had quieted down, the sexton said:

"Last night I had a curious dream. I dreamed that there was 'chometz' in the 'Aron Hakodesh.' At first I was undecided, but then, just to be sure, I dressed and went to the synagogue to investigate. Although I made a complete inspection, I found nothing. I returned home and went back to sleep. But again I had the same dream, and this time, on investigating, I noticed that the wine in the compartment of the 'Aron Hakodesh,' had a queer color. I took the bottle out and poured some of the contents into a glass. I immediately realized that it was blood. I could not imagine at first how such a thing could happen, but then I remembered that two nights ago a stranger had asked for permission to sleep in the synagogue because he had no other lodging for the night. I gave him permission and the next morning I found the synagogue empty. I did not think anything of it at the time, but when I saw the bottle of blood I realized what had happened. That man had substituted blood for the wine, hoping to provide evidence that we use the blood of gentiles on 'Pesach.' I quickly poured out the contents of the bottle and refilled it with wine. The two men who were here tonight were agents of the police."

SEFIRAS HA'OMER—THE COUNTING OF THE OMER

COUNTING THE DAYS. We all know the feeling of anticipation. How often have we counted the days before going off to summer camp. How anxious we are a month before graduation when we count the weeks, the days, and sometimes even the hours, until the great event. Our Sages tell us that when the Israelites left Egypt on their journey to the Promised Land they were very anxious. They knew that somewhere along the way they would camp and witness the most thrilling event ever experienced by human beings: the revelation of G-D to man. Even in their wildest flight of imagination they could not picture what was going to happen. There was only one way to find out: wait and see.

But waiting without any idea as to how long they would have to wait would be too much. The Israelites approached Moses and asked him how long they would journey in the wilderness before the time came for G-D's revelation. Moses told them they would not have to wait very long. It would only be a forty-nine-day wait from the second day after they left Egypt. On the fiftieth day they were to receive the Torah, revealed by G-D. And so they counted the days. Day by day they came closer and closer to the historic moment. Day by day they came closer and closer to understanding their divine mission.

According to the Torah, when the Israelites reached

Canaan, they were to make it a holy land. In the springtime when the first sheaves of grain were to be harvested, thanks were to be given to G-D. Before any of the new grain could be eaten, a special "omer" (measure of grain) offering was to be brought to the Temple. This "omer" offering was to be brought on the second day of Passover. From that day seven weeks were to be counted. This was called "counting the omer." On the fiftieth day another offering was to be brought to the Temple; the offering of the first fruits, the "Bikurim." The days of the "omer" were days of great joy and celebration. For what could make one happier than looking in the sunlight at a field of golden brown grain waving in the wind?

Unfortunately, these days of happiness were changed to days of sadness many years later in the time of Rabbi Akiva. It was during the days of the "omer" that a terrible plague attacked the students of this great Rabbi. Many of his twenty-four-thousand students died. From that time on the days of the "omer" are remembered and observed as days of mourning in consideration of the great tragedy.

LAWS OF THE "OMER." The "omer" is counted for seven full weeks beginning with the second night of Passover. It is counted in the evening after the "Ma'ariv" service. The blessing praising G-D's name and acknowledging the fulfillment of the commandment is recited. This is followed by counting the number of weeks and days that have passed in the "omer."

LAWS OF COUNTING. If one has forgotten to count the "omer" at night he must count it on the following day, without the blessing. The following night, however, he is to count again normally. If he accidentally skipped an entire day, he should still count, but he should no longer recite the blessing. At the conclusion of the Sabbath or Passover, the "omer" is counted before the "Havdolah" service is recited.

LAG BA'OMER. In contrast to the other days of the "omer," the thirty-third day is a day for rejoicing. History tells us that for some unknown reason, none of Rabbi Akiva's students died of the terrible plague on this day. It was also on this day that Bar Kochba, a famous Jewish general living in the time of Rabbi Akiva, won a great victory in the revolution of the Jews against the Romans. On this day none of the laws of mourning apply. This festival is called in Hebrew "Lag Ba'omer," "Lag" being the Hebrew letters for thirty-three, "Ba'omer" meaning "in the omer."

THE TORAH—A GIFT FOR ALL

The great news that G-D would soon give to the children of Israel the Torah, flashed through the camp of Israel. Moses had told his people to prepare for that great event—the Revelation of G-D on the Mount of Sinai. For three days they were to keep themselves pure and holy and then they would get that divine gift.

Moses wished to see how his brethren were preparing themselves for the receiving of the Torah, and set out on a tour of the camp of Israel. He passed by the tents of the Righteous and saw that they were happy and rejoicing.

"What is all this jubilation about?" asked Moses.

"Why, of all men, you, dear Master, should ask such a question?" the Righteous exclaimed. "Could there be a greater gift for G-D to give us? How could we worship G-D without it? Small wonder we are rejoicing with the Torah!"

"Truly spoken!" said Moses approvingly. "You, my righteous and pious brethren ought surely to rejoice with the holy Torah."

Moses continued on his way, and stopped near the tents of the Scholars. They, too, were rejoicing. "What is the cause of all this joy?" Moses asked the Scholars.

"We are rejoicing with the Torah, of course!" was the answer.

"And what makes you feel so happy about it?"

"Because there is no greater pleasure than the study of the Torah, and we are going to enjoy it. The Torah is wonderful! Every time you study it you discover something new. When you think you have grasped its meaning, then you read it again and realize how much more there is to learn from it. For a moment you think it very puzzling, so you concentrate all your mental faculties and delve further into it and you see the light again. Oh, it is wonderful, it is boundless . . . !"

"You are quite right, honorable Scholars," said Moses, nodding his head and smiling happily.

On went Moses until he came to the tents of the Merchants and Workers. They were sitting and talking about unimportant things, showing no sign of rejoicing with the coming event.

"Aren't you happy you are going to receive the Torah?" Moses inquired reproachfully.

"What share have we in the Torah?" they replied. "We are busy all day and have no time to study the Torah, nor can we understand it, so why should we rejoice?"

"But you do have a share in the holy Torah," Moses said. "It will be up to you to support the Yeshivoth and Talmud Torahs where the Torah will be studied. Your contributions to the Torah institutions and support of the Torah scholars will enable them to study the holy Torah, and it will be deemed that you have a share in their studies. Moreover, after you finish your day's work or business, you are going to join some Torah circle in the evening, you are going to attend the services at the "Shul" daily and Sabbath and "Yom Tov," you are going to follow the teachings and precepts of the holy Torah just the same as the others. Oh yes, my friends, you too have a share in the holy Torah—and an important one!" Moses concluded.

The faces of the Merchants and Workers lit up and they too, joined in the general preparations.

On went Moses and saw the women folk sitting and gossiping and not busy with preparations for the "Festival of the Giving of the Torah."

"You lazy women," Moses rebuked them, "why aren't you busy preparing puddings and pastry and other nice things in honor of the 'Festival of the Giving of Our Torah'?"

"But what have we to do with the Torah?" they replied.

"Weren't you the first to be told about the giving of the Torah?"
Moses said. "Why, your responsibility is even greater than your
husbands'! You will have to bring up your dear children to love
the Torah; you will take them to the Talmud Torah and Yeshivah.
You will also help support those Torah institutions. It will be
up to you to make your home a real Jewish home, and there are
many precepts of the Torah which only you alone have been
privileged to do. Rest assured, your part in the holy Torah is
very important!"

Thereupon the women got busy preparing for "Yom Tov."
They went to milk the cows, churn butter, knead the dough, and
bake in honor of the "Festival of the Giving of the Torah."

Moses continued his quest in the camp of Israel and presently
came upon the children flying kites, playing ball, sailing paper
boats, and doing a hundred and one other common things, but
none showed any sign of the real festive spirit.

"Aren't you ashamed to waste your time like this when you
should be getting ready for the receiving of the wonderful Torah?"
Moses said sternly.

"Oh, dear Master Moses!" the youngsters exclaimed, "but we
cannot understand the Torah. Guess we'll have to wait till we
grow up. Is there any other Torah for small children?"

"Certainly there is!" said Moses. "Go to the Talmud Torah or
Yeshivah, and you will see. Your teachers will teach you many
beautiful and wise things. You will learn 'Chumosh,' Scripture
and later also Talmud. Do you know that G-D loves your study
even more than the study of the grownups?"

Up jumped the children in great excitement. "Hurray!" they
cried, "we too are going to learn the Torah!"

At that time a sobbing child—he was four years old—came up
to Moses. "Dear Moses," the child said with tears in his eyes, "I
also want to have some of the Torah. Everybody is so happy about
it, and I cannot even read or write!"

Moses lifted the child in his arms. "Don't cry, my dear child.
You too will learn the Torah. When you learn the Aleph-Beth

and learn to read our sacred languages; Kometz Aleph-oh, Kometz-Beth-Boh, and so on, do you know what G-D will be doing at that time? He will gather up every sound that comes out from your pure little mouth, and He will play with them as you do with sparkling marbles. And He will love you for it, and love your dear parents too, for your sake."

Then every one in the camp of Israel, young and old, rich and poor, joined in the preparations for the holy day when G-D would reveal Himself on Mount Sinai and give them His holy Torah. And all the people of Israel said in one voice: "All that G-D will command us we will do!"

SHAVUOS: WHEN WE RECEIVED
OUR CONSTITUTION

> "We, the people of the United States, in order to form a more
> perfect Union, establish justice, insure domestic tranquility,
> provide for the common defense, promote the general wel-
> fare, and secure the blessings of liberty to ourselves and
> our posterity, do ordain and establish this Constitution for
> the United States of America." (*Preamble to the Constitution
> of the United States*)

WHAT IS FREEDOM? We all recognize this quotation as the
preamble to the Constitution of the United States. It is a
document that guarantees to every one of us the greatest
freedom ever given by a country to its citizens. We, in
America, have achieved liberty; we are free.

But, what is freedom? Is freedom the right for everyone
to do whatever he pleases? If so, people could destroy private property, rob or even kill, if they had the desire to do
so. This would be complete freedom to the ones who do these
things. But what would happen to the freedom of the others,
those to whom these things were done? People would have
to live behind locked doors, not knowing from one moment
to the next what might happen. It is obvious that this sort
of freedom is not true freedom. True freedom must be freedom for all.

In order to establish true freedom, a nation must adopt a set of laws, a constitution. This constitution must guarantee freedom and equal rights to all. No one may be persecuted because of his race, color or creed; everyone has the right to express an opinion and to be heard. Everyone must learn to respect the rights and personal property of his neighbor. Most important, the citizens must agree to accept allegiance to this constitution and abide by all its laws. Without a constitution to guide and protect, there can be no freedom.

The newly freed children of Israel faced an important problem when they left Egypt. They had been freed from slavery and were on their way to the Promised Land, Canaan. They were a nation of six hundred thousand males with women and children. What was to be their guide during the long journey? How were they to assure freedom and equal rights to all? Even more important, how were they to be governed when they reached Canaan and established their homeland?

The time had come for the adoption of a constitution and a way of life. The Israelites were to receive their law, the Torah, from G-D through their leader Moses. They would not have to draw up a constitution that would have to be changed and modified according to the times. Their constitution was to be a permanent set of laws for every generation. The Torah was to be so flexible that it could meet the needs and problems of all people everywhere at all times without being changed.

It would be a difficult and perhaps even an impossible task for Moses to make the Israelites understand that this Law was to come directly from G-D and that it would never need change or modernization. The people might believe him in the beginning, but in years to come when Moses would no longer be with them they might change their minds about the Torah and begin to abolish laws that they didn't understand. The people needed proof that the Torah was given to them by G-D; a proof that would win their loyalty and the loyalty of Jews throughout the generations. And so G-D made known His will to Moses that the Israelites would be privileged to witness the greatest event in human history: the revelation of the Torah on Mount Sinai.

It was about six weeks after they had left Egypt that the Israelites camped in a place called Sinai. After communion with G-D, Moses called the Israelites together for this message from G-D:

> *"You have seen what I did to the Egyptians and how I bore you on eagles' wings and brought you to Myself. Now, therefore, if you will listen to My voice and keep My Covenant then you will be a treasure to Me among all peoples: for all the earth is Mine. And you will be to Me a kingdom of priests and a holy nation."*
>
> (*Shmos 19:4–6*)

The people heard the message from G-D and accepted the covenant. They promised to obey all the laws without question. "Na'aseh V'nishma" was their cry; "we will follow and observe the laws even before we hear any reasons for them." After Moses returned with their reply to G-D, he told them to prepare themselves for the great event. After three days of preparation, the people gathered at the foot of Mount Sinai and waited. Moses alone went up.

> *"And it came to pass on the third day, in the morning, that there was thundering and lightning and a thick cloud upon the mount and the voice of the trumpet exceedingly loud so that all the people trembled . . . and Mount Sinai was altogether in a smoke because the Lord descended upon it in fire . . . and the whole mountain quaked greatly."*
>
> (*Shmos 19:16*)

At that moment six hundred thousand Israelites and their families heard a voice from G-D proclaiming the first and second commandments:

> *"I am the Lord your G-D who has brought you out of the land of Egypt from the house of bondage.*
> *You shall have no other gods before Me."*
>
> (*Shmos 20:1–2*)

The Israelites always remembered this historic event; it made a lasting impression upon them. This story was handed down from father to son throughout the generations to this very day. Our Sages tell us that our ancestors were not the only ones who surrounded Mount Sinai, but the soul of every human being that ever lived and that was yet to be born was there with them. And when our ancestors made the promise to accept the Torah without any conditions, we, too, made that promise. Perhaps that is why every Jew deep down in his heart believes in his religion and its teachings and wants to show his allegiance to it in some way.

THE EFFECT OF THE TORAH ON THE WORLD. But what is the importance of the Torah to the rest of the world? Has the Torah had any effect upon it or is it just a book for Jews?

Although the Torah was given to the Jews, its teachings have influenced millions of people all over the world. The Ten Commandments in particular are an example of laws that have been accepted by our western civilization and by much of the rest of the world. The Torah has been translated into more than a thousand different languages and it is recognized in almost every country of the world as the greatest contribution to world literature. Many of the stories in the Torah are told to children all over the world regardless of their religion because of their beauty, fascination and moral lessons. The story of Joseph so inspired the famous novelist,

Thomas Mann, that he wrote a series of novels based upon it. Many of the Torah stories have served as springboards for poems and plays written by some of the greatest authors and poets in the world.

The Torah, however, is not just a book of great literature. It is primarily a book of laws and ethics. As such a book, it has influenced millions of people the world over. It teaches some of the greatest social ideals. Justice is interwoven with kindness and mercy to make up the Jewish pattern of living. These high ideals of the Torah have inspired so many people that they have been used by nations all over the world as a basis for social justice in their lands. Our own country, the United States, has utilized many of the laws of the Torah and the Talmud in the Constitution and in Supreme Court rulings.

So you see, the Torah is truly a "tree of life" that nourishes all those who wish to partake of its fruits. It is a living Torah, one that is constantly bearing new fruit for those who obey and study it. This treasure serves to enlighten the world and teach man how to live better and more happily with his fellow man. This was our contribution to the world. The Torah was G-D's gift to humanity on the sixth day in the month of Sivan, seven weeks after the Israelites left Egypt. It is this historic event that we celebrate joyously and proudly on the holiday of "Shavuos."

LAWS OF SHAVUOS. The festival of "Shavuos" occurs on the sixth and seventh days of the Hebrew month "Sivan." The English translation of "Shavuos" is "weeks." As you remember, this holiday is celebrated at the end of seven full weeks of counting the "Omer" from the second day of Passover.

"Shavuos" is also known by three other names. "Z'Man Matan Toroseinu," "The Time of the Giving of our Torah"; "Chag Hakotsir," "The Holiday of Reaping"; and "Chag Habikurim," "The Holiday of the First Fruits."

Since "Shavuos" is a harvest festival, it is customary to decorate the home and the synagogue with tree branches, fruits and flowers.

DAIRY MEALS. Eating dairy products, rather than meat, for the main meal is a popular custom on this holiday. Some of our Sages attribute this custom to the verse in the Song of Songs by Solomon which likens the Torah to milk and honey. Others infer this custom from a verse in the Book of Ruth which is read on this holiday. Still others maintain that we mark Shavuos with dairy dishes because at this time of year dairy products are plentiful.

REVIEWING THE TORAH. On the first night of "Shavuos" it is customary to review selected parts of the Torah and the Oral Law. This is to renew our appreciation of this precious gift from G-D.

AKDOMUS. On the first day of "Shavuos" it is customary in all synagogues to read a poem called in Hebrew, "Akdomus." It is read after the "Shacharis" service, right before the reading of the Torah. In beautiful poetic language it tells us of the greatness of G-D and His creations. It tells how happy we should feel that we were chosen by G-D to receive the Torah. In the second part of this poem the author tells of the heroism that the Jewish people exhibited and their sacrifices for the upholding of the Torah.

One of the most popular and most frequently quoted phrases of the "Akdomus" is its expression of the greatness of the glory of G-D. Let us read from this beautiful poetry, in translation.

> *"Were the sky of parchment made,*
> *A quill each reed, each twig and blade,*
> *Could we with ink the oceans fill,*
> *Were every man a scribe of skill,*

The marvelous story
Of G-D's great glory
Would still remain untold;
For He, Most High,
The earth and sky
Created alone of old."

THE BOOK OF RUTH. On the second day of "Shavuos" it is customary to read the Book of Ruth after the "Shacharis" service. It is a story of devotion. It tells how the heroine, Ruth, was devoted to her husband, her mother-in-law, and above all the Jewish religion that she adopted through marriage. It teaches us that anyone who accepts the Torah and obeys it with sincerity will be a better person for it; his reward will be great. In the case of Ruth, her reward was realized not only in her lifetime, but even more so in later generations, for it was her great-grandson, David, who became the second kind of Israel. The Book of Ruth should be a lesson to all the world and to Jews in particular. Just as our ancestors, standing around Mount Sinai, took it upon themselves to obey the Torah, so, many years later, Ruth took upon herself this same obligation. True happiness and a rewarding life can only be achieved by living according to G-D's law and fulfilling His commandments.

YIZKOR. On the second day of "Shavuos" the special memorial prayer, "Yizkor" is recited before the "Musaf" service. As mentioned previously, this prayer is recited on each of the three pilgrimage festivals; "Succos," "Pesach," and "Shavuos," and also on Yom Kippur.

THE DAY OF DAYS

These are solemn days in the camp of Israel in the desert of Sinai. As you walk among the tents, you will see no idlers. Everyone is busy washing clothes, cleaning the camp, and preparing for the great event. You will hear no idle conversation, or vain laughter. Young and old alike are preoccupied with the great event about to take place.

Day of all days! Never has the sun risen so gloriously! Never has the sky been so blue, or the air so fresh! A holy light fills the whole world, as Moses leads his people out of the camp, while G-D raises Mount Sinai, so that its peak is lost in the heavens.

As the people stood below at a respectful distance, Moses fearlessly ascended the mountain until he too was engulfed by the heavens, and could no longer be seen.

Then G-D said to Moses: "Now I will give Israel the Torah. Today, the wonders of heaven shall be revealed to My chosen people. But since you are here on the mountain with Me, how will the people know it is I who speak and not you? Therefore, go down and join the people!"

At that instant, just as Moses turned to descend, the heavens opened, and the glories of Heaven were revealed to a spellbound Israel, for one unforgettable and awe-inspiring second.

Then Moses brought G-D's words to the people: "I am not like the earthly kings, the rulers and princes of the nations. I need no servant to clear the way for Me; nor attendants to lay green carpets for Me to tread upon. I need no candles to brighten My palace, nor purple tapestries need hang over My walls!

"I have spread the blue heaven above Me, and the whole wide

world is My palace, brightened by My own brilliant light! The green grass and fragrant flowers are My royal carpet, and the sun is but one of My torches. The world is Mine, and I am its King!

"Now, therefore, if you will hearken to My voice, and obey My commandments, I will make you a kingdom of priests and a holy nation, worthy subjects of the King of Kings!"

And Israel knew that true indeed were the words of G-D; that never a king breathed upon this earth who could compare with Him, for G-D is all-powerful, His wisdom boundless, and His mercy unending.

II

As the echoes of these words grew fainter and fainter, a great silence descended upon the earth. All movement ceased and everything stood still. No birds twittered, and no ox lowed in the meadow. The waters of the seas lay still, and not a wave rose or fell. No leaf fluttered in the wind, for no wind blew. The whole world was breathless with suspense. Bird, beast, and man, all were under the spell of the great event about to take place.

And then in the midst of this deep silence, the words of G-D burst forth like thunder, "I AM THE LORD THY G-D."

These words shook the world to its very foundations! They completely filled the universe and resounded throughout the earth. The tiniest babe, and the grayest head trembled alike before so much glory and holiness. The mountains trembled, and the sea rumbled. Lightning flashed in the heavens, and thunder rang out. And the words, once G-D had spoken them, became a burning flame, that floated in the air. As Israel stood in awe before Mount Sinai, the angels descended from Heaven, bearing G-D's commandments. As one lovingly presents precious jewels, the angels presented the commandments to Israel, showing them the beauties of every law, the reward for obeying it, or punishment if it be disobeyed. And only after every Jew had accepted the commandments, did G-D inscribe them upon the Tablets.

The flame issuing from G-D's words grew brighter and brighter, blinding Israel with its brilliance, and filling their hearts with terror. When the Torah looked down and saw Israel standing, nearly lifeless with terror, she turned to G-D and said, "What good will it do to give me to lifeless corpses? I am to be a source of life for them, not the cause of their death! Revive them, O, G-D, so that they will be able to rejoice with Thy great Gift."

Then a sweet dew fell upon Israel, reviving them, and giving them courage and strength to hear the rest of G-D's words.

III

The people of Israel were not alone in their fright caused by the tremor that shook the earth and the flame that floated in the air. The rulers and kings of all the nations were overcome with fear, and hastened to inquire of Balaam as to what strange phenomenon was occurring. "Is G-D going to destroy the world with another flood?" they asked.

"No," replied Balaam. "He is giving Israel the Torah." Content with this reply, the princes of the nations returned to their palaces.

In the meantime Moses brought to Israel the Ten Commandments which G-D had inscribed upon tablets of stone. When Moses had concluded reading the Ten Commandments to his people, Israel replied as one man, "We will do and listen!"

At that moment, six hundred thousand angels descended from Heaven, addressing each Jew: "You have made a wise choice. G-D rejoices that you are prepared to obey His every command, the smallest as well as the greatest. And because you have chosen to do so, behold the beautiful gifts we bring unto you!"

Then the angels placed on the head of each Jew two crowns of glory. One for promising "to do," and the other for promising "to listen" to the words of G-D.

A great thick cloud lay over Mount Sinai. Ascending the mountain to receive the Torah, Moses thought, "How shall I pass the cloud?" But suddenly, the cloud parted and bore Moses up to

Heaven. As Moses neared the gates of Heaven, the angels who guarded the portals of the divine kingdom asked him, "Moses, are you not afraid to enter Heaven? Don't the angels and their holy fire frighten you?" On went Moses, and presently the angels drew near, surrounding him with flame, threatening to engulf him. But Moses called out G-D's name, and the angels fled before him.

Still riding on the cloud, Moses saw a terrifying sight. Hadarniel, the angel whose every word shot twelve thousand darts of lightning into the air, appeared before him. Moses was struck dumb with fear. He could scarcely utter a syllable. Then G-D said to him, "You have addressed Me before, fearlessly, and without terror; why do you tremble now before an angel who is merely one of my servants?" New courage returned to Moses, and once again he called upon G-D. He had barely uttered a word, when Hadarniel approached Moses and said, "Blessed son of Amram! I will lead you through our kingdom." They had gone a little way, when Hadarniel turned to Moses and said, "I can go no further with you. I must turn back lest the great flame of the angel Sandalphon consume me!"

When Moses heard these words, his heart grew faint, and he turned to G-D with tears in his eyes, "Save me, G-D!"

Then Moses witnessed what no other human being ever witnessed before. Over a great river of fire, Moses passed. He shaded his eyes with his hands, for he beheld a light that surpassed all the others in brilliance. Bright angels, the brightest angels in Heaven, stood surrounding the Divine Throne. And only because G-D had endowed Moses with heavenly powers, could he endure to look upon these heavenly wonders.

IV

"Shall we let Moses take the Torah from us?" the angels in Heaven asked one of another.

"Moses!" said G-D. "The angels claim the Torah for themselves. Speak to them, and show why the Torah should be given to you."

"But I am afraid they will consume me with their fires."

"Have no fear. Hold on to My Throne and I will protect you."

Moses did so, and turning to the angels he replied: "Thus it is written in G-D's Torah: 'I am G-D, thy G-D, who hath taken thee out of Egypt. Thou shalt have no other gods. Remember the Sabbath to keep it holy. Thou shalt not steal. Thou shalt not murder.' Tell me, were you enslaved in Egypt? Will you, who daily look upon the glory of G-D, turn to worship heathen gods, idols of wood and stone? Are you ever tempted to steal or harm one another? No! The Torah is not for you, but for us, human beings!"

When Moses had ended, every angel saw the justice and wisdom of his words. "The will of G-D be done!" they replied. Then Moses heard wonderful and glorious strains of music ringing in his ears, the music of Heaven, for the angels were singing praises to Almighty G-D.

THE FAST DAYS:
HISTORICAL REMINDERS

In addition to Yom Kippur, there are five more fast days which Jews all over the world observe. One of these fast days, "Taanis Esther," we have already discussed in connection with Purim. In this chapter we will study the other four.

As you know from your study of history, the Jews were always devoted to the Land of Israel. When they were exiled from their homeland, they took an oath never to forget it. They vowed that they would remember Jerusalem even on their happiest occasions. How beautifully this idea is expressed in Psalm 137.

> *"By the waters of Babylon we sat down and wept when we remembered Zion. . . . How shall we sing the Lord's song in a foreign land? If I forget you, O Jerusalem, let me forget my right hand! May my tongue cleave to the roof of my mouth if I do not remember you, if I do not set Jerusalem above my highest joy!"*

The allegiance, which the Jews swore to the Land of Israel together with the prophecies that they would eventually return to it, gave them courage to exist as a nation despite the fact that they were scattered throughout the world. The fast days have served the Jews as reminders of the land that once belonged to their people.

With the arrival of each of the three fast days that bear directly on the destruction of the Temples and the city of Jerusalem, memories are reawakened. We remind ourselves that it was the sins of our ancestors that led to this destruction. In fasting and prayer we express the sorrow and pain we feel at our great loss. The many prayers and laments that are recited on these fast days help to keep the memory of our religious homeland fresh in our minds.

But more than this, the fast days remind us of the first and second Temples in Jerusalem that stood for devotion to G-D and to His law. With the destruction of the Temple came the destruction of the Land of Israel. For Israel could exist as a people in their land only when the Temple, the House of G-D, was their guide to living. With the rebuilding of Israel must come the rebuilding of the Temple. For only with the establishment of Torah as its guide can Israel set an example to the rest of the world.

In our joy as well as in our sorrow we look to the rebuilding of our Temple in Jerusalem. It will shine forth as a spiritual light that will be admired by all the nations of the world. "For out of Zion shall go forth the Law," said the prophet Isaiah, "and the word of the Lord from Jerusalem." And as our tradition tells us at that time all our fast days will change from days of sorrow to days of joy and celebration.

THE FAST OF THE NINTH OF "AV." The most important of the four fast days is "Tisha B'Av," the ninth day of the month of "Av." It commemorates the destruction of the first and second Temples.

With regard to food, "Tisha B'Av" has the same laws as Yom Kippur. Like Yom Kippur, "Tisha B'Av" is a twenty-four-hour fast from evening to evening.

KINOS. On the night of "Tisha B'Av" special services are held in the synagogue. The curtain is removed from the Holy Ark as a sign of mourning. Many synagogues use only sufficient light to be able to read the prayers. Many congregants remove their shoes or wear soft-soled shoes as a sign of mourning. The "Ma'ariv" service is recited in a soft mournful chant. When the evening service is over, the people in many congregations sit on the floor to put themselves in the mood for the lamentations that are to be recited. These lamentations are called in Hebrew, "Kinos"; they are recited in a tearful tone.

SERVICES. The following morning the services are the same as on the weekdays. Since the "Tallis" and the "Tephillin" are considered adornments, we do not wear them during the "Shacharis" service on "Tisha B'av," a day of mourning.

The Torah scroll is taken from the Ark at the "Shacharis" service and three people are called up for honors. The third person also recites the "Haftorah" for "Tisha B'Av"; it is chanted in a mournful tone. The Torah scroll is then returned to the Ark and special lamentations are again recited.

In the afternoon service, "Mincha," the "Tallis" and the "Tephillin" are put on and the benedictions for them are recited as usual. The Torah scroll is again read, and the "Haftorah" that is recited on all other fast days is chanted.

If "Tisha B'av" occurs on the Sabbath, it is postponed to Sunday.

THE FAST OF GEDALIAH. After the destruction of the first Temple by Nebuchadnezzar, the king of Babylonia, the Jews were governed by a man named Gedaliah ben Achikom, who was appointed by Nebuchadnezzar. On the third day of the Hebrew month "Tishrei," Gedaliah was killed, a murder which was cleverly instigated by the Ammonite king, Baalis, for certain military reasons. This meant more disaster to the Jews, for Nebuchadnezzar exiled them to Babylonia.

Ever since that day, the third day of "Tishrei" has been regarded as a day of sorrow. The Fast of Gedaliah is the day following Rosh Hashonah.

THE FAST OF THE TENTH OF TEIVES. This fast day commemorates the beginning of the siege of Jerusalem by Nebuchadnezzar, king of Babylonia. This siege finally led to the destruction of the first Temple.

THE FAST OF THE SEVENTEENTH OF "TAMUZ." This day commemorates four sorrowful events in the history of the Jewish People.

1. When Moses descended from Mount Sinai, it was the seventeenth day of "Tamuz." On that day the Tablets of the Law were broken.
2. The daily sacrifice in the Temple was abolished on this day.
3. Apostemus, the wicked, burned the Torah on that day and placed an idol in the Temple.
4. The walls of the city of Jerusalem were broken through on that day by the Romans, which led to the destruction of the second Temple by Titus.

Three weeks elapse from the seventeenth day of "Tamuz" to the ninth day of "Av." These days are known as days of mourning. No weddings or other joyous celebrations are held during this period. The last nine days are especially marked as mournful. Many people abstain from eating meat during the nine days since eating meat was always considered a sign of festivity.

The above three fast days begin as usual the preceding

evening. The actual fasting, however, does not begin until the morning. The morning services on these days are the same as the weekday morning service.

During the afternoon service, the Torah scroll is read and a special "Haftorah" is recited. Three people are called to the Torah, and in the "Shmoneh Esrei" the prayer of "Aneinu" is added.

If any of these fast days occur on Sabbath, it is postponed to Sunday.

THE LESSON OF TISHA B'AV

Shoshanna looked up from the book she was reading and spotted the red hair of her friend, Malka. She shouted to her. "Malka, Malka, I'm over here, on top of the hill."

It took Malka practically no time at all to race up the hill in her sneakers and sit down beside her friend on the grass.

"Hi," said Shoshanna. "Are you fasting?"

"Of course," said Malka. "It's Tisha B'av, isn't it."

"I know that, silly, but this is my first time. I was twelve in May so now mom permitted me to fast."

"Isn't it great?" Malka said. "I feel wonderful and fabulously grown up."

"Oh, Malka," Shoshanna cried. "You're all mixed up. You're supposed to feel sad not happy."

"I can't help it, Shoshanna. I feel very excited about it. If you promise you won't tell anyone I'll tell you a secret."

Shoshanna promised and Malka continued. "I don't even know the story of Tisha B'av or why we're fasting," she whispered.

Shoshanna stared at Malka in absolute shock. "You don't know the story—well, all right, I'll tell it to you."

And she told her friend of a glorious nation that devoted itself to G-D and of the beautiful and magnificent temple that stood as a symbol to the world, of that devotion. "And the people of the nation forgot their place as an example to the world and they were bad and didn't obey G-D's words as commanded in the Torah."

"See, here it is in my translation of the Lamentations."

She read the line aloud to Malka. "Jerusalem has grievously sinned; and so she has become an abomination." (1:8)

"What's an abomination?" asked Malka.

"It means something hateful and disgusting." She read another line to her friend. " 'Is this the city that men call the perfection of beauty, the joy of the earth?'

"And that's why," Shoshanna continued, "G-D allowed the enemies of the Jews to destroy the Temple and Jerusalem, just like this."

She plucked a handful of grass and showed it to her friend.

"I can just picture the burning of the Temple," she whispered sadly. "That's how the Temple was destroyed, you know. The flames must have been seen for miles around and all the people must have been screaming and crying."

Shoshanna swallowed the hard lump that had come into her throat as she recounted the tragedy of her people.

"Read this, Malka." Malka read the lines to which Shoshanna had pointed. "My eye runs down with rivers of water for the destruction of the daughter of my people." (3:48)

"Who is the daughter," Malka asked, her voice now quiet with the solemnity of the words to which she was listening.

Shoshanna's eyes were filled with tears as she softly answered Malka.

"The daughter means Jerusalem, of course; the people are sad because of her destruction."

"But Shoshanna, can't we ever rebuild the Temple and Jerusalem?"

"Just as that patch I made bare by pulling up the grass can blossom again with the right nourishment and sunlight so the Jews can be reborn as a nation and rebuild the Temple with the sunlight of G-D and the nourishment of the Torah as their guide," said Shoshanna.

"Oh, Shoshanna, that's wonderful. I hope it will happen soon, perhaps by the time we really grow up."

They sat in silence for a moment and Malka spoke up again.

"I just thought of something. I still don't know why we should have to fast on this day. After all, the burning took place so long ago."

"That's true," Shoshanna answered. "But there's one thing you have forgotten, many of our people today still do not obey the Torah. The fasting is to make us repent and remind us that we can become better persons."

"I see," said Malka. "If every person fasts and repents then the nation as a whole would be repenting, and then we would deserve the Temple."

"Exactly," Shoshanna said. She took Malka's hand and in her mind she saw a beautiful vision of the Temple that would some-day be rebuilt and serve as a light to the world.

"SHABBOS": A DAY OF FREEDOM

Are we slaves or are we free men?

Are we living the same kind of life our ancestors lived in Egypt or have we learned a better way of life?

LIFE IN EGYPT. As you remember from your history studies, the Israelites were enslaved by Pharaoh. They were subjected to his cruel rule every moment of their lives. Day after day, seven days a week, they labored in the hot sun, building the great cities of Pithom and Rameses.

The Israelites lived in a world where freedom was the privilege of the master, not of the slave. One free day to spend with the family, to put the week's worries aside, to relax in the comforts of home, and to devote oneself to holy things, was unheard of in those days. Pharaoh did not realize that had he given the Israelites a day of rest, once a week, they would return to their labor with new strength and vigor. He did not realize that after a day of rest they would be able to work harder, much better.

A NEW WAY OF LIFE. The time came, however, for the Israelites to give up this way of life. The Torah was to be their guide and Moses was to be their teacher.

The Israelites spent forty years in the wilderness learning the "Mitzvos" of the Torah from Moses, their leader. Day after day they came to him with their problems and quarrels, and he judged them according to the laws he had learned from G-D. The Torah that Moses taught them was a new way of life for the Israelites. Each "Mitzvah" they learned was a new and wonderful experience.

THE MITZVAH OF SHABBOS. But among all the "Mitzvos" that the Israelites learned there was one that shone out brighter than all the others, as the moon among the stars. It was the "Mitzvah" of "Shabbos." Not only did this "Mitzvah" revolutionize the life of the Israelites, but it was destined to revolutionize the life of almost the entire civilized world.

> *"Six days shall you labor and do all your work but the seventh day shall be the sabbath in honor of the Lord your G-D; on it you shall not do any work. . . . And you shall remember that you were a servant in the land of Egypt and that the Lord your G-D brought you out from there by a mighty hand and an outstretched arm; therefore has the Lord your G-D commanded you to observe the sabbath day."*
>
> (*D'vorim 5:13–16*)

What a wonderful idea! Do not work seven days a week, as you did in Egypt, devoting all your time and energy to toil. There are things in life so much more important than earning a living. *Don't neglect them!* Set aside one day as a sabbath. It is a day that will beautify your life; a day that will make you free; a day to which you will look forward six days a week.

But haven't we in the United States always had a day of rest? Not at all!

Did you know that until just a few decades ago people worked twelve and fourteen hours a day, seven days a week, right here in New York City?

Ask your parents or grandparents if they remember the sweat shops in the early years of the 20th century. Some of your grandparents may have worked in them. Anyone who worked in those sweat shops can tell you that it was Egyptian slavery right here in the United States. It took years of hard work, blood, sweat, and tears before the labor unions, with the aid of the government, convinced the bosses that the workers were entitled to a day of rest once a week. And it took many years before the bosses realized that the six-day-week would be just as beneficial to them as it would be to their employees.

Just think how far advanced our Torah is to have introduced the seventh day as a day of spiritual and physical rest more than three thousand years ago. How long it took humanity to learn this lesson taught to us by G-D!

What is the beauty of "Shabbos"?

How can it make us free?

The answer to these questions is given to us in the first book of the Torah, "Bareishis."

> "And the heavens and the earth and all their host were finished. And G-D had finished *on the seventh day His work which He had made,* and He rested *on the seventh day from all His work which He had made.* And G-D blessed *the seventh day* and made *it* holy *because on it He rested from all His work. . . .*"
>
> (*Bareishis 2:1–3*)

Sabbath, "Shabbos," in Hebrew, is a three letter word. The three letters remind us of the three phrases in the Torah that describe the first Sabbath which came at the end of the six days of creation. These three phrases are the key to Sabbath observance. (The three phrases are underlined in the above quotation.) Let us analyze these phrases one by one.

And G-D Had Finished. (1) It is a "Mitzvah" to walk in the ways of G-D. Just as He is merciful so must we be merciful. Just as He is forgiving so must we be forgiving. It is a "Mitzvah" to learn and practice all the wonderful virtues we learn from the Torah of G-D.

This "Mitzvah" also applies to "Shabbos." Just as G-D created the world in six days and finished His work at the close of the sixth day so must we do all our work and conduct our business in six days and finish them for the week at the close of the sixth day.

Although most of us have accepted the Sabbath day as a holiday, few of us know how to make it a real change in our weekday routine. In order to benefit from the true holiday spirit of "Shabbos" we must free ourselves of our weekday worries and concerns. We must forget our jobs, our professions and our businesses. We must give our mind and body freedom from the work they have done during the week. In order to make "Shabbos" a real holiday, a day of freedom, we should refrain from all creative work such as building or writing. For creative work is part of our weekday routine; it would spoil the spirit of "Shabbos." As G-D refrained from creating on the seventh day so must we refrain from creative work on this day.

And G-D Rested. (2) Just as G-D rested on the seventh day, the Sabbath, so must we rest on that day. The Sabbath should be a day of relaxation from the physical work we did during the week. In this way we can start the new week alert and fresh. What a blessing the Sabbath is to a man or woman who has worked hard all week long. How they look forward to their day of rest and relaxation. To them, "Shabbos" is truly a day of freedom.

But is this day a holiday for men and women alone?

Of course not. The Torah tells us:

> *"But the seventh day is the sabbath in honor of the Lord your G-D; on it you shall not do any work, neither you, nor your son, nor your daughter, nor your man servant, nor your maid*

servant, nor your ox, nor your donkey, nor the stranger who
is within your gates. . . ."

(*D'vorim 5:14*)

"Shabbos" is a holiday for the whole family. All deserve this day of rest once a week. Mother should rest from her week-day routine of cleaning, washing and cooking. Everything should be prepared before "Shabbos," so that on this holy day mother also will be a free person. As a son or daughter, you are also privileged to celebrate the Sabbath. It should be your day of rest, too. The servants or maids should be given the day off so that they too can relax and enjoy themselves. Even farm animals that are used to draw wagons or plows should be allowed to graze in the fields to rest from the week's labor.

"And G-D Blessed . . . and Made It Holy." The principal feature of "Shabbos" is its holiness. Just as G-D blessed the Sabbath day and made it holy so must we bless it and make it holy.

Make "Shabbos" a family day. Spend the whole day with the family enjoying each other's company. Discuss your schoolwork with father, with whom you hardly get a chance to talk during the week. Spend some time discussing your personal problems or religious questions with your parents.

Make "Shabbos" a day for learning. Study your "Chumosh" with father and mother. Share with them what you have learned in Hebrew school. They may have ideas to contribute that your teacher may not have mentioned.

Above all, attend services on Friday night and "Shabbos" morning. Spend part of this holy day in prayer and thanks-giving to G-D. Thank Him for the happiness He has given you. Thank Him for the privilege of living in America, the land of the free. Thank Him for giving the world its greatest blessing, the Sabbath.

So you see, one who observes the Sabbath is truly free. By observing the laws of Sabbath he frees himself from the weekday routine. He gives himself a real vacation, once a week. He devotes this day to the more important things in life; the study of Torah and living with the family. In this way he becomes not only a better Jew, but a better human being.

LAWS AND CUSTOMS

PREPARATION. Preparation for "Shabbos" begins during the week. In order to sanctify and celebrate "Shabbos" properly, mother cleans the house. In this way the spirit of "Shabbos" is felt in every corner of every room.

On Friday, "Erev" Shabbos, mother is especially busy, for she must prepare all the special "Shabbos" foods for the three meals of "Shabbos": Friday night, "Shabbos" afternoon and "Shabbos" evening before sunset.

It is customary to bathe and dress in holiday clothes on Friday afternoon in order to greet the Sabbath in a dignified manner.

CANDLE LIGHTING. Late Friday afternoon, twenty minutes before sundown, the Sabbath candles are lit. The "Mitzvah" of lighting the Sabbath candles is very important. It belongs exclusively to the woman of the house. The custom is usually to light two candles although some families light more than two.

After she lights the candles the woman waves her outstretched hands over the flame three times, covers her eyes and recites the blessing, "Blessed art Thou O Lord our G-D, King of the universe, who has sanctified us with His commandments and commanded us to light the Sabbath candles." (You will find this blessing in the Appendix.)

If there is no woman in the house the candles should be lit by a man.

To make it apparent to the family and guests that the candles are in honor of "Shabbos," they should be placed on the dining room table before they are lit and the candlesticks should remain there for the entire Sabbath day even though the candles have long burned out.

With the lighting of the candles "Shabbos" officially begins in the home. It is proper for the father and the sons to go to the synagogue at this time, for the Sabbath services. Mother and the daughters remain home in order to arrange the table for the Sabbath meal.

FRIDAY NIGHT SERVICES. The Friday afternoon "Mincha" service is the usual weekday "Mincha," consisting of "Ashrei," "Shmoneh Esrei," and "Oleinu."

KABOLAS SHABBOS. Following the "Mincha" prayer, there is a special service of welcome to the Sabbath. It is called "Kabolas Shabbos," "The Greeting to the Sabbath." In this service there is a beautiful hymn written by the Hebrew poet Shlomo Halevi. It is called "L'choh Dodi." If you look at it in your "Siddur" you will notice that each stanza begins with a letter of his name. The first letters of all the stanzas form the poet's full name.

In "L'choh Dodi," the poet pictures the Sabbath as a beautiful bride, whom we greet graciously every week. Here is a quotation from this poem:

> "Come, let us go to meet the Sabbath, for it is a source of blessing. From the beginning it was ordained; last in Creation, first in G-d's thoughts.
> Come, my friend, to meet the bride; let us welcome the Sabbath."

"Kabolas Shabbos" is followed by the "Ma'ariv" service. The "Ma'ariv" for "Shabbos" is essentially the same as the one for weekdays except for the addition of a Biblical quotation about "Shabbos" and a special "Shmoneh Esrei."

THE SHABBOS TABLE. When father and the sons return from the synagogue they find everything prepared for the "Shabbos" meal. The table is set with the best silverware and dishes. At the head of the table, where father sits, is the "Kiddush" cup and the two "Challos" (plural for "Challa"). The "Challos" are loaves of white bread baked especially for "Shabbos" and "Yom Tov." They are covered with a special cover which is usually embroidered with phrases from the Torah dealing with the beauty and holiness of "Shabbos."

"Challa." The "Challos" symbolize the double portion of Manna that fell in the desert and which the Israelites gathered on Fridays. (The double portion was to sustain the Israelites for two days since no Manna fell on "Shabbos.") The "Challa" cover symbolizes the dew that covered the ground so that the Manna fell on the dew and was covered to keep it clean.

THE SHABBOS MEAL. The family gather around the table and sing the beautiful hymn "Sholom Aleichem." This hymn is a greeting to the Angels of Peace who are believed to visit us on the Sabbath. We ask them to grant us the blessing of peace, and declare that the Holy One, blessed be He, is the King of Kings.

After "Sholom Aleichem" father fills the "Kiddush" cup with wine and recites the "Shabbos Kiddush." The cup of wine is then passed around the table so that everyone may have a sip.

Next the family wash their hands and the father, followed by the rest of the family, recite the "Motsee" upon the "challa." Father then cuts the "challa" and gives a slice to each person at the table.

After the first course, which is the traditional "gefilte fish," the family join father in singing the beautiful "Shabbos" songs, or "Z'miros." The "Z'miros" are songs of praise to G-D thanking Him for His gift, the Sabbath.

THE SHABBOS MORNING SERVICES. The next morning the entire family goes to the synagogue to participate in the "Shabbos" services.

The first service, "Shacharis," is similar to the weekly "Shacharis" except for the addition of several Psalms and a "Shmoneh Esrei" for "Shabbos."

At the conclusion of the "Shacharis" service the Torah scroll is taken from the Ark and the portion of the week is read. It is called the "Sidrah" of the week. The first two "Aliyos" are, as usual, given to a "Kohein" and "Levi." In all, there are eight "Aliyos" given on "Shabbos." The last of the "Aliyos" is called "Maftir." Whoever receives this "Aliyah" also recites a special portion from the books of the Prophets. This portion is called the "Haftorah."

After the "Sidrah" of the week is completed, the Torah is rolled up and put aside until it is returned to the Ark. Two people are called to the "Bimah," the "platform," one to lift the Torah, which is called "Hagbah," and the other to roll it up, bind and dress it. This is called "G'liloh."

After the Torah reading three prayers are recited which are followed by the returning of the Torah scroll to the Ark. The additional service, the "Musaf," is then recited. (For additional information concerning the content of the services see UNIT ONE / *Chapter Nine.*)

THE SECOND MEAL. After the "Shabbos" morning service is over, the family returns home for the second of the "Sholosh S'udos," the "Three Meals." Again a "Kiddush" is recited and "Z'miros" are sung.

SHABBOS AFTERNOON. It is a custom among many Jewish families for the father to spend some time with his children discussing with them the things they learned in Hebrew school during the past week. If they studied well they are rewarded. The little children are given some candy while the elder children may receive more valuable gifts.

In many communities, the Jewish center organizes a special youth program for "Shabbos." It is called an "Oneg Shabbat" program. The children of the community get together at the center in the afternoon. They listen to interesting Jewish stories, and play games. Some children enjoy singing and form a choral group that rehearses at this time. Others enjoy dancing and form an Israeli dance group. After the activities, refreshments are served and the children return home having had a truly enjoyable "Shabbos," or as we would say in Hebrew, an "Oneg Shabbat."

During the long summer days it is customary in many synagogues for the rabbi to teach the congregation some of the wonderful and wise sayings of our Sages. They are found in the book "Ethics of the Fathers" which is called in Hebrew, "Pirkei Ovos."

SHOLOSH S'UDOS. After the "Mincha" service the final "Shabbos" meal takes place. It is the third of the "Sholosh S'udos." In some communities it is served right in the synagogue. The congregants seat themselves at a large table and enjoy the meal together. A favorite at this meal is pickled herring.

As we sit around the table and "Shabbos" draws to a close we express our regrets that so wonderful a day must finally end. In the beautiful "Z'miros" that are sung at this time we express our love and respect for the Sabbath and our sorrow that the "Sabbath Queen" is leaving.

MA'ARIV AND HAVDOLAH. When three stars appear in the sky, "Shabbos" is over. The weekday "Ma'ariv" is recited and a special prayer, "Ata Chonantonu," is added to the "Shmoneh Esrei." In this prayer we thank G-D for giving us the wisdom to differentiate between "Shabbos" and weekdays. We pray that the coming days will be peaceful ones; free from sins, evil deeds and worries. "Ata Chonantonu" is also recited at the end of each holiday.

"Shabbos" is officially concluded with the ceremony of "Havdolah," or "Division." In this ceremony we recite a prayer which praises G-D as the One who separates the holy from the unholy, light from darkness, Israel from the other nations, and "Shabbos" from the rest of the week.

Three objects are used in this ceremony: the candle, the spices and the wine.

First the wine cup is filled and the candle is lit. The spices, which are in a special container, are put on the table. Father recites the opening paragraph followed by the "Brocha" upon the wine, the "Brocha" upon the spices and the "Brocha" upon the light of the candle. He then recites a closing prayer. (You will find the "Brochos" of the "Havdolah" in the Appendix.)

"Shabbos" is the life of our people. It has kept the Jews as a nation for over three thousand years. Perhaps this idea is expressed best by the famous saying, "Not only has the Jew kept the Sabbath, but the Sabbath has kept the Jew."

Make "Shabbos" a part of your life. Celebrate it, enjoy it and make it holy. Make it a day to which you will look forward every day of the week.

THE DISTURBED "SHABBOS"

Anyone who knew the wealthy merchant Samuel for a number of years also knew that Samuel had known what it was like to be poor. But rich as he was now, he was the same pious, good Jew that he had been in the years of his poverty. He always remembered that it was G-D who decided man's fate and in Him must we trust.

And in case you want proof of Samuel's sincerity, here is a story which will convince you.

It was one Friday night, when all the family were sitting at the Sabbath table, all radiating that glow which only the Sabbath seems to bring to all those who observe it. Presently the maid appeared and said that a messenger had come from the governor and wished to see the master of the house immediately. The family had been singing the "Shabbos Z'miros" and their voices were now suddenly stilled. What could this unusual visit mean?

The messenger was called in and, apologizing for his interruption of their Sabbath meal, he explained that some foreign guests were expected at the governor's house and it was therefore necessary to purchase a number of rugs and spreads from Samuel's store.

"But this is impossible," protested Samuel. "It is our Sabbath and I never do business on the Sabbath. Please explain to the governor that I shall be happy to carry out his request tomorrow night, as soon as the Sabbath is over."

The messenger departed protesting that it would make trouble for all concerned, if this order was ignored.

"My dears," Samuel said, "let us not forget that tonight is 'Shabbos.' Do not look so worried. Let us continue with our singing. I think it would be nice to sing that new tune for 'Yoh Ribon Olam' (Lord Eternal Master of the World)." And Samuel began, in his musical voice, to bring the family into a singing mood again.

Try as they would, the family's singing seemed somewhat less spirited this evening. Only Samuel seemed able to shake off the serious and worried mood caused by the visit of the messenger.

The family had just finished the "Grace After Meal" when the maid came in again saying that the messenger had come back and that he wanted to see the master again.

The messenger handed Samuel a letter written in the governor's own handwriting. Samuel read it aloud.

"Dear Sir," it began. "I need hardly point out to you that I am one of your best customers. You also must know that I have a great deal of influence among my friends at the court. I have been perfectly satisfied with your attention to my orders until now, and it is for this reason that I am willing to give you an opportunity to make a good profit on this order for rugs and spreads which I need at once. As you say you do not do business on the Sabbath I shall not ask you for the account (itemized bill) now, but I insist that you send the merchandise to me immediately, with my messenger. The account may follow later, you may state your own prices. Surely you will admit that my offer is very generous.

"Should you, however, again refuse my request, I must tell you that not only will I stop doing business with you but I shall see to it that none of my friends does business with you either."

Samuel looked up at the messenger. "I am afraid that my answer remains the same as before," he said. "I do not do any business whatever on the holy Sabbath. If the governor cannot wait until tomorrow night, I must refuse his request. Please tell the governor that high as I esteem him and his orders, I must esteem G-D's orders still more."

You can be sure that there was little sleep for Samuel and his family that night. The next day, too, they could not banish that heavy feeling of disaster.

No sooner was "Shabbos" over, than another urgent summons came from the governor requesting Samuel to appear at the court right away. Samuel went off with a steady tread, but fear and trembling filled the hearts of his family. They prayed hard that G-D would be with him.

As Samuel and the messenger walked toward the governor's home, he thought to himself: "Why should I imagine that I am worthy to be a rich man forever? I was poor once, so what if I am poor again. But my children, they will find it hard to accept. For it is easier to get used to a rich life after being poor than to a poor life after being rich. However, rich or poor, we all have one G-D, he will surely take care of us all."

Imagine Samuel's astonishment and relief when, upon arrival at the governor's home, the governor himself came to meet him with outstretched hands and a broad smile on his face.

"Welcome my friend," he greeted him, shaking his hand. "You have made me very happy, indeed, by your obstinacy. You are surely a member of a 'stiff-necked people.' Come in and let me tell you what happened."

With that he led Samuel to his private study. When they were seated the governor began:

"I had some foreign princes visiting with me last week. During a conversation one of them mentioned the Jews and said that all Jews could think about was money and how to make more money. Nothing was more sacred to the Jew than wealth, he said.

"I denied that there was any truth in such a statement and had suggested that I would prove to this Jew hater the falsity of his accusation.

"And that, my dear friend, is the reason why I sent you that urgent order by special messenger, without even giving you a hint that you were being put to a test. Not only am I pleased that you have shown me what a sincerely religious man you are, putting your religion above all material gain, but you have shown this Jew hater that he is altogether wrong.

"As for you, dear Samuel, I shall see to it that all my friends hear about this story and I shall encourage them to give you their business. I shall point out to them that a man who thinks so little of money and profit will surely give them the best value and fair dealing. Good luck, my friend; you certainly deserve it."

Dear Pupils,

By the time you are ready for our closing chapter you will have read, and we hope learned well, the laws and customs of our people as given to us by G-D in our most precious possession, the Torah. We have tried, wherever possible, to give reasons for, and simple explanations of, the different laws and customs in order to make them clear and understandable. Our job as authors of this book and your teacher's job as instructor is over. But *your job* has only just begun.

Now that you have a general idea of the beauty of our religion and the responsibilities you have toward your people and your G-D, you must make up your mind to live up to these responsibilities. Read the book over on your own, not as a textbook, but rather as a handbook to guide you throughout your life. Remember well that as a Jew you were chosen by G-D to fulfill a mission in the world. When the Israelites encamped around Mount Sinai to receive the most important Code of Laws ever given to humanity, they were told by G-D, through Moses, that before they could receive so precious a gift, they would have to take upon themselves the fulfillment of all its commandments. They had to accept the mission of bringing the word of G-D to a world that refused even to listen. The Israelites were to serve as a "kingdom of priests and a holy nation," the Torah tells us. Each and every member was to take upon himself the obligations of a priest, a teacher; thus the whole nation would consist of priests.

And in this way, the nation was to become a holy one dedicated to the will of G-D as it is expressed in the Torah. What courage it must have taken to accept such a difficult task! Despite the difficulty and despite the long suffering that was bound to be involved, the Israelites accepted G-D's mission without question and without compromise. Their forthright reply was "all that G-D has spoken we will do."

It was this promise that gave them the right and the privilege to receive the Torah. It was only after they swore allegiance to Him and to their duty that they could attain a height never before and never again reached by any nation of the world. Yes, it was that day that all six hundred thousand of them reached the heights of prophecy and actually heard the voice from G-D recite the first and second of the Ten Commandments.

You, as future leaders in our religion, must always remember your great responsibility. You must never forget the promise that has been carried out, despite all obstacles, for thousands of years. Our people lived by the Torah and when it was necessary, died for it. Who will ever forget the six million of our brothers and sisters of Eastern European Jewry who were brutally murdered by the Nazis during World War II simply because they were Jews? They never lost their faith in G-D and they never forgot their promises. During their last moments, as they were led to their death, their voices rang out in song, "Ani Mamin Be'Emunoh Shleimoh," "I believe with perfect faith. . . ."

With such a noble heritage to look back upon, you can choose only to continue in the footsteps of our forefathers. Study the Torah and learn your obligations. Consult with your rabbis and teachers on the many problems that may come up. Show the world the beauty of G-D's Torah and the happiness it can bring to all that follow it. You, as members of the Jewish people, must accept this as your goal in life.

Only by living by the Torah can you show the world that this is the best way of life. And only when the world recognizes that this way of life is the one that it should follow will your mission as Jews be accomplished. As the prophet Micah foresaw:

"And it shall come to pass to the last days that the mountain of the Lord's house shall be firmly established on the top of the mountains. . . . And many nations shall come and say, Come, let us go up to the mountain of the Lord . . . that He may teach us of His ways, and we may walk in His paths . . . and they shall beat their swords into plowshares and their spears into pruning knives: nation shall not lift up sword against nation and they shall not learn war any more."
(Micah 4:1-4)

APPENDIX

UNIT ONE / *Chapter One*

1. Amen means _____ is a _____.
2. The table upon which we eat is compared by our Sages to an _____.
3. The first prayer we recite in the morning is called _____ _____.
4. It is proper to _____ our _____ before beginning the morning services.
5. Before eating or drinking we thank G-D by reciting a _____ _____.

Essay Questions

1. Why do we recite "Brochos?"
2. Why do we compare G-D to a king? Is it a good comparison? Why?

UNIT ONE / *Chapter Two*

1. "Tzitzis" are worn only on a) two cornered garments b) three cornered garments c) four cornered garments.
2. Each of the "Tzitzis" must have a) four strands b) eight strands c) seven strands.
3. The "Tallis" is a larger form of the a) אַרְבַּע כַּנְפוֹת b) פָּרֹכֶת c) קִיטְל.
4. The "Tallis" is worn by the congregation a) only on holi-

days b) only on the Sabbath c) every morning, Sabbath and holidays.

5. We learn the laws of the "Tzitzis" from a) the Torah b) the "Siddur" c) the Psalms.

6. "Tephillin" are worn a) by all males b) by males of thirteen and over c) by males after they marry.

7. The only time the "Tallis" is worn by the congregation in the evening is on a) יוֹם כִּפּוּר b) שַׁבָּת c) פֶּסַח.

8. We learn the law of the "Tephillin" from a) אַשְׁרֵי b) שְׁמַע c) שְׁמוֹנֶה עֶשְׂרֵה.

9. The "Tephillin" worn on the head is called a) שֶׁל רֹאשׁ b) סוֹפֵר c) שֶׁל יָד.

10. The "Tephillin" are not worn a) on weekdays b) on Sabbaths c) on Sabbaths and holidays.

11. The "Tephillin" are worn a) three times a day b) only during "Mincha" services c) only during "Schacharis" services.

12. The man who writes the parchments for the "Tephillin" and the "Mezuzah" is called a a) סוֹפֵר b) חַזָּן c) שׁוֹחֵט.

13. "Tephillin" are worn a) only during synagogue services b) only when we pray at home c) at home or in the synagogue on weekday mornings.

14. The "Mezuzah" is a) a reminder b) a lucky charm c) a decoration.

15. The "Mezuzah" must be a) worn around the neck b) put on the wall c) put on the door post.

16. The "Mezuzah" contains the passage a) שְׁמַע b) עָלֵינוּ c) מוֹדֶה אֲנִי.

17. The "Mezuzah" is put a) on every door of the house b) on every door except the bathroom c) only on the door of the entrance.

18. The "Mezuzah" is put on   a) the right side of the entrance
    b) the left side of the entrance   c) any side.

19. Three reminder symbols of the Jews are

    a) ‏תְּפִלִּין, מְזוּזָה, צִיצִית‏   b) ‏קִיטְל, תְּפִלִּין, מְזוּזָה‏

    c) ‏תְּפִלִּין, זְמִירוֹת, טַלִּית‏.

20. In putting on the "Tephillin"   a) the "Shel Rosh" is put on
    first   b) the "Shel Yod" is put on first   c) it doesn't make
    any difference.

Essay Questions

1. Would it be considered stealing to borrow a "Tallis" in the
   synagogue without permission? Why?
2. What is the purpose of the "Tzitzis," the "Tephillin," and
   the "Mezuzah"? How do they fulfill this purpose?
3. Explain how we learn the laws of "Tephillin" and "Mezuzah" and from where.
4. Why is the privilege of wearing "Tephillin" given to males
   above the age of thirteen?

UNIT ONE / *Chapter Three*

1. The first five books of the Bible are known as the   a) Torah
   b) "Mitzvos"   c) Prophets.
2. If someone drops the Torah   a) he must give to charity
   b) he must donate a new Torah   c) he may fast or give to
   charity.
3. One who copies the Torah scroll is called a   a) ‏סוֹפֵר‏
   b) ‏חַזָּן‏   c) ‏מוֹהֵל‏.
4. When the Torah scroll is no longer fit for use   a) it is
   thrown away   b) it is burned   c) it is buried.
5. When the Torah is carried, as a sign of respect we   a) rise
   b) bow down   c) remain seated.

Essay Questions

1. Explain: When we handle holy books with respect we are giving respect to G-d.
2. How do we show our respect to the Torah?
3. What is the meaning of the Torah blessings?
4. Show what influence the Bible has had on the world? Why?

UNIT ONE / *Chapter Four*

1. The signs of a kosher fish are   a) fins and scales   b) fins or scales   c) long fins.
2. A kosher animal must   a) chew its cud   b) have split hoofs   c) have split hoofs and chew its cud.
3. The word kosher means   a) holy   b) fit for use in accordance with Jewish law   c) tasty.
4. The man who slaughters the animal according to Jewish law is called a   a) שׁוֹחֵט   b) מוֹהֵל   c) בַּעַל תּוֹקֵעַ.
5. Nowadays   a) we eat all parts of the animal   b) we do not eat the hind quarters   c) we only eat the hind quarters.
6. After the animal is slaughtered the meat must be   a) salted   b) washed and salted   c) blessed by a rabbi.
7. Products which are neither meat nor dairy are called
   a) חַלָּה   b) חָמֵץ   c) פַּארְוֶע.
8. If we find a blood spot in an egg   a) the blood spot must be removed   b) the egg cannot be eaten   c) the egg must be salted.
9. Meat and dairy   a) may be eaten together   b) may not be eaten together   c) may not be cooked or eaten together.
10. a) Lobster   b) Crabs   c) all sea food are forbidden to be eaten according to Jewish law.
11. a) All   b) Most   c) No fowl are permitted to be eaten according to Jewish law.
12. Dietary laws come to us from   a) the Torah   b) the "Siddur"   c) the "Machzor."

13. According to Jewish law we must have separate dishes for
    a) meat and dairy   b) fish and dairy   c) fish and meat.

14. Vegetables   a) may only be eaten with meat   b) need no
    qualifications   c) should be examined to make sure they
    have no worms.

15. The term kosher can be applied   a) only to food   b) to
    food and religious articles   c) only to meat.

Essay Questions

1. Is there any purpose in observing the Dietary Laws without
   knowing the reason for them? Explain.

2. Follow an animal from the field until it appears on your plate
   telling all the necessary steps for it to be considered kosher.

3. What are the benefits of keeping a kosher home?

UNIT ONE / *Chapter Five*

1. The law of circumcision is mentioned in the _____.
   It is called in Hebrew, _____.

2. The man who performs the circumcision ceremony is called
   a _____, in Hebrew.

3. Circumcision occurs on the _____ day after birth.

4. The first man to perform circumcision was _____.

5. The circumcision must be performed even if the day falls
   on the _____.

6. The firstborn male child is redeemed by a _____.
   This ceremony occurs on the _____ day after birth.

7. If the day of redemption falls on a _____ or _____
   _____, the ceremony is postponed.

8. If one knows for certain that he was not _____ he
   must do so even if he is an adult.

9. The father of the child gives _____ dollars to the
   "Kohein" in the redemption ceremony.

10. The redemption ceremony is not necessary if the father of
    the child is a _____ or a _____ or the mother
    of the child is the daughter of a _____ or a _____
    _____.

Essay Questions

1. How is circumcision a treaty between God and Israel?
2. What was the reason for the dedication of the firstborn male to G-D?
3. How was the firstborn dedicated in the time of the Temples?
4. Explain: The firstborn male is to serve as a model of the Torah way of life.

UNIT ONE / *Chapter Six*

1. According to Jewish law animals are slaughtered by a
   a) healthy method   b) dangerous method   c) humane method.
2. If one injures his neighbor he cannot be fully forgiven until he   a) pays damages   b) asks forgiveness from him   c) asks forgiveness from G-d.
3. A law for which no reason is given in the Torah is called a
   a) מִצְוָה   b) חֹק   c) שַׁעַטְנֵז.
4. A law in the Torah prohibits wearing garments that contain a mixture of   a) silk and wool   b) wool and linen   c) cotton and linen.
5. Stolen money   a) may be accepted for charity   b) may never be accepted for charity   c) may sometimes be accepted for charity.
6. According to the Torah the use of animals for medical research purposes is   a) forbidden   b) sometimes permitted   c) always permitted.
7. A law in the Torah states that permanent tattoos   a) are forbidden for men   b) are forbidden for women   c) are forbidden for all.
8. Cheating in business is   a) always forbidden   b) permitted if it does not involve a loss of money   c) sometimes permitted.
9. It is forbidden to   a) buy from a thief   b) sell to a thief   c) talk to a thief.

10. Stealing is forbidden a) only from Jews b) only from nonJews c) from all people.

Essay Questions

1. What is the reason why some Jewish people wear beards?
2. What are the two purposes in looking for reasons? Which one would apply to Jewish law? How?
3. How does the Torah show kindness towards animals?

UNIT ONE / *Chapter Seven*

1. One of the nicest ways to give charity is to give it _____ _____.
2. One of the greatest blessings we can have is a good _____ _____.
3. The first five Commandments are between _____ and _____.
4. It is a beautiful custom to drop a few coins into the "Tzedoko" box before lighting the _____ _____.
5. For the Jewish people the saying "Love your neighbor as yourself?" is a _____. It is written in the _____.
6. The Hebrew word for charity is _____.
7. _____ to parents is equivalent to honor to _____.
8. The _____ has kept the Jews together throughout the generations.
9. The custom of visiting the sick is known, in Hebrew, as _____.
10. The prayer for the sick, recited in the synagogue, is only recited when the _____ is read.
11. _____ is the Yiddish word for anniversary. It is only used in reference to the anniversary of a death.
12. The "Kaddish" is recited for _____ months of the first year and every following year on the _____.
13. "Kaddish" is a prayer of _____ to G-d.
14. The day of the "Yahrtzeit" should be determined according to the _____ calendar.

15. It is customary for the immediate family of the one who passed away to light a _____ in his or her honor on the day of the "Yahrtzeit."

Essay Questions

1. In what ways do we show our respect to parents?
2. How have the Jewish people used the Torah as a weapon to protect them?
3. How does the word "Tzedoko" explain the concept of charity?
4. Explain: A visit to a sick person takes away one-sixtieth of his illness.
5. What do these two proverbs mean to the Jewish people? a) Practice what you preach b) Action speaks louder than words.

UNIT ONE / *Chapter Eight*

1. In the Jewish leap year a whole month is added to the calendar; it is called _____.
2. _____ is a special service of praise and thanksgiving that is recited on the first day of the month.
3. The Jewish people use a _____ calendar calculated according to the revolutions of the _____ around the _____.
4. The first day of the Hebrew month is called _____.
5. On the first day of the month, after the Torah reading, the additional holiday service called _____ is recited.

Essay Questions

1. Why do the Jewish people use a lunar calendar?
2. What is the purpose of "Adar Sheini" in relation to the Jewish holidays?
3. Discuss the additional prayers and ceremonies in connection with the new month.

UNIT ONE / *Chapter Nine*

1. The daily prayer book is called   a) מַחֲזוֹר   b) סִדוּר
   c) הַגָּדָה.

2. The morning service is called   a) שַׁחֲרִית   b) מִנְחָה
   c) מוּסַף.

3. The a) אַשְׁרֵי   b) מוֹדֶה אֲנִי   c) שְׁמוֹנֶה עֶשְׂרֵה   is an
   essential part of all services.

4. The afternoon service is called   a) מַעֲרִיב   b) מִנְחָה
   c) עָלֵינוּ.

5. The "Shema" is recited in the two services
   a) שַׁחֲרִית and מַעֲרִיב   b) מִנְחָה and מַעֲרִיב
   c) מִנְחָה and שַׁחֲרִית.

6. A Torah Honor is called   a) עֲלִיָּה   b) כֹּהֵן   c) סְדָרָה.

7. The Torah is read in the synagogue   a) every day   b) only
   on Sabbath   c) four times a week.

8. The first two "Aliyos" are given to the   a) "Kohein" and
   "Levi"   b) "Kohein" and Israelite   c) "Levi" and Israelite.

9. "Siddur" means   a) book of service   b) order   c) book of
   religious poems.

10. The Torah is read   a) after שַׁחֲרִית   b) before the שְׁמַע
    c) after מוּסַף.

Essay Questions

1. Explain The "Siddur" unites the Jewish people all over the
   world.

2. What is the content of the prayers of Praise, Thanksgiving,
   and Request?

UNIT ONE / *Chapter Ten*

1. The quorum of ten males needed for services is called
    a) בִּימָה b) גְּלִילָה c) מִנְיָן.

2. The synagogue as a house of worship (prayer) is called
    a) בֵּית תְּפִלָּה b) בֵּית מִדְרָשׁ c) בֵּית כְּנֶסֶת.

3. The ark where the Torah is kept is known as the
    a) בְּלֵי קֹדֶשׁ b) אֲרוֹן קֹדֶשׁ c) בִּימָה.

4. The crown that is placed over the Torah is called
    a) כֶּתֶר תּוֹרָה b) נֵר תָּמִיד c) פָּרֹכֶת.

5. The synagogue as a house of learning is known as the
    a) בֵּית מִדְרָשׁ b) בֵּית כְּנֶסֶת c) בֵּית תְּפִלָּה.

6. The silver pieces that are placed on top of the Torah are
    called a) בְּלֵי קֹדֶשׁ b) רִמּוֹנִים c) אֲרוֹן קֹדֶשׁ.

7. The light kept burning in the synagogue to commemorate
    the menorah that stood in the Temple is called a) מְנוֹרָה
    b) הַבְדָּלָה c) נֵר תָּמִיד.

8. The curtain that decorates the ark is called a) פָּרֹכֶת
    b) קִיטֶל c) כַּפָּרוֹת.

9. The synagogue as a community center is known as the
    a) בֵּית כְּנֶסֶת b) בֵּית תְּפִלָּה c) בֵּית מִדְרָשׁ.

10. The a) קַדִּישׁ b) קִידוּשׁ may be recited only when
    there is a "Minyan" present.

Essay Questions

1. How has the synagogue in your community fulfilled the
    three purposes for which it was made to serve?

2. Why is it important for every Jewish community to have
    a synagogue?

3. Which holiday synagogue service during the year impresses you most? Why?

UNIT ONE / *Chapter Eleven*

1. In the days of the Temple, the "challah" was given to the
   a) יִשְׂרָאֵל b) כֹּהֵן c) לֵוִי.

2. The Sabbath candles should be lit by a) the man of the house b) the woman of the house c) the youngest child.

3. According to Jewish law a girl should fulfill her obligation as a Jewess at the age of a) twelve b) thirteen c) twenty-one.

4. In Abraham's household the doors of hospitality were open as long as a) Deborah lived b) Sarah lived c) Isaac lived.

5. When the commandment for observing the Sabbath was given to Moses the words a) we will do and we will listen b) we will honor and respect c) observe and remember were heard at the same time.

Essay Questions

1. What is the significance of the lesson our rabbis taught us, about Abraham, Sarah, and Rebecca?

2. Why is it important for a girl to receive a Jewish education?

UNIT TWO / *Chapter One*

1. The Hebrew month in which Jews all over the world prepare for the High Holidays is called a) אֱלוּל b) תִּשְׁרֵי c) נִיסָן.

2. The special prayers of penitence recited beginning with the Saturday night before Rosh Hashonah are called
   a) סְלִיחוֹת b) יִזְכֹּר c) שְׁבָרִים.

3. One of the things of which we are reminded when we hear the Shofar is a) the sacrifice of Isaac b) the burning bush c) the splitting of the Red Sea.

4. Rosh Hashonah as the "Day of Remembrance" is called
   a) יוֹם הַזִּכָּרוֹן   c) יוֹם תְּרוּעָה   b) יוֹם הַדִּין.

5. The prayer book used on Rosh Hashonah is called the
   a) הַגָּדָה.   c) מַחֲזוֹר   b) סִדּוּר.

6. The man who sounds the shofar is called   a) סוֹפֵר
   b) בַּעַל תּוֹקֵעַ   c) חַזָּן.

7. The special cantor's prayer recited on Rosh Hashonah and
   Yom Kippur is called   a) סֵדֶר הָעֲבוֹדָה   b) וּנְתַנֶּה תֹּקֶף
   c) הִנְנִי הֶעָנִי מִמַּעַשׂ.

8. The prayer recited near a flowing river or stream is called
   a) נְעִילָה   b) סְלִיחוֹת   c) תַּשְׁלִיךְ.

9. If Rosh Hashonah occurs on the Sabbath   a) we blow the
   shofar   b) we don't blow the shofar   c) we blow the
   shofar twice.

10. Rosh Hashonah is celebrated for   a) one day   b) three
    days   c) two days.

Match the English in Column B to the Hebrew in
Column A.

A	B
1) שַׁבַּת שׁוּבָה	a) Prayers describing revelation
2) עֲשֶׂרֶת יְמֵי תְּשׁוּבָה	b) Three blasts on the Shofar
3) מַלְכִיּוֹת	c) Prayers describing the Glory of G-d's Kingdom
4) זִכְרוֹנוֹת	d) Symbolizes the resounding of the shofar
5) שׁוֹפָרוֹת	e) The Sabbath between Rosh Hashonah and Yom Kippur
6) לְשָׁנָה טוֹבָה תִּכָּתֵבוּ	f) Describes Rosh Hashonah in heaven

A	B
7) יוֹם הַדִּין	g) The "Day of Judgment"
8) וּנְתַנֶּה תֹּקֶף	h) "May you be inscribed for a good year"
9) שְׁבָרִים	i) The "Ten Days of Penitence"
10) יוֹם תְּרוּעָה	j) Prayers in which we remember the miracles G-d performed for our forefathers
	k) The opening service of the holiday

Essay Questions

1. What should Rosh Hashonah mean to you as a Jew?
2. How can we best make use of the trial period of "Aseres Ymai T'shuvah"?

UNIT TWO / *Chapter Two*

Match the English in Column B to the Hebrew in Column A.

A	B
1) כַּפָּרוֹת	a) To collect for charity on "Erev" Yom Kippur
2) סְעוּדָה הַמַפְסֶקֶת	b) The closing prayer of Yom Kippur
3) קַעֲרוֹת צְדָקָה	c) We symbolically transfer our sins
4) קִיטְל	d) White robe worn on Yom Kippur
5) כָּל נִדְרֵי	e) Opening prayer of Yom Kippur
6) סֵדֶר הָעֲבוֹדָה	f) The day on which the "Kaporos" ceremony is performed
7) אֵלֶּה אֶזְכְּרָה	g) Confessions recited on Yom Kippur
8) נְעִילָה	h) Last meal on "Erev" Yom Kippur

A	B
9) וִדּוּי	i) Description of the Temple Service
10) עֶרֶב יוֹם כִּפּוּר	j) Description of the martyrs as they were killed by Hadrian of Rome
	k) The cantor's prayer

Essay Questions

1. Explain the reasons for the following: a) fasting on Yom Kippur   b) not wearing shoes in the synagogue on Yom Kippur

2. Explain in detail the meaning of the sentence "The color of Yom Kippur is white."

UNIT TWO / *Chapter Three*

Match the English in Column B to the Hebrew in Column A.

A	B
1) חֲתַן תּוֹרָה	a) Material used for the roof of the "Succah"
2) חֲתַן בְּרֵאשִׁית	b) The one who recites the blessing upon beginning the Torah
3) כָּל הַנְּעָרִים	c) The citron
4) הַקָּפוֹת	d) The procession with the Torah around the synagogue
5) אֶתְרוֹג	e) The palm branch
6) לוּלָב	f) Prayer inviting our forefathers to the "Succah"
7) הֲדַס	g) The myrtle branch
8) עֲרָבָה	h) Torah honor given to all young children together
9) אוּשְׁפִּיזִין	i) The willow branch
10) סְכַךְ	j) The one who is honored to finish the Torah
	k) The last "Sidrah" of the Torah

Essay Questions

1. What is the meaning given to the four species used on "Succos"?
2. What is the lesson of "Succos"?
3. What is the importance of beginning reading the Torah again immediately after we finish reading it on "Simchas Torah"?

UNIT TWO / *Chapter Three*

1. During which month do we celebrate "Succos"? a) תִּשְׁרֵי
   b) כִּסְלֵו c) אֲדָר.

2. What is the meaning of the word "Succos"? a) huts
   b) temples c) gatherings.

3. What are the names of the three Pilgrimage Festivals?
   a) פֶּסַח, שָׁבְעוֹת, סֻכּוֹת b) פֶּסַח, חֲנוּכָּה, פּוּרִים
   c) סֻכּוֹת, יוֹם כִּפּוּר, רֹאשׁ הַשָּׁנָה.

4. "Succos" as a "Time of Rejoicing" is known as
   a) זְמַן חֵרוּתֵנוּ b) חַג הָאָסִף c) זְמַן שִׂמְחָתֵנוּ.

5. The seventh day of "Succos" is called a) שִׂמְחַת תּוֹרָה
   b) הוֹשַׁעְנָא רַבָּא c) שְׁמִינִי עֲצֶרֶת.

6. On the Sabbath, the four species a) are used b) are not used c) are used twice.

7. The ceremony of water drawing that took place in the days of the Temple is called a) זְמַן שִׂמְחָתֵנוּ b) שִׂמְחַת תּוֹרָה
   c) שִׂמְחַת בֵּית הַשּׁוֹאֵבָה.

8. On which day is the special prayer for rain recited?
   a) שְׁמִינִי עֲצֶרֶת b) הוֹשַׁעְנָא רַבָּא c) שִׂמְחַת תּוֹרָה.

9. On which day does the completion of the reading of the Torah take place? a) שְׁמִינִי עֲצֶרֶת b) שִׂמְחַת תּוֹרָה
   c) הוֹשַׁעְנָא רַבָּא.

10. The ceremony that officially ends the nine-day celebration
    of "Succos" is called   a) כָּל הַנְּעָרִים   b) מוּסָף
    c) הַבְדָּלָה.

UNIT TWO / *Chapter Four*

1. The symbol and reminder of the miracle of Chanukah is
   the   a) שַׁמָּשׁ   b) הַלֵּל   c) מְנוֹרָה.

2. Chanukah is celebrated for   a) four days   b) eight days
   c) seven days.

3. The additional prayer recited in the "Shmoneh Esrei" on
   Chanukah is called: a) יַעֲלֶה וְיָבֹא   b) עַל הַנִּסִּים
   c) שֶׁהֶחֱיָנוּ.

4. Chanukah is celebrated during the month of   a) כִּסְלֵו
   b) אֲדָר   c) נִיסָן.

5. On Friday night the Chanukah "menorah"   a) is not lit   b)
   is lit after the Sabbath candles   c) is lit before the Sabbath
   candles.

6. The leader of the Jewish army after the death of Mattathias
   was   a) Antiochus   b) Judah Maccabee   c) Jason the
   Priest.

7. Chanukah candles should burn for at least   a) one hour
   b) half hour   c) five minutes.

8. When lighting the "menorah"   a) the newest candle is lit
   first   b) the oldest candle is lit first   c) it does not make any
   difference.

9. On the first night of Chanukah the additional blessing recited while lighting the candles is called   a) שֶׁהֶחֱיָנוּ
   b) עַל הַנִּסִּים   c) שֶׁהַכֹּל.

10. The Hasmonean family were later called   a) rebels
    b) Maccabees   c) Sons of Mattathias.

Essay Questions

1. What made Antiochus think that he could convert the Jews to paganism?
2. How did the incident in the market place in Modin lead to the rebellion?
3. Explain: Not only did the Jews win a victory over Antiochus; they won a victory over themselves.

UNIT TWO / *Chapter Five*

1. "Tu Bishvat" is known in Hebrew as _____.
2. "Tu Bishvat" marks the beginning of the _____ season in Israel.
3. This holiday occurs on the _____ day of the Hebrew month _____.
4. _____ is the new year for trees.
5. In the United States it is customary to celebrate "Tu Bishvat" by eating _____ from _____.

Essay Questions

1. Explain the two reasons for "Tu Bishvat."
2. Plan a "Tu Bishvat" program for a class celebration.

UNIT TWO / *Chapter Six*

1. The day before Purim is a _____ day, called, in Hebrew, _____.
2. The meaning of the word "Purim" is _____.
3. Purim is celebrated on the _____ day of the Hebrew month _____.
4. The scroll from which the Purim story is read is called _____.
5. The Purim story is read _____ times during the holiday.
6. If Purim occurs on Sunday _____ is observed on the preceding Thursday.

7. The custom of giving gifts one to another on Purim is called in Hebrew _____.

8. In the days of the Temple half a _____ was collected during the month of _____ for the purchase of sacrifices.

9. _____ or _____ as it is known in Hebrew, is a favorite cake baked only for this holiday.

10. _____ is a special prayer added to the _____ of each of the daily services on Purim.

Essay Questions

1. Tell in your own words the main parts of the Purim story.

2. How does the idea "History repeats itself" apply to Purim? What lesson does this holiday teach?

UNIT TWO / *Chapter Seven*

1. Passover begins on the fifteenth of   a) אֲדָר   b) נִיסָן   c) שְׁבָט.

2. The middle four days of Passover are called
a) שָׁלֹשׁ רְגָלִים   b) יוֹם טוֹב   c) חֹל הַמּוֹעֵד.

3. The Passover fund for the poor is called   a) מִשְׁלוֹחַ מָנוֹת
b) מָעוֹת חִטִּים   c) שַׁבָּת הַגָּדוֹל.

4. The products that are forbidden on Passover are called
a) כַּרְפַּס   b) מָרוֹר   c) חָמֵץ.

5. The Sabbath before Passover is known as   a) שַׁבָּת שׁוּבָה
b) עֶרֶב פֶּסַח   c) שַׁבָּת הַגָּדוֹל.

6. The ceremony of burning the "Chometz" is called
a) הַסְבָּה   b) בְּדִיקַת חָמֵץ   c) בִּעוּר חָמֵץ.

7. The three holidays during which the Jews of Israel made pilgrimages to the Temple are called   a) שָׁלֹשׁ רְגָלִים
b) אַחֲרוֹן שֶׁל פֶּסַח   c) עֲשֶׂרֶת יְמֵי תְּשׁוּבָה.

8. The last piece of matzoh eaten at the "Seder" is called
   a) כַּרְפַּס b) יַחַץ c) אֲפִיקוֹמָן.

9. The prayer for dew that is recited on the last day of Passover
   is called a) גֶּשֶׁם b) טַל c) הַלֵּל.

10. The day before Passover is called a) עֶרֶב פֶּסַח
    b) שְׁמִינִי עֲצֶרֶת c) אַחֲרוֹן שֶׁל פֶּסַח.

1. The "Mitzvah" of eating matzoh is fulfilled on the _____
   night of Passover.

2. Selling "Chometz" products and utensils to a nonJew before
   Passover is known as _____.

3. The ritual of searching for "Chometz" on the night of "Erev
   Pesach" is known as _____.

4. A special service for the first born males held on "Erev
   Pesach" is known as the _____.

5. The book used at the "Seder" service is called the _____.

Match the English in Column B to the Hebrew in
Column A.

A	B
1) כַּרְפַּס	a) Reminder of the bitter times
2) מָרוֹר	b) Order of the Passover night
3) חֲרוֹסֶת	c) Parsley dipped in salt water
4) קִיטְל	d) White robe of purity
5) סֵדֶר	e) Reminder of the mortar
6) יַחַץ	f) Breaking the middle matzoh

Essay Questions

1. Tell in your own words the main points of the Passover
   story.

2. What is the significance of the two other names by which

Passover is known: "Chag Hapesach" and "Z'man Cheiruseinu"?

3. Discuss the following terms used at the "Seder" services:
    a) "Yachatz" b) "Magid" c) "Karpas."

UNIT TWO / *Chapter Eight*

Match the English in Column B to the Hebrew in
Column A.

A	B
עוֹמֶר (1	a) His students died during the "Omer"
לַ"ג בָּעוֹמֶר (2	b) Total amount of days in the "Omer"
סְפִירַת הָעוֹמֶר (3	c) Led the revolution against Rome
Rabbi Akiva (4	d) The "Omer" is counted after this
	service
לַ"ג (5	e) Measure of grain
מַעֲרִיב (6	f) The thirty-third day
49 (7	g) The "Counting of the 'Omer' "
50th day (8	h) Sacrifice of the first fruit
24,000 (9	i) Amount of students that died during
	the plague
Bar Kochva (10	j) The thirty-third day of the "Omer"
	k) The number of soldiers killed in the
	revolution against Rome

Essay Questions

1. Why did the Israelites count the "Omer"? a) in the wilder-
    ness b) in the days of the Temple.
2. Why should we count the "Omer" in our day?

UNIT TWO / *Chapter Nine*

1. The holiday of "Shavuos" occurs in the month of a) נִיסָן
    b) תִּשְׁרֵי c) סִיוָן.

2. "Shavuos" is celebrated for a) 1 day b) 2 days c) 7 days.

3. "Shavuos" means a) days b) months c) weeks.

4. "Shavuos" as the holiday of the Torah is called
   a) ‏זְמַן מַתַּן תּוֹרָתֵנוּ‎ b) ‏זְמַן שִׂמְחָתֵנוּ‎ c) ‏זְמַן חֵרוּתֵנוּ‎.

5. On the first day of "Shavuos" the poem a) ‏רוּת‎
   b) ‏לְכָה דוֹדִי‎ c) ‏אַקְדָּמוּת‎ is read in the synagogue.

6. "Shavuos" as the holiday of the first fruit is known as
   a) ‏חַג הַבִּכּוּרִים‎ b) ‏חַג הָאָסִף‎ c) ‏חַג הַקָּצִיר‎.

7. Which of the following is read on the second day of "Shavuos"? a) ‏רוּת‎ b) ‏אַקְדָּמוּת‎ c) ‏שׁוּבָה יִשְׂרָאֵל‎.

8. What is the name of the memorial prayer recited on "Shavuos"? a) ‏יִזְכֹּר‎ b) ‏קַדִּישׁ‎ c) ‏נְעִילָה‎.

9. On the first night of "Shavuos" it is customary a) to review the Torah b) to read the book of Ruth c) to read the book of Lamentations.

10. Which of the following is a popular custom on "Shavuos"?
    a) to eat dairy products b) to dip the "challah" in honey c) to eat a special holiday cake.

Essay Questions

1. Why is it necessary to have laws in a free country?
2. What was the problem Moses faced when he prepared himself to receive the Torah?
3. How has the Torah affected the rest of the world?
4. What is the lesson of the book of Ruth?

UNIT TWO / *Chapter Ten*

1. There are _____ fast days that deal directly with the destruction of the Temples and the city of Jerusalem.

2. _____ is the day on which the first and second Temples were destroyed.

3. The only two twenty-four-hour fast days in our religion are
   _____ and _____.

4. _____ is the Hebrew name given to the lamentations
   recited on "Tisha B'Av."

5. On "Tisha B'Av" the _____ and the _____
   are not worn during the "Shacharis" service.

6. On "Tisha B'Av" the Torah is read twice, at the _____
   and at the _____ service.

7. _____ ben _____ was appointed by Nebuchadnezzar as governor of Israel after the destruction of the
   first Temple.

8. The Fast of Gedaliah is on the day after _____. It
   commemorates the murder of _____ ben _____.

9. The fast day that commemorates the siege of Jerusalem by
   Nebuchadnezzar is the _____ of _____.

10. If any one of these four fast days occurs on _____ it
    is postponed to the following day.

Essay Questions

1. How have the fast days served as a reminder to the Jews of
   their homeland?

2. What are the four sorrowful events commemorated by the
   17th day of "Tamuz"?

UNIT TWO / *Chapter Eleven*

1. The law of "Shabbos" is a) one of the Ten Commandments
   b) comes from the books of Prophets c) is from the
   Ethics of the Fathers.

2. On the Sabbath we partake of a) סְעוּדָה הַמַּפְסֶקֶת

   b) שָׁלֹשׁ רְגָלִים c) שָׁלֹשׁ סְעוּדוֹת.

3. The Sabbath candles are lit on Friday a) before sunset
   b) after sunset c) late in the evening.

4. The "Mitzvah" of lighting the Sabbath candles belongs to
   a) the father b) the mother c) the youngest child in the
   family.

5. If there is no woman in the house the Sabbath candles a) are not lit   b) are lit by the man of the house   c) are placed on the table unlit.

6. The Sabbath candlesticks must remain on the table a) for at least an hour   b) until the candles burn out   c) for the entire Sabbath.

7. The special Sabbath Greeting Service is called
a) קַבָּלַת שַׁבָּת   b) שָׁלֹשׁ סְעוּדוֹת   c) מוּסָף.

8. L'choh Dodi is a poem recited as part of the a) מוּסָף
b) קַבָּלַת שַׁבָּת   c) שַׁחֲרִית.

9. The special loaves of bread used on the Sabbath are called
a) שָׁלֹשׁ סְעוּדוֹת   b) שָׁלוֹם עֲלֵיכֶם   c) חַלוֹת

10. The opening hymn of the Sabbath meal is called a) קִידוּשׁ
b) חַלוֹת   c) שָׁלוֹם עֲלֵיכֶם.

Match the English in Column B to the Hebrew in Column A.

A		B
זְמִירוֹת	1.	Sanctification recited on the wine
קִידוּשׁ	2.	The weekly portion read from the Torah on Sabbath
הַפְטוֹרָה	3.	The joy of Sabbath
סְדָרָה	4.	Special Sabbath hymns
מוֹצִיא	5.	The portion read from the books of the Prophets
עוֹנֶג שַׁבָּת	6.	Ethics of the Fathers
פִּרְקֵי אָבוֹת	7.	The blessing recited on the bread
הַבְדָּלָה	8.	Torah honors
עֲלִיוֹת	9.	The additional service for Sabbath and holidays

Match the English in Column B to the Hebrew in Column A.

A		B
אַתָּה חוֹנַנְתָּנוּ	10.	Friday
הַגְבָּהָה	11.	Ceremony which ends the Sabbath
גְּלִילָה	12.	Lifting the Torah
מוּסָף	13.	The special Sabbath and holiday loaf
חַלָּה	14.	Rolling up, binding and dressing the Torah
עֶרֶב שַׁבָּת	15.	Prayer in the "Shmoneh Esrei" recited Saturday eve and holidays
	16.	Mourners' prayer recited in the synagogue

Essay Questions

1. Explain a) "Not only has the Jew kept the Sabbath but the Sabbath has kept the Jew."

   b) One who observes the Sabbath fully enjoys more freedom than the one who does not.

2. How can we bring true holiness to our home on the Sabbath?

VOCABULARY

א

אֲדָר שֵׁנִי	Adar Sheini	The additional month added to the Jewish Leap Year
אוּשְׁפִּיזִין	Ooshpizin	Special service recited in the "Succah"
אָזְנֵי הָמָן	Oznei Homon	The Hebrew name for the cake baked on Purim
אַחֲרוֹן שֶׁל פֶּסַח	Achron Shel Pesach	The last day of Passover
אֵלֶּה אֶזְכְּרָה	Aileh Ezkeroh	"These I Will Remember" part of the "Musaf" service of Yom Kippur
אָמֵן	Amen	G-D is a Faithful King
אֲפִיקוֹמָן	Afikomon	Piece of matzoh eaten at the end of the "Seder" on Passover
אַשְׁרֵי	Ashrei	First prayer recited in the "Mincha" service
אַקְדָמוּת	Akdomus	Poem recited on "Shavuos" before the Torah reading
אַרְבַּע כַּנְפוֹת	Arba Kanfos	Four cornered garment on which we put the "Tzitzis"
אַתָּה הָרְאֵתָ	Atoh Horeiso	Opening prayer of the "Simchas Torah" processions
אֶתְרוֹג	Esrog	Citron used on "Succos"

247

אֲרוֹן קוֹדֶשׁ	Aron Kodesh	The Holy Ark
בְּדִיקַת חָמֵץ	B'dikas Chometz	Searching for the "chometz"
בִּעוּר חָמֵץ	Biur Chometz	Burning of the "chometz"
בִּקּוּר חוֹלִים	Bikur Cholim	Visiting the sick
בֵּית הַכְּנֶסֶת	Beis Hakneses	The synagogue
בַּעַל תּוֹקֵעַ	Baal Tokaya	The man who sounds the shofar
בְּרָכָה	Brocha	Blessing
בְּרִית	Bris	Circumcision ceremony
בַּר מִצְוָה	Bar Mitzvah	When a boy reaches the age where he is required to fulfill the "Mitzvos"
בַּת מִצְוָה	Bas Mitzvah	When a girl reaches the age where she is required to fulfill certain "Mitzvos"
בִּימָה	Bimah	The platform where the Cantor stands and the Torah scroll is read

בְּרֵאשִׁית	Bereishis	The first portion of the Torah
בֵּית תְּפִלָּה	Beis Tfilloh	A house of prayer
בֵּית מִדְרָשׁ	Beis Midrosh	A house of learning
גְּלִילָה	G'lilah	Rolling up the Torah
דְּבָרִים	D'vorim	The last (fifth) book of the Torah
הַבְדָּלָה	Havdolah	The dividing ceremony that officially ends the Sabbath and holidays
הַגָּדָה	Haggadah	The book used for the "Seder" service on Passover
הֲדַס	Hadas	The myrtle branch attached to the "Lulov" on the holiday of "Succos"
הוֹשַׁעֲנוֹת	Hoshanos	The service added after "Musaf" during the holiday of "Succos"
הוֹשַׁעֲנָא רַבָּא	Hoshanoh Rabboh	The seventh day of "Succos" on which all of the "Hoshanos" that have been recited during the holiday are recited again

הַלֵּל	Hallel	Special service of praises to G-D added to the holiday services after "Shacharis"
הָמָן טַאשֶׁן	Hamantashen	Special cake baked for Purim
הִנְנִי הֶעָנִי מִמַּעַשׂ	Hinini Heoni Meemaas	Cantor's prayer beginning the "Musaf" service for Rosh Hashonah and Yom Kippur
הַסִּבָּה	Hasiba	Reclining during the Passover "Seder"
הַהַפְטָרָה	Haftorah	Portion of the Prophets read after the Torah reading on Sabbath and holidays
הַקָּפוֹת	Hakofos	Procession of Torahs around the synagogue on "Simchas Torah"
הַגְבָּהָה	Hagbohoh	Lifting up the Torah

וַיִּקְרָא	Vayikro	The third book of the Torah
וּרְחַץ	Urchatz	Part of the "Seder" service of Passover in which we wash our hands

וּנְתַנֶּה תֹּקֶף	Unisaneh Tokef	One of the prayers in the "Musaf" for Rosh Hashonah and Yom Kippur
וְזֹאת הַבְּרָכָה	V'zos Habrocha	The last of the "Sidras" in the Torah
ז		
זִכְרוֹנוֹת	Zichronos	Part of the "Musaf" service for Rosh Hashonah in which we recall Biblical history
זְמַן חֵרוּתֵנוּ	Zman Cheiruseinu	The Time of Our Freedom (Passover)
זְמַן מַתַּן תּוֹרָתֵנוּ	Zman Matan Toroseinu	The Time Our Torah Was Given (Shavuos)
זְמַן שִׂמְחָתֵנוּ	Zman Simchoseinu	The Time of Our Rejoicing (Succos)
זְמִירוֹת	Z'miros	Hymns sung on the Sabbath
ח		
חַג הָאָבִיב	Chag Ho'Oviv	The Holiday of Spring (Passover)
חַג הָאָסִיף	Chag Ho'Osif	The Holiday of Gathering (Succos)
חַג הַפֶּסַח	Chag Ha'Pesach	The Holiday of Passover

חַג הַמַּצּוֹת	Chag Ha'Matzos	The Holiday of Matzohs (Passover)
חַג הַקָּצִיר	Chag Ha'Kotzir	The Holiday of Reaping (Shavuos)
חוֹל הַמּוֹעֵד	Chol Hamoed	The middle four days of the holidays Passover and "Succos"
חַזָּן	Chazan	Cantor
חֻקִּים	Chukim	Laws in the Torah for which no reason was given
חֻמָּשׁ	Chumosh	The Five Books of Moses
חַלָּה	Challah	Special loaves of white bread baked only for Sabbath and holidays
חָמֵץ	Chometz	Products that may not be eaten on Passover
חֲנֻכָּה	Chanukah	The holiday of Dedication
חֹק	Chok	Singular for "Chukim"
חֲרוֹסֶת	Charoses	Mixture of wine, apple, and nuts used at the Passover "Seder" service
חֲתַן בְּרֵאשִׁית	Chasan Breishis	The Torah Honor given to the one who begins the Torah anew
חֲתַן תּוֹרָה	Chasan Torah	The Torah Honor given to the one who finishes the Torah

252

חֲצִי	Yachatz	Part of the Passover "Seder" service in which we break the middle matzoh
יאָרצײַט	Yohrtzeit	Anniversary of a death
יִזְכֹּר	Yizkor	Memorial prayer for parents or close relatives
יִשְׂרָאֵל	Yisroel	Israelite, one who is neither a "Kohein" nor a "Levi"
יוֹם הַדִּין	Yom Hadin	"The Day of Judgment," another name for Rosh Hashonah
יוֹם הַזִּכָּרוֹן	Yom Hazikoron	"The Day of Remembrance," another name for Rosh Hashonah
יוֹם טוֹב	Yom Tov	Holiday
יוֹם כִּפּוּר	Yom Kippur	"The Day of Atonement"
יוֹם תְּרוּעָה	Yom T'ruah	"The Day of Sounding," another name for Rosh Hashonah
יוֹד	Yod	Pointer used by the Torah reader
יַעֲלֶה וְיָבֹא	Ya'aleh V'yovo	Special prayer recited on the three festivals and Rosh Chodesh

253

כֹּהֵן	Kohein	Descendant of the priestly family of Aaron
כֹּהֲנִים	Kohanim	Plural of "Kohein"
כָּל הַנְּעָרִים	Kol Han'orim	The "Aliyah" on "Simchas Torah" which includes all the children
כָּל נִדְרֵי	Kol Nidre	Opening prayer of Yom Kippur
כַּפָּרוֹת	Kaporos	Ceremony on "Erev" Yom Kippur in which we symbolically offer a fowl as atonement for our sins
כֹּרֵךְ	Korech	Part of the Passover "Seder" in which we eat a sandwich of matzoh and bitter herbs
כַּרְפַּס	Karpas	Part of the "Seder" service in which we eat a piece of parsley or potato
כָּשֵׁר	Kosheir	Fit for use according to Jewish law
כְּלֵי קֹדֶשׁ	Klei Kodesh	Holy vessels used to decorate the Torah
כֶּתֶר תּוֹרָה	Keser Torah	Crown put on the Torah scroll

254

The thirty-third day of the "Omer"	Lag Ba'Omer	לַ"ג בָּעֹמֶר
Descendant of the tribe of Levi	Levi	לֵוִי
Palm branch used on the holiday of "Succos"	Lulov	לוּלָב
"Poor Man's Bread" another name given to the matzoh eaten on Passover	Lechem Oni	לֶחֶם עֹנִי
A night watched by G-D (first two nights of Passover)	Leil Shimurim	לֵיל שִׁמּוּרִים
Greeting on Rosh Hashonah, "May you be inscribed for a good year"	L'shono Tovo Tikoseivu	לְשָׁנָה טוֹבָה תִּכָּתֵבוּ
Poem welcoming the "Sabbath Bride" recited Friday night	L'cho Dodi	לְכָה דוֹדִי

Part of the "Seder" service of Passover in which the "Haggadah" is read telling the story	Maggid	מַגִּיד
The scroll of the Purim story	Megillah	מְגִלָּה
The one who performs the circumcision ceremony	Moheil	מוֹהֵל

255

מ

מוּסָף	Musaf	The service added on Sabbaths and holidays
מְזוּזָה	Mezuzah	The case containing the "Shema" put on the doorpost
מַחֲזוֹר	Machzor	Prayer book used on the High Holidays, Rosh Hashonah and Yom Kippur
מְכִירַת חָמֵץ	M'chiras Chometz	Selling of the "Chometz" to a non-Jew before Passover
מַלְכִיּוֹת	Malchiyos	Portion of the "Musaf" of Rosh Hashonah that praises G-D as King of the universe
מְנוֹרָה	Menorah	The candelabra used on Chanukah
מִנְחָה	Mincha	The afternoon service
מִנְיָן	Minyan	Ten male quorum needed for services
מָעוֹת חִטִּים	Maos Chittim	Money given to the poor before Passover to buy supplies for the holiday
מַעֲרִיב	Maariv	The evening service
מַצָּה	Matzoh	Unleavened bread eaten on Passover
מִצְוָה	Mitzvah	A commandment in the Torah

מַפְטִיר	Maftir	The last of the Torah Honors on Sabbath and holidays
מָרוֹר	Moror	The bitter herbs eaten during the "Seder" on Passover
מִשְׁלוֹחַ מָנוֹת	Mishloach Monos	Sending of gifts on Purim
מוֹצִיא	Motsee	The prayer for bread, also the part of the "Seder" service on Passover where the blessing on the matzoh is recited
מִקְדָּשׁ מְעַט	Mikdosh M'at	The name given to the synagogue, the small Temple
נֵר תָּמִיד	Neir Tomid	Eternal light
נְעִילָה	N'eilah	The concluding prayer of the Yom Kippur service
נַעֲשֶׂה וְנִשְׁמָע	Naaseh V'nishma	The words uttered by the Israelites as they accepted the responsibility of the Torah, "We will do and we will hear"
נִרְצָה	Nirtso	At the conclusion of the "Seder" service of Passover we pray that our service will be accepted by G-D
נִחוּם אֲבֵלִים	Nichum Aveilim	Comforting of the Mourners

ס

סֵ֫דֶר	Seder	Order, the service on the first and second nights of Passover
סִדּוּר	Siddur	The prayer book
סִדְרָה	Sidroh	The Torah portion of the week read on the Sabbath
סֵ֫דֶר הָעֲבוֹדָה	Seder Hoavodah	The section of the "Musaf" for Yom Kippur that describes the Temple Service at this time
סִיּוּם בְּכוֹרִים	Siyum Bechorim	The service for the firstborn on "Erev Pesach"
סוֹפֵר	Sofeir	One who writes Torahs, "Mezuzos," and "Tephillin"
סְכָךְ	S'chach	Covering for the roof of the "Succah"
סֻכּוֹת	Succos	Huts, the name of the holiday
סְעֻדָּה הַמַּפְסֶ֫קֶת	S'udah Hamafsekes	The last meal before a fast
סְפִירַת הָעֹ֫מֶר	S'firas Haomer	Counting of the "Omer" between Passover and "Shavuos"

עֲלִיָה	Aliyah	Torah Honor
עֲלִיוֹת	Aliyos	Plural for "Aliyah"
עַל הַנִּסִים	Al Haneesim	The name of the special prayer added to the "Shmoneh Esrei" on Purim and Chanukah
עָלֵינוּ	Oleinu	Concluding prayer of all services
עֶרֶב	Erev	The day before a holiday or Sabbath
עֲרָבָה	Arovah	The willow branch attached to the "Lulov" used on "Succos"
עֲשֶׂרֶת יְמֵי תְּשׁוּבָה	Asseres Y'mai T'shuvah	The ten days from Rosh Hashonah to Yom Kippur
עֹנֶג שַׁבָּת	Oneg Shabbos	Special party on Sabbath afternoon

פָּרֹכֶת	Poroches	Ark Curtain
פִּדְיוֹן הַבֵּן	Pidyon Habein	Ceremony of redemption of the firstborn male child
פּוּרִים	Purim	The Feast of Lots

259

פֶּסַח	Pesach	Passover
פִּרְקֵי אָבוֹת	Pirkei Ovos	"Ethics of the Fathers" studied on Sabbath afternoons during summer months.
קַבָּלַת שַׁבָּת	Kabolas Shabbos	Sabbath-greeting service on Friday night
קַדֵּשׁ	Kadesh	Part of the "Seder" service on Passover in which the males recite the blessing over wine
קִדּוּשׁ	Kiddush	The blessing over wine recited on Sabbath and holidays
קַדִּישׁ	Kaddish	Memorial prayer for the dead
קִינוֹת	Kinos	Lamentations recited on "Tisha B'Av"
קִדּוּשׁ לְבָנָה	Kiddush Lvono	Sanctification of the new moon
קִיטְל	Kittel	White robe worn at the "Seder" and on Yom Kippur, symbolizing purity
קְעָרַת צְדָקָה	K'aros Tz'dokoh	Plates used for collecting charity on "Erev" Yom Kippur

רֹאשׁ הַשָּׁנָה	Rosh Hashonah	The Head of the Year, the Jewish New Year
רֹאשׁ חֹדֶשׁ	Rosh Chodesh	The first day of the Hebrew month
רֹאשׁ הַשָּׁנָה לָאִילָנוֹת	Rosh Hashonah Lo'ilonos	The New Year for Trees on "Tu Bishvat"
רְחַץ	R'chatz	Part of the "Seder" service meaning "wash the hands"
רִמּוֹנִים	Rimonim	Silver crowns placed on the rollers of the Torah scroll as decoration

שְׁמַע	Shema	Excerpt from the Torah recited three times a day—contains the laws of "Tzitzis," "Mezuzah" and "Tephillin"
שַׁעַטְנֵז	Shatnez	Mixture of wool and linen
שֶׁקֶל	Shekel	A coin used in the time of the Temple
שָׁלוֹם עֲלֵיכֶם	Sholom Aleichem	The song of welcome to the angels sung on Friday night
שָׁלֹשׁ סְעֻדּוֹת	Shalosh S'udos	The three Sabbath meals

שִׁבְעָה	Shiva	Seven days of mourning
שָׁבֻעוֹת	Shavuos	The Holiday of Weeks
שַׁבָּת	Shabbos	The Sabbath
שַׁבָּת הַגָּדוֹל	Shabbos Hagodol	The Sabbath before Passover
שְׁבָרִים	Shevorim	Three blasts on the shofar
שַׁבָּת שׁוּבָה	Shabbos Shuva	The Sabbath between Rosh Hashonah and Yom Kippur
שׁוּבָה יִשְׂרָאֵל	Shuvo Yisroel	The "Haftorah" recited on "Shabbos Shuva"
שׁוֹחֵט	Shochet	The man who slaughters animals according to Jewish law
שׁוֹפָר	Shofar	Ram's born sounded on Rosh Hashonah
שׁוֹפְרוֹת	Shofros	Section of the "Musaf" service on Rosh Hashonah that describes the revelation of God on Mount Sinai
שֶׁהֶחֱיָנוּ	Shehecheyonu	Blessing recited upon doing certain things for the first time
שַׁחֲרִית	Shacharis	The first of the daily services
שֶׁל יָד	Shel Yod	One of the "Tephillin" that goes on the arm

שֶׁל רֹאשׁ	Shel Rosh	One of the "Tephillin" that goes on the head
שֻׁלְחָן עוֹרֵךְ	Shulchon Orech	Part of the "Seder" service on Passover in which the meal is eaten
שָׁלֹשׁ רְגָלִים	Sholosh Regolim	Three Pilgrimage Festivals: "Pesach," "Shavuos," and "Succos"
שִׂמְחַת תּוֹרָה	Simchas Torah	The holiday of the "Rejoicing of the Law"
שְׁמוֹת	Shmos	The second book of the Torah
שְׁמוֹנֶה עֶשְׂרֵה	Shmoneh Esrei	The section of eighteen blessings recited in every service
שִׂמְחַת בֵּית הַשּׁוֹאֵבָה	Simchas Beis Hashoevah	"Celebration of the Water Drawing"
שְׁמִינִי עֲצֶרֶת	Shmini Atseres	The eighth day of "Succos"

ת

תַּלְמוּד	Talmud	Books of the oral law

UNIT ONE / *Chapter Nine*

בָּרְכוּ אֶת יְיָ הַמְבֹרָךְ. בָּרוּךְ יְיָ הַמְבֹרָךְ לְעוֹלָם וָעֶד.

בָּרוּךְ אַתָּה, יְיָ אֱלֹהֵינוּ, מֶלֶךְ הָעוֹלָם, אֲשֶׁר בָּחַר בָּנוּ מִכָּל

הָעַמִּים, וְנָתַן לָנוּ אֶת תּוֹרָתוֹ. בָּרוּךְ אַתָּה, יְיָ, נוֹתֵן הַתּוֹרָה.

Bless ye the Lord who is to be blessed. Blessed be the Lord, who
is to be blessed for ever and ever. Blessed art Thou, O Lord our
G-D, King of the universe, who hast chosen us from all peoples,
and hast given us Thy Law. Blessed art Thou, O Lord, who
givest the Law.

בָּרוּךְ אַתָּה, יְיָ אֱלֹהֵינוּ, מֶלֶךְ הָעוֹלָם, אֲשֶׁר נָתַן לָנוּ תּוֹרַת

אֱמֶת, וְחַיֵּי עוֹלָם נָטַע בְּתוֹכֵנוּ. בָּרוּךְ אַתָּה, יְיָ, נוֹתֵן הַתּוֹרָה.

Blessed art Thou, O Lord our G-D, King of the universe, who
has given us the Law of truth, and hast planted everlasting life
in our midst. Blessed art Thou, O Lord, who givest the Law.

UNIT TWO / *Chapter Six*

בָּרוּךְ אַתָּה, יְיָ אֱלֹהֵינוּ, מֶלֶךְ הָעוֹלָם, אֲשֶׁר קִדְּשָׁנוּ בְּמִצְוֹתָיו

וְצִוָּנוּ עַל מִקְרָא מְגִלָּה.

Blessed art Thou, O Lord our G-D, King of the universe, who
hast sanctified us by Thy commandments, and hast given command concerning the reading of the Megillah.

בָּרוּךְ אַתָּה, יְיָ אֱלֹהֵינוּ, מֶלֶךְ הָעוֹלָם, שֶׁעָשָׂה נִסִּים

לַאֲבוֹתֵינוּ בַּיָּמִים הָהֵם בַּזְּמַן הַזֶּה.

Blessed art Thou, O Lord our G-D, King of the universe, who
wrought miracles for our fathers in days of old, at this season.

UNIT ONE / *Chapter One*

בָּרוּךְ אַתָּה, יְיָ אֱלֹהֵינוּ, מֶלֶךְ הָעוֹלָם, שֶׁהֶחֱיָנוּ וְקִיְּמָנוּ
וְהִגִּיעָנוּ לַזְּמַן הַזֶּה.

Blessed art Thou, O Lord our G-D, King of the universe, who
hast kept us in life, and hast preserved us, and enabled us to reach
this season.

UNIT ONE / *Chapter Two*

בָּרוּךְ אַתָּה, יְיָ אֱלֹהֵינוּ, מֶלֶךְ הָעוֹלָם, אֲשֶׁר קִדְּשָׁנוּ בְּמִצְוֹתָיו
וְצִוָּנוּ לְהִתְעַטֵּף בַּצִּיצִת.

Blessed art Thou, O Lord our G-D, King of the universe, who
hast sanctified us by Thy commandments, and hast commanded
us to enwrap ourselves in the fringed garment.

בָּרוּךְ אַתָּה, יְיָ אֱלֹהֵינוּ, מֶלֶךְ הָעוֹלָם, אֲשֶׁר קִדְּשָׁנוּ בְּמִצְוֹתָיו
וְצִוָּנוּ לְהָנִיחַ תְּפִלִּין.

Blessed art Thou, O Lord our G-D, King of the universe, who
hast sanctified us by Thy commandments, and hast commanded
us to put on the Tephillin.

בָּרוּךְ אַתָּה, יְיָ אֱלֹהֵינוּ, מֶלֶךְ הָעוֹלָם, אֲשֶׁר קִדְּשָׁנוּ בְּמִצְוֹתָיו
וְצִוָּנוּ עַל מִצְוַת תְּפִלִּין.

Blessed art Thou, O Lord our G-D, King of the universe, who
hast sanctified us by Thy commandments, and hast given us
command concerning the precept of the Tephillin.

בָּרוּךְ שֵׁם כְּבוֹד מַלְכוּתוֹ לְעוֹלָם וָעֶד.

Blessed be His name, whose glorious kingdom is for ever and ever.

בָּרוּךְ אַתָּה, יְיָ אֱלֹהֵינוּ, מֶלֶךְ הָעוֹלָם, אֲשֶׁר קִדְּשָׁנוּ בְּמִצְוֹתָיו וְצִוָּנוּ לִקְבּוֹעַ מְזוּזָה.

Blessed art Thou, O Lord our G-D, King of the universe, who hast sanctified us by Thy commandments, and commanded us to affix the Mezuzah.

UNIT ONE / Chapter Eleven

בָּרוּךְ אַתָּה, יְיָ אֱלֹהֵינוּ, מֶלֶךְ הָעוֹלָם, אֲשֶׁר קִדְּשָׁנוּ בְּמִצְוֹתָיו וְצִוָּנוּ לְהַדְלִיק נֵר שֶׁל שַׁבָּת.

Blessed art Thou, O Lord our G-D, King of the universe, who hast sanctified us by Thy commandments, and commanded us to kindle the Sabbath Light.

בָּרוּךְ אַתָּה, יְיָ אֱלֹהֵינוּ, מֶלֶךְ הָעוֹלָם, אֲשֶׁר קִדְּשָׁנוּ בְּמִצְוֹתָיו וְצִוָּנוּ לְהַפְרִישׁ חַלָּה מִן הָעִסָּה.

Blessed art Thou, O Lord our G-D, King of the universe, who hast sanctified us by Thy commandments, and commanded us to separate the challah from the dough.

בָּרוּךְ אַתָּה, יְיָ אֱלֹהֵינוּ, מֶלֶךְ הָעוֹלָם, אֲשֶׁר קִדְּשָׁנוּ בְּמִצְוֹתָיו וְצִוָּנוּ לְהַדְלִיק נֵר שֶׁל שַׁבָּת וְשֶׁל יוֹם הַכִּפֻּרִים.

Blessed art Thou, O Lord our G-D, King of the universe, who hast sanctified us by Thy commandments, and commanded us to kindle (the Sabbath and) the Day of Atonement light.

UNIT TWO / Chapter Three

בָּרוּךְ אַתָּה, יְיָ אֱלֹהֵינוּ, מֶלֶךְ הָעוֹלָם, אֲשֶׁר קִדְּשָׁנוּ בְּמִצְוֹתָיו וְצִוָּנוּ לֵישֵׁב בַּסֻּכָּה.

Blessed art Thou, O Lord our G-D, King of the universe, who hast sanctified us by Thy commandments, and commanded us to dwell in the Tabernacle.

בָּרוּךְ אַתָּה, יְיָ אֱלֹהֵינוּ, מֶלֶךְ הָעוֹלָם, אֲשֶׁר קִדְּשָׁנוּ בְּמִצְוֹתָיו וְצִוָּנוּ עַל נְטִילַת לוּלָב.

Blessed art Thou, O Lord our G-D, King of the universe, who hast sanctified us by Thy commandments, and commanded us concerning the taking of the Lulov.

UNIT ONE / *Chapter Two*

בָּרוּךְ אַתָּה, יְיָ אֱלֹהֵינוּ, מֶלֶךְ הָעוֹלָם, אֲשֶׁר קִדְּשָׁנוּ בְּמִצְוֹתָיו וְצִוָּנוּ עַל מִצְוַת צִיצִת.

Blessed art Thou, O Lord our G-D, King of the universe, who hast sanctified us by Thy commandments, and commanded us concerning the precept of fringes.

UNIT ONE / *Chapter Eleven*

בָּרוּךְ אַתָּה, יְיָ אֱלֹהֵינוּ, מֶלֶךְ הָעוֹלָם, אֲשֶׁר קִדְּשָׁנוּ בְּמִצְוֹתָיו וְצִוָּנוּ לְהַדְלִיק נֵר שֶׁל שַׁבָּת וְשֶׁל יוֹם טוֹב.

Blessed art Thou, O Lord our G-D, King of the universe, who hast sanctified us by Thy commandments and commanded us to kindle (on Friday add: the Sabbath and) the Festival light.

UNIT ONE / *Chapter One*

מוֹדֶה אֲנִי לְפָנֶיךָ, מֶלֶךְ חַי וְקַיָּם, שֶׁהֶחֱזַרְתָּ בִּי נִשְׁמָתִי בְּחֶמְלָה; רַבָּה אֱמוּנָתֶךָ.

I thank Thee O Living and eternal King for returning my soul to me, Thou art very faithful.

בָּרוּךְ אַתָּה, יְיָ אֱלֹהֵינוּ, מֶלֶךְ הָעוֹלָם, אֲשֶׁר קִדְּשָׁנוּ בְּמִצְוֹתָיו
וְצִוָּנוּ עַל נְטִילַת יָדַיִם.

Blessed art Thou, O Lord our G-D, King of the universe, who
hast sanctified us by Thy commandments, and commanded us
concerning the washing of the hands.

Prayer recited on bread:

בָּרוּךְ אַתָּה, יְיָ אֱלֹהֵינוּ, מֶלֶךְ הָעוֹלָם, הַמּוֹצִיא לֶחֶם מִן
הָאָרֶץ.

Blessed art Thou, O Lord our G-D, King of the universe, who
brings forth bread from the earth.

Prayer recited on fruits that grow on trees:

בָּרוּךְ אַתָּה, יְיָ אֱלֹהֵינוּ, מֶלֶךְ הָעוֹלָם, בּוֹרֵא פְּרִי הָעֵץ.

Blessed art Thou, O Lord our G-D, King of the universe, who
createst the fruit of the tree.

Prayer recited on all foods that grow in or on the ground:

בָּרוּךְ אַתָּה, יְיָ אֱלֹהֵינוּ, מֶלֶךְ הָעוֹלָם, בּוֹרֵא פְּרִי הָאֲדָמָה.

Blessed art Thou, O Lord our G-D, King of the universe, who
createst the fruit of the earth.

Prayer recited on water, fish, eggs, milk and other products
for which there is no special blessing:

בָּרוּךְ אַתָּה, יְיָ אֱלֹהֵינוּ, מֶלֶךְ הָעוֹלָם, שֶׁהַכֹּל נִהְיֶה בִּדְבָרוֹ.

Blessed art Thou, O Lord our G-D, King of the universe, by whose
word all things exist.

Prayer recited on all types of cake and pastry:

בָּרוּךְ אַתָּה, יְיָ אֱלֹהֵינוּ, מֶלֶךְ הָעוֹלָם, בּוֹרֵא מִינֵי מְזוֹנוֹת.

Blessed art Thou, O Lord our G-D, King of the universe, who
createst various kinds of food.

UNIT TWO / *Chapter Four*

בָּרוּךְ אַתָּה, יְיָ אֱלֹהֵינוּ, מֶלֶךְ הָעוֹלָם, אֲשֶׁר קִדְּשָׁנוּ בְּמִצְוֹתָיו
וְצִוָּנוּ לְהַדְלִיק נֵר שֶׁל חֲנֻכָּה.

Blessed art Thou, O Lord our G-D, King of the universe, who
hast sanctified us by Thy commandments, and commanded us
to kindle the light of Chanukah.

בָּרוּךְ אַתָּה, יְיָ אֱלֹהֵינוּ, מֶלֶךְ הָעוֹלָם, שֶׁעָשָׂה נִסִּים
לַאֲבוֹתֵינוּ בַּיָּמִים הָהֵם בַּזְּמַן הַזֶּה.

Blessed art Thou, O Lord our G-D, King of the universe, who
wroughtest miracles for our fathers in days of old, at this season.

UNIT TWO / *Chapter Seven*

בָּרוּךְ אַתָּה, יְיָ אֱלֹהֵינוּ, מֶלֶךְ הָעוֹלָם, אֲשֶׁר קִדְּשָׁנוּ בְּמִצְוֹתָיו
וְצִוָּנוּ עַל בְּעוּר חָמֵץ.

Blessed art Thou, O Lord our G-D, King of the universe, who
hast sanctified us by Thy commandments and hast commanded
us concerning the burning of the leaven.

בָּרוּךְ אַתָּה, יְיָ אֱלֹהֵינוּ, מֶלֶךְ הָעוֹלָם, בּוֹרֵא פְּרִי הַגָּפֶן.

Blessed art Thou, O Lord our G-D, King of the universe, who
createst the fruit of the vine.

בָּרוּךְ אַתָּה, יְיָ אֱלֹהֵינוּ, מֶלֶךְ הָעוֹלָם, אֲשֶׁר קִדְּשָׁנוּ בְּמִצְוֹתָיו
וְצִוָּנוּ עַל אֲכִילַת מַצָּה.

Blessed art Thou, O Lord our G-D, King of the universe, who hast
sanctified us by Thy commandments and hast commanded us
concerning the eating of Matzoh.

בָּרוּךְ אַתָּה, יְיָ אֱלֹהֵינוּ, מֶלֶךְ הָעוֹלָם, אֲשֶׁר קִדְּשָׁנוּ בְּמִצְוֹתָיו
וְצִוָּנוּ עַל אֲכִילַת מָרוֹר.

Blessed art Thou, O Lord our G-D, King of the universe, who
hast sanctified us by Thy commandments and hast commanded
us concerning the eating of bitter herbs.

UNIT TWO / *Chapter Eight*

בָּרוּךְ אַתָּה, יְיָ אֱלֹהֵינוּ, מֶלֶךְ הָעוֹלָם, אֲשֶׁר קִדְּשָׁנוּ בְּמִצְוֹתָיו
וְצִוָּנוּ עַל סְפִירַת הָעֹמֶר.

Blessed art Thou, O Lord our G-D, King of the universe, who
hast sanctified us by Thy commandments, and hast commanded
us concerning the counting of the Omer.

THE JEWISH CALENDAR YEAR

TISHREI תִּשְׁרֵי	CHESHVAN חֶשְׁוָן	KISLEIV כִּסְלֵו	TEIVEIS טֵבֵת
Dates 1–Rosh Hashonah 2–Rosh Hashonah 3–Fast of Gedaliah 10–Yom Kippur 15–21–Succos 22–Shmini Atseres } 9 days 23–Simchas Torah }		25–29–Chanukah (8 days)	1–3–Chanukah 10–Fast of the Tenth of Teiveis

SHEVAT שְׁבָט	ADAR אֲדָר	NISSAN נִיסָן	IYAR אִיָּר
15–Tu Bishvat	13–Fast of Esther 14–Purim	15–22–Pesach (8 days)	18–Lag Baomer

SIVAN סִיוָן	TAMUZ תַּמּוּז	AV אָב	ELUL אֱלוּל
6, 7–Shavuos (2 days)	17–Fast of the Seventeenth day of Tamuz	9–Fast of the Ninth of Av	29–Erev Rosh Hashonah

271